Essential .NET
Volume 1

Microsoft .NET Development Series

John Montgomery, *Series Advisor*
Don Box, *Series Advisor*
Martin Heller, *Series Editor*

"This Microsoft .NET series is a great resource for .NET developers. Coupling the .NET architects at Microsoft with the training skills of DevelopMentor means that all the technical bases, from reference to 'how-to,' will be covered."
—JOHN MONTGOMERY, Group Product Manager
for the .NET platform, Microsoft Corporation

"The Microsoft .NET series has the unique advantage of an author pool that combines some of the most insightful authors in the industry with the actual architects and developers of the .NET platform."
—DON BOX, Architect, Microsoft Corporation

Titles in the Series

Keith Ballinger, *.NET Web Services: Architecture and Implementation with .NET*, 0-321-11359-4

Don Box with Chris Sells, *Essential .NET Volume 1: The Common Language Runtime*, 0-201-73411-7

Microsoft Common Language Runtime Team, *The Common Language Runtime Annotated Reference and Specification*, 0-321-15493-2

Microsoft .NET Framework Class Libraries Team, *The .NET Framework CLI Standard Class Library Annotated Reference*, 0-321-15489-4

Microsoft Visual C# Development Team, *The C# Annotated Reference and Specification*, 0-321-15491-6

Damien Watkins, Mark Hammond, Brad Abrams, *Programming in the .NET Environment*, 0-201-77018-0

Shawn Wildermuth, *Pragmatic ADO.NET: Data Access for the Internet World*, 0-201-74568-2

http://www.awprofessional.com/msdotnetseries/

Essential .NET
Volume 1

The Common Language Runtime

- **Don Box**
  with Chris Sells

♦♦Addison-Wesley

Boston • San Francisco • New York • Toronto • Montreal
London • Munich • Paris • Madrid
Capetown • Sydney • Tokyo • Singapore • Mexico City

The publisher offers discounts on this book when ordered in quantity for bulk purchases and special sales. For more information, please contact:

U.S. Corporate and Government Sales
(800) 382-3419
corpsales@pearsontechgroup.com

For sales outside of the U.S., please contact:

International Sales
(317) 581-3793
international@pearsontechgroup.com

Visit Addison-Wesley on the Web:
www.awprofessional.com

ISBN 0-201-73411-7
Text printed on recycled paper
1 2 3 4 5 6 7 8 9 10—MA—0605040302
First printing, October 2002

Box, Don, 1962–
    Essential .NET : the common language runtime
/ Don Box with Chris Sells.
        p.   cm.
    Includes bibliographical references and index.
    ISBN 0-201-73411-7 (alk. paper)
    1. Microsoft .NET.   2. Component software.
    3. Programming languages (Electronic
    computers).   I. Sells, Chris.   II. Title.

    QA76.76.M52 B69 2002
    005.13—dc21

                        2002026087

Contents

Figures

Chapter 2:   Advanced Methods

Chapter 8:   Domains

Chapter 9:   Security

Chapter 10:   CLR Externals

Tables

Chapter 10: CLR Externals

Foreword

I WORKED FOR THE World Wide Web Consortium in its early days at the Massachusetts Institute of Technology (MIT). We decided we needed to learn about both COM and CORBA, at that time the leading frameworks for object-oriented programming over the network.

I called our Microsoft representative and asked who he could send to teach the Consortium staff the fundamentals of COM. I explained that the Consortium staff were very technical and were interested in the "why" of things at least as much as the "how." I explained that we were designing the next generation Web protocols and knew just about everything there was to know about application protocols on the Internet, and that we'd built some very large object-oriented programs in C++ and Objective C.

I fully expected him to suggest someone from Microsoft. Instead he said, "The best person in the world is Don Box." And that's how I met Don, one of the finest teachers I know. Don not only explained well and ran labs well and wrote well, but he never broke down under endless detailed questioning, ranging from the high-level "Why would you build the architecture that way?" to the low-level "Where does that bit ever get set?" So Don taught me (along with hundreds of thousands of others) what COM is, why COM is, and what the problems with COM are. Along the way, just off-hand 'cause he thought we might be interested, he also did an amazingly good comparison to the CORBA technology and to the Web technology we were designing and building.

I left the MIT and the Web Consortium to come to Microsoft to work on a top-secret project called "COM+ Services." My business card read "Program Manager, Garbage Collection and Related Rubbish" because all we could say (even internally at Microsoft) was that it had something to do with programming languages and distributed systems, and it had a garbage collector. I'm still on that same project at Microsoft, working almost four years to help design and build what is now the Common Language Runtime. I've worked on the IL design, four different JITs, the metadata, the garbage collector, the execution engine, and the ECMA (and soon, hopefully, ISO) standards.

I was sure that I'd be able to turn around and teach Don something I'd learned in this process (I'm not a bad teacher myself). But Don beat me to the punch. He told me to read this book. And (darn it) he's taught me stuff I didn't know about my own product! And I bet he'll teach you something, too.

Dr. James S. Miller
Microsoft Corporation
Lead Program Manager
Common Language Runtime

Preface

What Happened?

In 1998, Microsoft held a Professional Developer's Conference (PDC) in San Diego. COM luminary Charlie Kindel stood up in a general session and proclaimed "no more GUIDs—no more HRESULTs—no more IUnknown." He and Mary Kirtland proceeded to show the basic architecture of the CLR, then known as the COM+ Runtime. Later in the session, Nat Brown and David Stutz stood up and demonstrated cross-language inheritance using Visual Basic and Java. Attendees actually went home with CDs containing primitive versions of compilers that could reproduce this very odd demonstration. It is now February 2002, and this technology has finally shipped in release form.

There are two days that will forever demarcate the evolution of the Microsoft platform. On July 27, 1993, Windows NT 3.1 was released, marking the end of the DOS era. On February 13, 2002, the Common Language Runtime (CLR) was released as part of the .NET Framework, marking the end of the COM era.

The .NET Framework is a platform for software integration. Fundamentally, the .NET Framework provides two core integration technologies. The Common Language Runtime (CLR) is used to integrate software within a single operating system process. XML Web Services are used to integrate software at Internet scale. Both rely on similar ideas, that is, strongly typed contracts and encapsulation. Fundamentally, though, they are two distinct technologies that one can elect to adopt independently of one another. It is completely reasonable to adopt XML Web Services prior to the CLR (in fact, many production Web services have already done this). It is also reasonable to adopt the CLR in the absence of XML Web Services in order to access CLR-specific features such as code access security or superior memory management facilities. Going forward, however, both the CLR and XML Web Services will be central to the Microsoft development platform, and it is only a matter of time before both of these technologies play a role in everyone's development experience.

The CLR and XML Web Services are both focused on strongly typed contracts between components. Both technologies require developers to describe component interactions in terms of type definitions or contracts. In both technologies, these contracts share two key ideas that tend to permeate their use: metadata and virtualization.

Both the CLR and XML Web Services rely on high-fidelity, ubiquitous, and extensible metadata to convey programmer intention. Metadata conveys the basic structure and type relationships to the developers who will consume a CLR component or XML Web Service.

Equally important, ubiquitous metadata informs the tools and underlying platform of what the component developers had in mind when they were authoring the code.

This metadata-directed "clairvoyance" allows the platform to provide richer support than would be possible if the component were completely opaque. For example, various aspects of object-to-XML mapping are captured in metadata for use by the CLR's XML serializer. How the developer intended the XML to look is conveyed through declarative metadata extensions rather than through explicit labor-intensive coding.

The second key idea that permeates CLR and XML Web Service contracts is the notion of virtualization. Both technologies emphasize the separation of semantic intentions from physical implementation details. Specifically, the metadata for both technologies work at an abstract structural level rather than in terms of low-level data representations and implementation techniques. When developers specify intercomponent contracts at this "virtual" level, the underlying platform is free to express the contracts in the most appropriate manner available. For example, by expressing Web Service contracts in terms of an abstract data model, the plumbing is free to use an efficient binary data representation for performance or to use the text-based XML 1.0 representation for maximum interoperability.

Because contracts are virtualized, this specific detail of the contract can be bound at runtime based on post-development characteristics.

Because this volume focuses exclusively on the CLR, a working definition of the CLR is in order. The CLR is fundamentally a loader that brings your components to life inside an operating system process. The CLR replaces COM's `CoCreateInstance` and Win32's `LoadLibrary` as the primary loader for code.

The CLR loader provides a number of services beyond what COM and Win32 offered before it. The CLR loader is version-aware and provides flexible configuration of version policies and code repositories. The CLR loader is security-aware and is a critical part of the enforcement of security policy. The CLR loader is type-aware and provides a rich runtime environment for the explicit management and creation of types independent of programming language. In short, the CLR loader is an advanced component technology that supplants COM as Microsoft's primary in-memory integration strategy.

The CLR is made accessible through compilers that emit the CLR's new file format. Program language wonks view the CLR as providing key building blocks for compiler writers, building blocks that reduce the complexity of compiler implementations. In contrast, systems wonks often view programming languages as facades or "skins" over the underlying constructs of the CLR. The author falls firmly into the latter camp. However, programming languages are a necessary lens through which even low-level systems plumbers view the CLR. To that end, examples in this book are written in various programming languages because binary dumps of metadata and code are arcane to the point of being incomprehensible.

About This Book

I try very hard to make a book readable and accessible to a wide array of readers, but invariably, my terse writing style tends to make a "Don Box book" a challenge to get through. Experience has shown me that I am horrible at writing tutorials or primers. What I can do reasonably well is convey how I see the world in book form. To that end, it is not uncommon to need to read a Don Box book more than once to get the intended benefits.

As the previous paragraph implied, this book is by no means a tutorial. If you try to learn .NET Framework programming from a standing start using this book, the results may not be pretty. For readers looking for a good tutorial on .NET programming techniques or the C# language, please read Stan Lippman's *C# Primer* (Addison-Wesley, 2002) or Jeffery Richter's *Applied .NET Framework Programming* (Microsoft Press, 2002) before taking on this book.

This book is divided into two volumes. Volume 1 focuses on the Common Language Runtime. Volume 2 will focus [ST3]on XML Web Services. Although the two technologies share a fair number of core concepts, the thought of covering them both in a single book made my head spin.

This book was written against Version 1 of the CLR. Some of the internal techniques used by the CLR may evolve over time and may in fact change radically. In particular, the details of virtual method dispatch are very subject to change. They are included in this book largely as an homage to COM developers wondering where the vptr went. That stated, the basic concepts that are the focus of this book are likely to remain stable for years to come.

Throughout the book, I use assertions in code to reinforce the expected state of a program. In the CLR, assertions are performed using `System.Diagnostics.Debug.Assert`, which accepts a Boolean expression as its argument. If the expression evaluates to false, then the assertion has failed and the program will halt with a distinguished error message. For readability, all code in this book uses the short form, `Debug.Assert`, which assumes that the `System.Diagnostics` namespace prefix has been imported.

My perspective on .NET is fairly agnostic with respect to language. In my daily life, I use C# for about 50 percent of my CLR-based programming.

I use C++ for about 40 percent, and I resort to ILASM for the remaining 10 percent. That stated, most programming examples in this book use C# if for no other reason than it is often the most concise syntax for representing a particular concept or technique. Although some chapters may seem language-focused, none of them really is. The vast majority of this book could have used C++, but, given the tremendous popularity of C#, I elected to use C# to make this book as accessible as possible.

This book focuses on the Common Language Runtime and is divided into 10 chapters:

• Chapter 1—The CLR as a Better COM: This chapter frames the discussion of the CLR as a replacement for the Component Object Model (COM) by looking at the issues that faced COM developers and explaining how the CLR addresses those issues through virtualization and ubiquitous, extensible metadata.

• Chapter 2– Components: Ultimately, the CLR is a replacement for the OS and COM loaders. This chapter looks at how code is packaged and how code is loaded, both of which are done significantly differently than in the Win32 and COM worlds.

• Chapter 3—Type Basics: Components are containers for the code and metadata that make up type definitions. This chapter focuses on the CLR's common type system (CTS), including what constitutes a type and how types relate. This is the first chapter that contains significant chunks of source code.

• Chapter 4—Programming with Type: The CLR makes type a first-class concept in the programming model. This chapter is dedicated to the explicit use of type in CLR programs, with an emphasis on the role of metadata and runtime type information.

• Chapter 5—Instances: The CLR programming model is based on types, objects, and values. Chapter 4 focused on type; this chapter focuses on objects and values. Specifically, this chapter outlines the difference between these two instancing models, including how values and objects differ with respect to memory management.

• Chapter 6—Methods: All component interaction occurs through method invocation. The CLR provides a broad spectrum of techniques for making method invocation an explicit act. This chapter looks at those techniques, starting with method initialization through JIT compilation and ending with method termination via strongly typed exceptions.

• Chapter 7—Advanced Methods: The CLR provides a rich architecture for intercepting method calls. This chapter dissects the CLR's interception facilities and its support for aspect-oriented programming. These facilities are one of the more innovative aspects of the CLR.

• Chapter 8—Domains: The CLR uses AppDomains rather than OS processes to scope the execution of code. To that end, this chapter looks at the role of AppDomains both as a replacement for the underlying OS's process model as well as an AppDomain's interactions between the assembly resolver or loader. Readers with Java roots will find the closest analog to a Java class loader here.

• Chapter 9—Security: One of the primary benefits of the CLR is that it provides a secure execution environment. This chapter looks at how the CLR loader supports the granting of privileges to code and how those privileges are enforced.

• Chapter 10—CLR Externals: The first nine chapters of this book are focused on what it means to write programs to the CLR's programming model. This concluding chapter looks at how one steps outside of that programming model to deal with the world outside of the CLR.

Acknowledgments

As always, my wife and children made unreasonable sacrifices for me to complete this book. In acknowledgment of this, I am taking at least a year off before I tackle another book project.

This book would never have been completed had it not been for Chris Sells. Chris was my writing partner on this project and pulled me through some very rocky times during 2001, both personally and professionally. Although Chris contributed no paragraphs to this book, his efforts are visible on every page.

Thanks go out to Jim Miller of the CLR team at Microsoft. Jim was nice enough to write the foreword for this book, and for that I am personally grateful. More importantly, however, Jim was the lead author on what I consider the most important writing on the CLR, which is the five-part ECMA specification for the CLI. These five Microsoft Word documents reside in the Tools Developer's Guide folder in the .NET Framework SDK and give more insight into the CLR than anything else I have read. Readers familiar with my COM background may recall that I considered the COM specification to be must-reading. For the CLR, I believe the ECMA specifications are even more vital.

A lot of the insights I gained while writing this book were a result of conversations that took place on the DOTNET mailing list at http://discuss.develop.com/. This list is the center of the universe for developers and architects who are active in the CLR programming community. Specific listers who helped my thinking include Brian Harry, Jim Miller, Dennis Angeline, Steven Pratchner, Brent Rector, John Lam, Mike Woodring, Keith Brown, Peter Drayton, Brad Wilson, Jay Freeman, and Sam Gentile.

This book would have considerably more errors had it not been for my reviewers. Thanks go out to Dan Sullivan, Peter Drayton, Mike Woodring, Chris Sells, Stuart Celarier, Jay Freeman, Steve Vinoski, Stan Lippman, Robert Husted, Peter Jones, Mike Giroux, Vishwas Lele, Dan Green, Paul Gunn, and Fumiaki Yoshimatsu. Arguably the most critical review was from Brian Kernighan early on in the project. That review made me reevaluate where I wanted the book to go and how I was going to get it there. Had it not been for Brian's review, I am not certain I would have survived the process. Thanks, Brian.

As always, it takes a village to be Don Box. For this book, that village consisted of Helga Thomsen, Sandy Deason, Barbara Box, Judith Swerling, David Baum, David Stromberg, Martin Gudgin, Mike Woodring, Fritz Onion, Shannon Ahern Ikeda, Ron Sumida, Tim Ewald, and Aaron Skonnard.

Don Box
February 2002
Yarrow Point, WA

1

The CLR as a Better COM

M Y FIRST BOOK, *Essential COM* (Addison-Wesley 1998), began by describing the problems that plagued the pre-COM world and then proceeded to describe an architecture for solving those problems. Because the CLR is the heir apparent to COM, it seems fitting that this book begin with a similar treatment, this time looking at the world that COM has wrought.

COM Revisited

Component technologies focus on the **contracts** between independently developed and deployed programs. The Component Object Model (COM) was Microsoft's first attempt at formalizing these contracts both as a design paradigm and through supporting platform technology. The design paradigm of COM was that component contracts are expressed as **type definitions**. This was a step forward from the world COM replaced, in which contracts were expressed only as simple functional entry points. In this respect, COM was a major advance because it brought the dynamic loading of code and the type system together in a fairly self-consistent manner.

The COM programming model itself has stood the test of time extremely well. COM combined existing ideas such as encapsulation, polymorphism, and separation of interface from implementation into a unified programming discipline that has left an indelible mark on the field of software engineering. Rather than rehash that model here, I will point you to

Chapter 1 of either *Essential COM* or *Design Patterns* (Erich Gamma et al., Addison-Wesley 1995) for two very different descriptions of essentially the same programming model.

Remember, however, that COM is both a programming model and a supporting platform technology. On that latter front, COM has not held up nearly as well as the programming model I know and love. Unfortunately, a solid platform technology is needed to make COM more than just an idea or programming discipline. For that reason, the COM era is coming to a close.

Most if not all of the problems with the COM platform can be traced back to the nature of contracts between **components**. In an ideal world, the contracts between components would be expressed purely in terms of the semantic guarantees and assumptions that exist between the consumer and the component. Unfortunately, the field of software engineering has yet to define a way to express semantics that has been proven commercially (or technically) viable for large-scale industry-wide deployment. The closest we have come as a profession is to use programmatic type definitions along with human-readable documentation that describes the semantics of those types. This is how it was done before COM. This is how it will be done long after the last COM component on earth is finally wiped out of existence.

COM expressed component contracts in terms of types; however, a component contract in COM had two key problems that made COM-based contracts sub-optimal for expressing semantics. One of these problems was related to the description of a COM contract. The other problem was related to the contract itself.

The first problem with COM relates to how contracts are described. The COM specification bent over backwards to avoid mandating an interchange format for contract definitions. This meant that if one adhered to only the COM specification, there was no standardized way to describe a contract; rather, the COM specification assumed that the type definitions of a contract would be communicated via some out-of-band technique that was outside the scope of COM proper. Of course, this is viable only in the world of specifications. To make COM a useful technology, a concrete solution was needed; otherwise, it would have been impossible to build compilers, tools, and supporting infrastructure.

Microsoft defined and supported not one but two interchange formats for COM contract descriptions: **Interface Definition Language (IDL)** and **type library (TLB)** files. That in itself would not have been a problem; however, the two formats were not isomorphic. That is, there were constructs that could be expressed in one format that had no meaningful representation in the other format. Worse, the constructs supported by one format were not a proper subset of the constructs supported by the other, so it was impossible to view either of these formats as the "authoritative" or "normative" format for contract descriptions.

An argument could have been made for simply defining a third format based on the union of constructs supported by both formats. However, there were at least two other critical problems with the way contracts were described in COM. For one, COM made no attempt to describe component **dependencies**. At the time of this writing, there is no way to walk up to a COM component (or its contract definition) and determine which other components are required to make this component work. The lack of dependency information made it difficult to determine which DLLs would be needed to deploy a COM-based application. This also made it impossible to statically determine which versions of a component were needed, which made diagnosing versioning problems extremely difficult.

The second major problem and the ultimate death knell for COM's contract description format was its lack of extensibility. In the early 1990s, the **Microsoft Transaction Server (MTS)** team was working on a new programming model based on the ideas now known as **aspect-oriented programming (AOP)**. AOP takes aspects of the code that are not domain-specific and hoists them out of the developer's source code. AOP-based systems rely on alternative mechanisms for declaring these aspects to make the intention of the programmer explicit rather than implicit.

The MTS team wanted to allow developers to express their requirements for concurrency, transactioning, and security as **aspects** rather than as calls to API functions. Because of the broad adoption of COM, the MTS developers used augmentations to COM contract descriptions as the mechanism for expressing these aspects. Developers using MTS simply annotate their COM class, interface, and method definitions with attributes that inform the MTS executive of the requirements and assumptions of the underlying code. To make these attributes useful, the MTS executive replaced the COM loader and injected interceptors based on the aspects of the class being loaded. The MTS interceptor (called a **context wrapper**) would do whatever work was necessary to ensure that the developer's assumptions were met prior to dispatching the method call. As a point of interest, this model of using declarative attributes and interception was later used as the basis for Enterprise Java Beans, an homage to MTS from Sun Microsystems.

Unfortunately, the MTS team couldn't rely on either of COM's contract formats as a reliable way to convey and store attributes. One of the contract formats, Interface Definition Language (IDL), was a text-based format that was rarely deployed with the component itself. Moreover, IDL was typically used only by C++ developers, which meant that IDL-based contract definitions were largely useless given the relatively small number of C++ developers building the enterprise systems for which MTS was designed. The second format, type library (TLB) files, had very rudimentary (and buggy) extensibility hooks. The ultimate downfall of TLBs, however, was the fact that the mainstream developer using Visual Basic had no way to directly influence the TLB. Rather, the Visual Basic IDE and compiler insulated the developer from TLB generation, making it impossible for VB programmers to specify MTS attributes during the development process. Although VB 5.0 finally added support for one of the MTS attributes (`Transaction`), the MTS team was beholden to the VB team to make its technology available to the masses. Understandably, the VB team had its own agenda, and that caused the MTS and COM teams to abandon TLBs and IDL once and for all and define a new contract definition format that would be extensible in a cleaner, more accessible way than TLBs. That new contract format is the focus of most of the remainder of this book.

The previous discussion focused on the problems with how component contracts are described. Even if a perfect unified description format were to emerge, COM will still have a fundamental problem with the way contracts work. That problem has nothing to do with the way the contract is described. Rather, the problem is rooted deeply in the contract itself.

A component contract in COM is based on type descriptions. The type system used in these contracts is based on a subset of C++ that is guaranteed to be portable across compilers. This portability guarantee is not just in terms of the lexical programming language. Rather, the portability guarantee is in terms of the data representations used by most modern compilers. And therein lies the problem.

A component contract in COM is a **physical** (also known as **binary**) contract. That is, a COM component has hard requirements on how inter-component invocations must work. A COM contract mandates precise vtable offsets for every method. A COM contract mandates the exact stack discipline (e.g., __stdcall) to use during method invocation. A COM contract mandates the exact offset of every data structure that is passed as a method parameter. A COM contract mandates exactly which memory allocator to use for callee-allocated memory. A COM contract mandates the exact format of an object reference (called an **interface pointer**), including the exact format of the vptr and vtbl to be used. As far as the underlying technology of COM is concerned, a component contract is ultimately just a protocol for forming stack frames in memory, utterly free of semantic content.

The physical nature of a component contract in COM has its downsides. For one, a considerable amount of attention to detail is needed to make sure things work properly. This made COM a difficult technology to use even for developers with above-average attention spans, let alone casual programmers. Attempts by tool developers to hide this complexity have only compounded the problem, as any VB programmer who has dealt with VB's binary compatibility mode can attest.

The physical nature of a COM component contract is especially problematic in the face of component versioning. Versioning is hard enough when only semantic changes must be accounted for. When minute details such as vtable ordering or field alignment cause runtime errors, it only makes the problem worse. Granted, the precision of a contract definition in COM allowed for extremely efficient code to be generated; however, the brittleness exhibited by this code was arguably an unacceptable trade-off.

The Common Language Runtime

To address the problems with COM contracts and their definitions, the COM and MTS teams at Microsoft set out to develop a new component platform called COM3. Soon after that name was chosen, various parties within Microsoft discovered that COM3 was not a legal directory name under certain Microsoft platforms, so they quickly changed the name to the Component Object Runtime (COR). Other names used during the development cycle included the COM+ Runtime, Lightning, and the Universal Runtime (URT), and then finally, just prior to its first public beta, the technology was renamed to the **Common Language Runtime (CLR)**.

It is difficult to talk about the CLR without discussing the difference between a **specification** and an **implementation**. As part of the .NET initiative, Microsoft has submitted large parts of the platform to various standards organizations. In particular, Microsoft has submitted the Common Language Infrastructure (CLI) to the ECMA (http://www.ecma.org). The CLI includes the common type system (CTS), the Common Intermediate Language (CIL), and the underlying file and metadata formats. However, the CLR itself is not part of the ECMA submission. Rather, the CLR is an implementation of the CLI that is owned and controlled exclusively by Microsoft. In general, this book will not distinguish between the CLI specification and the CLR, as, at the time of this writing, no other implementations of the CLI were widely available.

Like the COM platform it replaces, the CLR focuses on the contracts between components. As with COM, these contracts are based on type. However, that is all the two contracts have in common.

Unlike COM, the CLR begins its life on Earth with a fully specified format for describing component contracts. This format is referred to generically as **metadata**. CLR metadata is machine-readable, and its format is fully specified. Additionally, the CLR provides facilities that let programs read and write metadata without knowledge of the underlying file format. CLR metadata is cleanly and easily extensible via custom attributes, which are themselves strongly typed. CLR metadata also contains component dependency and version information, allowing the use of a new range of techniques to handle component versioning. Finally, the presence of CLR metadata is mandatory; you cannot deploy or load a component without having access to its metadata, something that makes building CLR-based infrastructure and tools considerably easier than in environments (e.g., COM) where metadata is optional.

The second way that CLR contracts differ from COM contracts is in the very nature of the contract itself. In COM, a component contract implies a precise in-memory representation of a stack frame, a vtable, and any data structures that are passed as method parameters. In this respect, the CLR and COM could not be more different.

Contracts in the CLR describe the logical structure of types. Contracts in the CLR specifically do not describe the in-memory representation of anything. The CLR postpones the decisions regarding in-memory representations until the type is first loaded at runtime. This **virtualization** of contracts greatly reduces the brittleness of COM's binary contracts because no in-memory representations are assumed between components.

Because a CLR type definition is logical rather than physical, the precise code sequence for accessing a field or method is not baked into the contract. This gives the CLR a great deal of flexibility with respect to virtual method table layout, stack discipline, alignment, and parameter passing conventions, all of which could change between versions of the CLR without the need to recompile components. By referring to fields and methods by name and signature rather than by their offsets, the CLR avoids the order-of-declaration problems that plague COM. The actual address/offset of a member cannot be determined until the type is loaded and initialized at runtime.

The virtualization of data representations and method addressing has one significant requirement. Because the exact physical aspects of a contract (e.g., method table/field offsets) are not known when the consumer of the component is compiled, some mechanism is needed to defer the resolution of these offsets until the code is actually deployed against the final versions of the components on a particular processor architecture. To make this possible, components written for the CLR rarely contain machine code.

Rather, CLR-based components use **Common Intermediate Language (CIL)** for their method implementations.

It is easy to dismiss CIL as a processor-neutral instruction set. However, even if only one processor architecture were ever anticipated, CIL is important because of its ability to abstract away the physical data representation issues inherent in native machine code. To this end, the opcodes used by CIL to access fields and invoke methods do not use absolute offsets or addresses. Rather, those CIL instructions contain references to the metadata for the field or method they operate on. These references are based solely on the name and signature of the field or method and not on its location or offset. As long as the target component has a field or method that matches the name and signature, the physical offsets chosen by the CLR are immaterial.

It is important to note that the CLR never executes CIL directly. Rather, CIL is always translated into native machine code prior to its execution. This translation can be done either when the component is loaded into memory or preemptively when the component is installed on the deployment machine. In either case, when the CIL-to-native translation is done, the actual in-memory representations of any data types or method tables are used to generate the native machine code, resulting in efficient code with relatively little indirection.

The native code produced by the CLR yields the same high-performance physical coupling that is used in C++ and COM. However, unlike C++ and COM, which calculate this physical coupling at development time, the CLR does not resolve the details of the physical binding until CIL-to-native translation takes place. Because this translation is done on the deployment machine, the type definitions that are needed from external components will match the ones found on the deployment machine and not those on the developer's machine. This greatly reduces the brittleness of cross-component contracts without compromising performance.

Finally, because the CIL-to-native translation occurs on the deployment machine, any processor-specific layout or alignment rules that are used will match the processor architecture that the code will execute on. This is especially important at a time when the industry faces another processor shift as the installed base moves from the existing IA-32/Pentium architecture to the IA-64/Itanium architecture.

The Evolution of the Programming Model

The nature of CLR contracts naturally lends itself to a programming model that is independent of task or programming language. The programming model implied by the CLR is a refinement of the COM programming model and is very **type-centric** because every entity your program can deal with is affiliated with a type. This applies to objects, values, strings, primitives, and arrays. The type-centricity of the programming model is a necessity because one of the key services provided by the CLR is that code can be verifiably type-safe. This prevents malicious code from hijacking an object reference and invoking methods that are not part of the object's contract.

Although developers can recompile existing C++ programs for the CLR, most new programs written for the CLR are written at a higher level of abstraction. The CLR encourages a worldview in which everything is a type, an object, or a value. To this end, the CLR provides a range of services that collectively are called **managed execution**. Under managed execution, the CLR is omniscient and has complete information about all aspects of a running program. This includes knowledge of the state and liveness of local variables in a method. This includes knowledge of where the code for each stack frame originated. This includes knowledge of all extant objects and object references, including reachability information.

Programmers who target the CLR are encouraged to abandon the unmanaged programming style of the past. In particular, programmers are encouraged to give up the explicit management of memory and instead allocate and use instances of types. Similarly, programmers are encouraged to give up manual thread management and instead use the CLR's facilities for concurrent method execution.

For those readers who naturally resist giving up control to a body of software written by someone else, it is important to look back at the move from the DOS-based platform to Windows NT. Initially, there were developers who felt that moving from physical memory and interrupts to virtual memory and threads would either be too slow or too limiting to be practical for all but the most casual programmer. Many of those same arguments will be leveled against the CLR. Only time will tell whether the CLR is "too much abstraction"; however, it is the author's belief that the shift to managed execution environments such as the CLR or the Java virtual machine (JVM) is a step forward, not backward. As always, when programmers are faced with a choice between productivity and control, technologies that make them more productive tend to win out over time. Figure 1.1 shows the relationship between these two factors.

Another key aspect of the new programming model is the heavy reliance on metadata. Independent of the fact that metadata is required to translate CIL to native code, metadata is also made accessible to any program running inside or outside the CLR. The ability to reflect against metadata enables programming techniques in which programs are generated by other programs, not humans. **Generative programming** is a fairly new discipline. However, most applications of generative programs typically take one program's metadata as input and emit another program as output. The easy accessibility of the input program's metadata makes building generative architectures considerably easier.

The CLR also supports generative programming via a facility called the **CodeDOM**. The CodeDOM allows C#, VB.NET, and JavaScript programs to be constructed in memory as a strongly typed object model rather than as a text stream. The CodeDOM enables generative programs that emit source code to postpone the decision as to output language until the last

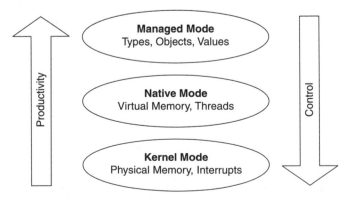

Figure 1.1: *The Move toward Managed Execution*

minute. Additionally, the CodeDOM supports in-memory compilation of code, and that allows new generative technologies (including compilers for new programming languages) to deal in a familiar high-level programming language rather than the low-level aspects of CIL and metadata attributes.

The CLR is a platform for loading and executing code. However, it is difficult to discuss the CLR (or its implied programming model) without addressing programming languages. In general, the CLR supports any programming language that has a compiler that emits CLR metadata and CIL. Programming languages are like flavors of ice cream in that what attracts a person to one language may repulse another person's esthetic sensibilities. To that end, this book will avoid language-specific discussions whenever possible. Unfortunately, some programming language must be used to demonstrate various facets and features of the CLR.

Examples in this book typically use C#. C# is used simply because it is the de facto standard language for the platform, as is evidenced by numerous support tools, documentation, and SDK samples. Note that although C# has its own unique syntax that is largely derived from C, C++, and Java, C# is ultimately just another programming language that imposes its own set of conventions and constructs over the underlying CLR. Table 1.1 shows the trade-offs between the five programming languages explicitly supported by Microsoft in Version 1.0 of the .NET Framework software development kit (SDK).

Where Are We?

The CLR is an evolutionary step in component software. Like its predecessor, COM, the CLR supports the integration of components based on strongly typed contracts. Unlike COM, however, these contracts are based on logical structure and imply no underlying physical data representation. This virtualization gets us one step closer to the Holy Grail of purely semantic contracts. Component contracts are described by CLR metadata, an extensible, machine-readable interchange format that is ubiquitous in CLR-based programs and architectures.

TABLE 1.1 .NET Language Features

Feature	VB.NET	JScript	C#	C++	ILASM
Compiler	VBC.EXE	JSC.EXE	CSC.EXE	CL.EXE	ILASM.EXE
CodeDOM support	Yes	Yes	Yes	No	No
Dynamic member addition	No	Yes	No	No	No
Late binding	Automatic	Automatic	Manual	Manual	Manual
User-defined value types	Yes	No	Yes	Yes	Yes
Case-sensitive	No	Yes	Yes	Yes	Yes
Unsigned integral types	No	Yes	Yes	Yes	Yes
Method overloading	Yes	Yes	Yes	Yes	Yes
Operator overloading	No	No	Yes	Yes	N/A
C-style pointers	No	No	Yes	Yes	Yes
Native/unmanaged methods	No	No	No	Yes	No
Code verification	Always	Always	Optional	Never	Optional
Opaque/unmanaged types	No	No	No	Yes	Yes
Templates/generics	No	No	No	Yes	No
Multiple inheritance	No	No	No	Yes	No

▛ 2 ▪

Components

T HE CLR HAS its own set of concepts and techniques for packaging, deploying, and discovering component code. These concepts and techniques are fundamentally different from those used by technologies such as COM, Java, or Win32. The difference is best understood by looking closely at the CLR loader, but first one must look at how code and metadata are actually packaged.

Modules Defined

Programs written for the CLR reside in **modules**. A CLR module is a byte stream, typically stored as a file in the local file system or on a Web server.

As shown in Figure 2.1, a CLR module uses an extended version of the PE/COFF executable file format used by Windows NT. By extending the PE/COFF format rather than starting from scratch, CLR modules are also valid Win32 modules that can be loaded using the LoadLibrary system call. However, a CLR module uses very little PE/COFF functionality. Rather, the majority of a CLR module's contents are stored as opaque data in the .text section of the PE/COFF file.

CLR modules contain code, metadata, and resources. The code is typically stored in common intermediate language (CIL) format, although it may also be stored as processor-specific machine instructions. The module's metadata describes the types defined in the module, including names, inheritance relationships, method signatures, and dependency

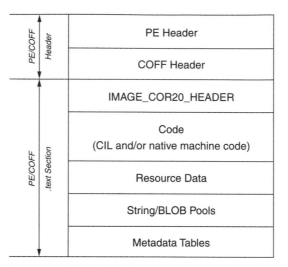

Figure 2.1: *CLR Module Format*

information. The module's resources consist of static read-only data such as strings, bitmaps, and other aspects of the program that are not stored as executable code.

The file format used by CLR modules is fairly well documented; however, few developers will ever encounter the format in the raw. Even developers who need to generate programs on-the-fly will typically use one of the two facilities provided by the CLR for programmatically generating modules. The IMetaDataEmit interface is a low-level COM interface that can be used to generate module metadata programmatically from classic C++. The System.Reflection.Emit namespace is a higher-level library that can be used to generate metadata and CIL programmatically from any CLR-friendly language (e.g., C#, VB.NET). The CodeDOM works at an even higher layer of abstraction, removing the need to know or understand CIL. However, for the vast majority of developers, who simply need to generate code during development and not at runtime, a CLR-friendly compiler will suffice.

The C# compiler (CSC.EXE), the VB.NET compiler (VBC.EXE), and the C++ compiler (CL.EXE) all translate source code into CLR modules. Each of the compilers uses command-line switches to control which kind of module to produce. As shown in Table 2.1, there are four possible options. In C# and VB.NET, one uses the /target command-line switch (or its

TABLE 2.1 Module Output Options

C#/VB.NET	C++	Directly Loadable?	Runnable from Shell?	Access to Console?
`/t:exe`	`/CLR`	Yes	Yes	Always
`/t:winexe`	`/CLR /link /subsystem:windows`	Yes	Yes	Never
`/t:library`	`/CLR /LD`	Yes	No	Host-dependent
`/t:module`	`/CLR:NOASSEMBLY /LD`	No	No	Host-dependent

shortcut, `/t`) to select which option to use. The C++ compiler uses a combination of several switches; however, one always uses the `/CLR` switch to force the C++ compiler to generate CLR-compliant modules. The remainder of this discussion will refer to the C# and VB.NET switches, given their somewhat simpler format.

The `/t:module` option produces a "raw" module that by default will use the `.netmodule` file extension. Modules in this format cannot be deployed by themselves as stand-alone code, nor can the CLR load them directly. Rather, developers must associate raw modules with a full-fledged component (called an assembly) prior to deployment. In contrast, compiling with the `/t:library` option produces a module that contains additional metadata that allows developers to deploy it as stand-alone code. A module produced by compiling with `/t:library` will have a `.DLL` file extension by default.

Modules compiled with `/t:library` can be loaded directly by the CLR but cannot be launched as an executable program from a command shell or the Windows Explorer. To produce this kind of module, you must compile using either the `/t:exe` or the `/t:winexe` option. Both options produce a file whose extension is `.EXE`. The only difference between these two options is that the former assumes the use of the console UI subsystem; the latter option assumes the GUI subsystem. If no `/t` option is specified, the default is `/t:exe`.

Modules produced using either the /t:exe or the /t:winexe option must have an **initial entry point** defined. The initial entry point is the method that the CLR will execute automatically when the program is launched. Programmers must declare this method static, and, in C# or VB.NET, they must name it Main. Programmers can declare the entry point method to return no value or to return an int as its exit code. They can also declare it to accept no parameters or to accept an array of strings, which will contain the parsed command-line arguments from the shell. The following are four legal implementations for the Main method in C#:

```
static void Main() { }
static void Main(string[] argv) { }
static int Main() { return 0; }
static int Main(string[] argv) { return 0; }
```

These correspond to the following in VB.NET:

```
shared sub Main() : end sub
shared sub Main(argv as string()) : end sub
shared function Main() : return 0 : end function
shared function Main(argv as string())
  return 0
end function
```

Note that these methods do not need to be declared public. Programmers must, however, declare the Main method inside a type definition, although the name of the type is immaterial.

The following is a minimal C# program that does nothing but print the string Hello, World to the console:

```
class myapp {
  static void Main() {
    System.Console.WriteLine("Hello, World");
  }
}
```

In this example, there is exactly one class that has a static method called Main. It would be ambiguous (and therefore an error) to present the C# or VB.NET compiler with source files containing more than one type having a static method called `Main`. To resolve this ambiguity, programmers can use the `/main` command-line switch to tell the C# or VB.NET compiler which type to use for the program's initial entry point.

Assemblies Defined

In order to deploy a CLR module, developers must first affiliate it with an **assembly**. An assembly is a logical collection of one or more modules. As just described, modules are physical constructs that exist as byte streams, typically in the file system. Assemblies are logical constructs and are referenced by location-independent names that must be translated to physical paths either in the file system or on the Internet. Those physical paths ultimately point to one or more modules that contain the type definitions, code, and resources that make up the assembly.

The CLR allows developers to compose assemblies from more than one module primarily to support deferred loading of infrequently accessed code without forming separate encapsulation boundaries. This feature is especially useful when developers are using code download because they can download the initial module first and download secondary modules only on an as-needed basis. The ability to build multimodule assemblies also enables mixed-language assemblies. This allows developers to work in a high-productivity language (e.g., Logo.NET) for the majority of their work but to write low-level grunge code in a more flexible language (e.g., C++). By conjoining the two modules into a single assembly, developers reference, deploy, and version the C++ and Logo.NET code as an atomic unit.

Parenthetically, though an assembly may consist of more than one module, a module is generally affiliated with only one assembly. As a point of interest, if two assemblies happen to reference a common module, the CLR will treat this as if there are two distinct modules, something that results in two distinct copies of every type in the common module. For that reason, the remainder of this chapter assumes that a module is affiliated with exactly one assembly.

Assemblies are the "atom" of deployment in the CLR and are used to package, load, distribute, and version CLR modules. Although an assembly may consist of multiple modules and auxiliary files, the assembly is named and versioned as an atomic unit. If one of the modules in an assembly must be versioned, then the entire assembly must be redeployed because the version number is part of the assembly name and not the underlying module name.

Modules typically rely on types from other assemblies. At the very least, every module relies on the types defined in the mscorlib assembly, which is where types such as System.Object and System.String are defined. Every CLR module contains a list of assembly names that identifies which assemblies are used by this module. These external assembly references use the logical name of the assembly, which contains no remnants of the underlying module names or locations. It is the job of the CLR to convert these logical assembly names into module pathnames at runtime, as is discussed later in this chapter.

To assist the CLR in finding the various pieces of an assembly, every assembly has exactly one module whose metadata contains the **assembly manifest**. The assembly manifest is an additional chunk of CLR metadata that acts as a directory of adjunct files that contain additional type definitions and code. The CLR can directly load modules that contain an assembly manifest. For modules that lack an assembly manifest, the CLR can load them only indirectly, by first loading a module whose assembly manifest refers to the manifest-less module. Figure 2.2 shows two modules: one with an assembly manifest and one without one. Note that of the four /t compiler options, only /t:module produces a module with no assembly manifest.

Figure 2.3 shows an application that uses a multimodule assembly, and Listing 2.1 shows the MAKEFILE that would produce it. In this example, code.netmodule is a module that does not contain an assembly manifest. To make it useful, one needs a second module (in this case, component.dll) that provides an assembly manifest that references code.netmodule as a subordinate module. One achieves this using the /addmodule switch when compiling the containing assembly. After this assembly is produced, all the types defined in component.dll and

/t:module

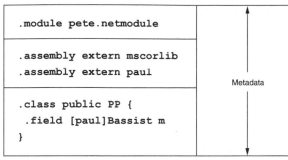

/t:library

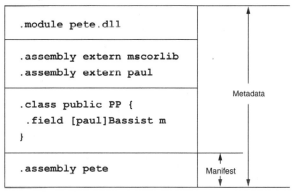

Figure 2.2: *Modules and Assemblies*

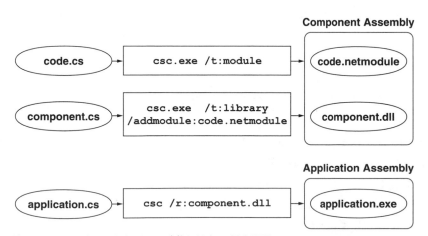

Figure 2.3: *Multimodule Assemblies Using CSC.EXE*

code.netmodule are scoped by the name of the assembly (component). Programs such as application.exe use the /r compiler switch to reference the module containing the assembly manifest. This makes the types in both modules available to the referencing program.

Listing 2.1: *Multimodule Assemblies Using CSC.EXE an1d NMAKE*

```
# code.netmodule cannot be loaded as is until an assembly
# is created
code.netmodule : code.cs
  csc /t:module code.cs

# types in component.cs can see internal and public members
# and types defined in code.cs
component.dll : component.cs code.netmodule
  csc /t:library /addmodule:code.netmodule component.cs

# types in application.cs cannot see internal members and
# types defined in code.cs (or component.cs)
application.exe : application.cs component.dll
  csc /t:exe /r:component.dll application.cs
```

The assembly manifest resides in exactly one module and contains all of the information needed to locate types and resources defined as part of the assembly. Figure 2.4 shows a set of modules composed into a single assembly, as well as the CSC.EXE switches required to build them. Notice that in this example, the assembly manifest contains a list of file references to the subordinate modules pete.netmodule and george.netmodule. In addition to these file references, each of the public types in these subordinate modules is listed using the .class extern directive, which allows the complete list of public types to be discovered without traversing the metadata for each of the modules in the assembly. Each entry in this list specifies both the file name that contains the type as well as the numeric metadata token that uniquely identifies the type within its module. Finally, the module containing the assembly manifest will contain the master list of externally referenced assemblies. This list consists of the dependencies of every module in the assembly, not just the dependencies of the current module. This allows all of the assembly's dependencies to be discovered by loading a single file.

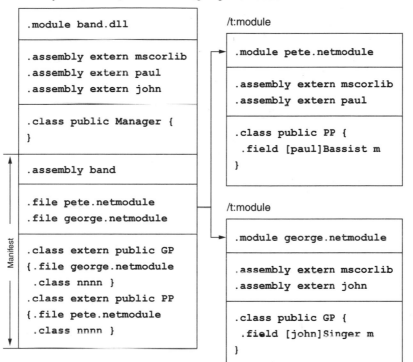

Figure 2.4: *A Multimodule Assembly*

Finally, the module containing the assembly manifest will contain the master list of externally referenced assemblies. This list consists of the dependencies of every module in the assembly not only the dependencies of the current module. This allows all of the assembly's dependencies to be discovered by loading a single file.

Assemblies form an **encapsulation boundary** to protect internal implementation details from interassembly access. Programmers can apply this protection to members of a type (e.g., fields, methods, constructors) or to a type as a whole. Marking a member or type as `internal` causes it to be available only to modules that are part of the same assembly. Marking a type or member as `public` causes it to be available to all code (both inside and outside the current assembly). Individual members of a type (e.g., methods, fields, constructors) can also be marked as `private`, which restricts access to only methods and constructors of the declaring type. This supports classic C++-style programming, in which intracomponent encapsulation is desired. In a similar vein, programmers can mark members of a type as `protected`, which broadens the access allowed by `private` to include methods and constructors of derived types. The `protected` and `internal` access modifiers can be combined, something that provides access to types that are either derived from the current type or are in the same assembly as the current type. Table 2.2 shows the language-specific modifiers as they apply both to types and to individual members. Note that members marked `protected internal` in C# require only that the accessor be in the same assembly or in a derived type. The CLR also supports an access modifier that requires the accessor to be both in the same assembly and in a derived type (marked `famandassem` in the metadata). However, VB.NET and C# do not allow programmers to specify this access modifier.

Assemblies scope the type definitions of a component. CLR types are uniquely identified by their assembly name/type name pair. This allows two definitions of the type `Customer` to coexist inside the runtime without ambiguity, provided that each one is affiliated with a different assembly. Although it is possible for multiple assemblies to define the type `Customer` without confusing the runtime, it does not help the programmer who

TABLE 2.2 Access Modifiers

		C#	VB.NET	Meaning
Type		`public`	`Public`	Type is visible everywhere.
		`internal`	`Friend`	Type is visible only inside assembly.
Member		`public`	`Public*`	Member is visible everywhere.
		`internal`	`Friend`	Member is visible only inside assembly.
		`protected`	`Protected`	Member is visible only inside declaring type and its subtypes.
		`protected internal`	`Protected Friend`	Member is visible only inside declaring type and its subtypes or other types inside assembly.
		`private`	`Private*`	Member is visible only inside declaring type.

*   VB.NET defaults to `Public` for methods and `Private` for fields declared using the Dim keyword.

wants to use two or more definitions of the same type name in a single program because the symbolic type name is always `Customer` no matter which assembly defines it. To address this limitation of most programming languages, CLR type names can have a **namespace prefix**. This prefix is a string that typically begins with either the organization name of the developer (e.g., `Microsoft`, `AcmeCorp`) or `System` if the type is part of the .NET framework. An emerging convention is to name the assembly based on the namespace prefix. For example, the .NET XML stack is deployed in the `System.Xml` assembly, and all of the contained types use the `System.Xml` namespace prefix. This is simply a convention and not a rule. For example, the type `System.Object` resides in an assembly called `mscorlib` and not in the assembly called `System`, even though there actually is an assembly called `System`.

Assembly Names

Each assembly has a four-part name that uniquely identifies it. This four-part name consists of the friendly name, culture, developer, and version of the component. These names are stored in the assembly manifest of the assembly itself as well as all assemblies that reference it. The CLR uses the four-part assembly name to find the correct component at load time. The CLR provides programmatic access to assembly names via the `System.Reflection.AssemblyName` type, which is easily accessed via the `System.Reflection.Assembly.GetName` method.

The `Name` property of the assembly name typically corresponds to the underlying file name of the assembly manifest sans any file extension that may be in use. This is the only part of the assembly name that is not optional. In simple scenarios, the `Name` property is all that the CLR needs to locate the correct component at load time. When one builds an assembly, this part of the name is automatically selected by your compiler based on the target file name.

All assembly names have a four-part version number (`Version`) of the form `Major.Minor.Build.Revision`. If you do not set this version number explicitly, its default value will be 0.0.0.0. The version number is set at build time, typically using a custom attribute in the source code. The `System.Reflection.AssemblyVersion` attribute accepts a variety of string

TABLE 2.3 Inside the AssemblyVersion Attribute

Attribute Parameter	Actual Value
1	1.0.0.0
1.2	1.2.0.0
1.2.3	1.2.3.0
1.2.3.4	1.2.3.4
1.2.*	1.2.d.s
1.2.3.*	1.2.3.s
‹absent›	0.0.0.0

*   Where *d* is the number of days since Feb. 1, 2000, and *s* is the number of seconds since midnight /2

formats, as shown in Table 2.3. When you specify the version number, the Major version number is mandatory. Any missing parts are assumed to be zero. At build time, the Revision can be specified as * (asterisk), and that causes the compiler to use the wall clock to produce a monotonically increasing revision number for each compilation. If an * is specified for the Build number, the number emitted into the assembly manifest is based on the number of days that have elapsed since February 1, 2000, ensuring that each day has its own unique build number but that a given build number will be applied only for a given 24-hour period. You cannot specify an * for the Major or Minor part of the version number. Later, this chapter discusses how the assembly loader and resolver use the Version of the assembly.

Assembly names can contain a CultureInfo attribute that identifies the spoken language and country code that the component has been developed for. Developers specify CultureInfo using the System.Reflection.AssemblyCulture attribute, which accepts a two-part string as specified by Internet Engineering Task Force (IETF) Request for Comments (RFC) 1766. The first part of the string identifies the spoken language using a two-character lowercase code. The (optional) second part of the string identifies the geographic region using a two-character uppercase code. The string `"en-US"` identifies U.S. English. Assemblies that contain a `Culture-Info` cannot contain code; rather, they must be **resource-only** assemblies (also known as **satellite** assemblies) that can contain only localized strings and other user-interface elements. Satellite assemblies allow a single DLL containing code to selectively load (and download) localized resources based on where they are deployed. Assemblies containing code (that is, the vast majority of assemblies) are said to be **culture-neutral** and have no culture identifier.

Finally, an assembly name can contain a **public key** that identifies the developer of the component. An assembly reference can use either the full 128-byte public key or the 8-byte public key token. The public key (token) is used to resolve file name collisions between organizations, allowing multiple `utilities.dll` components to coexist in memory and on disk provided that each one originates from a different organization, each of which is guaranteed to have a unique public key. The next section discusses public key management in detail.

Because assembly references occasionally must be entered by hand (for example, for use in configuration files), the CLR defines a standard format for writing four-part assembly names as strings. This format is known as the **display name** of the assembly. The display name of the assembly always begins with the simple `Name` of the assembly and is followed by an optional list of comma-delimited properties that correspond to the other three properties of the assembly name. If all four parts of the name are specified, the corresponding assembly reference is called a **fully qualified reference**. If one or more of the properties is missing, the reference is called a **partially qualified reference**.

Figure 2.5 shows a display name and the corresponding CLR attributes used to control each property. Note that if an assembly with no culture is desired, the display name must indicate this using `Culture=neutral`. Also, if an assembly with no public key is desired, the display name must indicate this using `PublicKeyToken=null`. Both of these are substantially different from a display name with no `Culture` or `PublicKeyToken` property. Simply omitting these properties from the display name results

Display Name of Assembly Reference

yourcode, **Version**=1.2.3.4, **Culture**=en-US, **PublicKeyToken**=1234123412341234

└──── or Neutral   └──── or Null

C# Code

```
using System.Reflection;
[assembly: AssemblyVersion("1.2.3.4") ]
[assembly: AssemblyCulture("en-US") ] // resource-only assm
[assembly: AssemblyKeyFile("acmecorp.snk") ]
```

Figure 2.5: *Fully Specified Assembly Names*

in a partially specified name that allows any `Culture` or `PublicKeyToken` to be matched.

In general, you should avoid using partially specified assembly names; otherwise, various parts of the CLR will work in unexpected (and unpleasant) ways. However, to deal with code that does not heed this warning, the CLR allows partial assembly names to be fully qualified in configuration files. For example, consider the following application configuration file:

```
<configuration>
  <runtime>
    <asm:assemblyBinding
     xmlns:asm="urn:schemas-microsoft-com:asm.v1"
    >
      <asm:qualifyAssembly partialName="AcmeCorp.Code"
          fullName="AcmeCorp.Code,version=1.0.0.0,
          publicKeyToken=a1690a5ea44bab32,culture=neutral"
      />
    </asm:assemblyBinding>
  </runtime>
</configuration>
```

This configuration allows the following call to `Assembly.Load`:

```
Assembly assm = Assembly.Load("AcmeCorp.Code");
```

The preceding call behaves identically to a call such as this one:

```
Assembly assm = Assembly.Load("AcmeCorp.Code, "+
    "version=1.0.0.0,publicKeyToken=a1690a5ea44bab32,"+
    "culture=neutral");
```

The `partialName` attribute must match the parameter to `Assembly`. `Load` completely; that is, each property specified in the call to `Assembly.Load` must also be present in the `partialName` attribute in the configuration file. Also, each property specified in the `partialName` attribute must be present in the call to `Assembly.Load`. Later, this chapter discusses how configuration files are located.

Public Keys and Assemblies

The CLR uses public key technology both to uniquely identify the developer of a component and to protect the component from being tampered with once it is out of the original developer's hands. Each assembly can have a public key embedded in its manifest that identifies the developer. Assemblies with public keys also have a **digital signature** that is generated before the assembly is first shipped that provides a secure hash of the assembly manifest, which itself contains hashes of all subordinate modules. This ensures that once the assembly ships, no one can modify the code or other resources contained in the assembly. This digital signature can be verified using only the public key; however, the signature can be generated only with the corresponding **private key**, which organizations must guard more closely than their source code. The current builds of the CLR use RSA public/private keys and Secure Hash Algorithm (SHA) hashing to produce the digital signature. Although the private key used to sign the assembly is a unique fingerprint for each organization, it does not provide the same level of **nonrepudiation** that digital certificates provide. For example, there is no way to look up the developer's identity based solely on an assembly's public key. The CLR does provide support for embedding digital certificates into assemblies, but that is outside the scope of this chapter (for more information, see Chapter 9).

The .NET SDK ships with a tool (`SN.EXE`) that simplifies working with public and private keys during development and deployment. Running `SN.EXE` with the `-k` option creates a new file that contains a newly generated public/private key pair. This file contains your private key, so it is critical that you practice safe computing and do not leave this file in an unsecured location. Because the private key is so critical, most organizations postpone the actual signing of the assembly until just before shipping, a practice called **delay signing**. To allow all developers in an organization to access the public key without having access to the private key, SN.EXE supports removing the private key portion using the -p option. This option creates a new file that contains only the public key. The conventional file extension for both public/private and public-only key files is .SNK.

The public key produced by SN.EXE is a 128-byte opaque algorithm-specific structure with an additional 32 bytes of header information. To keep the size of assembly references (and their display names) compact, an assembly reference can use a **public key token**, which is an 8-byte hash of the full public key. The assembly references emitted by most compilers use this token in lieu of the full public key to keep the overall size of the manifest small. You can calculate the token for a public key by using SN.EXE's -t or -T options. The former calculates the token based on an .SNK file containing only a public key. The latter calculates the token based on a public key stored in an assembly's manifest. Figure 2.6 shows the SN.EXE tool in action.

Development tools that support the CLR must provide some mechanism for developers to sign their assemblies, either via custom attributes or

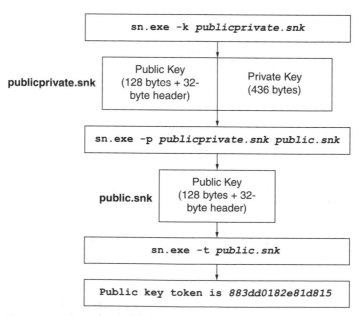

Figure 2.6: *Managing Public/Private Keys Using SN.EXE*

command-line switches. The `System.Reflection.AssemblyKeyFile` attribute tells the compiler where to find the `.SNK` file that contains the developer's public key. This attribute will work with either the public/private key pair or the public-only key, something that allows developers to build, test, and debug their components without access to the organization's private key. In order to build an assembly using only a public key, you must also use the `System.Reflection.AssemblyDelaySign` attribute to inform the compiler that no private key is present and that no meaningful digital signature can be produced. When delay signing is used, space is reserved for the digital signature so that a trusted member of the organization can re-sign the assembly without having to replicate the original developer's build environment. In general, assemblies that have a public key but do not have a valid signature cannot be loaded or executed. To allow delay-signed assemblies to be used during development, this policy can be disabled for a particular assembly or public key using the `-Vr` option to `SN.EXE`. Figure 2.7 shows the `AssemblyKeyFile` attribute used from C#. This figure also shows the resultant assembly as well as another assembly that references it. Note that the 128-byte public key is stored in

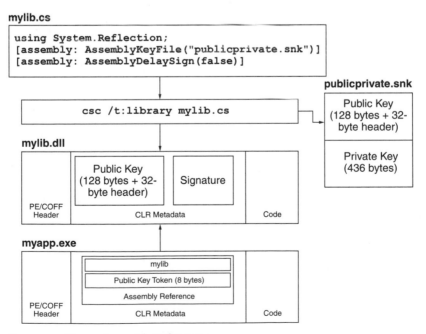

Figure 2.7: *Strong Assembly References*

the target's assembly manifest along with a digital signature to protect the assembly from tampering. Also note that the second assembly, which references the target, contains only the 8-byte public key token. Because the target assembly was built with delay signing turned off, the assembly can now be deployed and loaded in secured environments. In contrast, the target assembly produced by the C# compiler shown in Figure 2.8 is not suitable for deployment because it is built with delay signing turned on. However, after a trusted individual signs the assembly with the private key, the assembly is ready to be deployed. Note that in this example, the SN.EXE tool is used with the -R option, which overwrites the digital signature in the target assembly with one based on the public/private key provided on the command line. To manually verify that an assembly has been signed, you can use SN.EXE with the -v or -vf option. The latter overrides any configured settings that might disable signature verification.

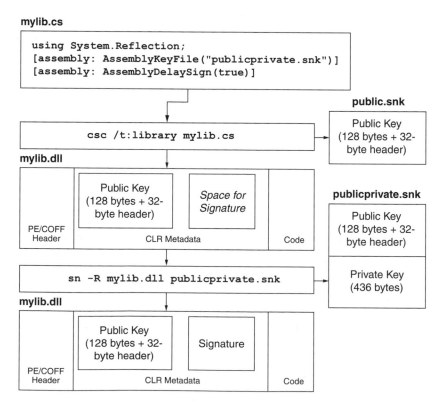

Figure 2.8: *Delay Signing an Assembly*

The CLR Loader

The **CLR loader** is responsible for loading and initializing assemblies, modules, resources, and types. The CLR loader loads and initializes as little as it can get away with. Unlike the Win32 loader, the CLR loader does not resolve and automatically load the subordinate modules (or assemblies). Rather, the subordinate pieces are loaded on demand only if they are actually needed (as with Visual C++ 6.0's delay-load feature). This not only speeds up program initialization time but also reduces the amount of resources consumed by a running program.

In the CLR, loading typically is triggered by the just in time (JIT) compiler based on types. When the JIT compiler tries to convert a method body from CIL to machine code, it needs access to the type definition of the declaring type as well as the type definitions for the type's fields. Moreover, the JIT compiler also needs access to the type definitions used by any local variables or parameters of the method being JIT-compiled. Loading a type implies loading both the assembly and the module that contain the type definition.

This policy of loading types (and assemblies and modules) on demand means that parts of a program that are not used are never brought into memory. It also means that a running application will often see new assemblies and modules loaded over time as the types contained in those files are needed during execution. If this is not the behavior you want, you have two options. One is to simply declare hidden static fields of the types you want to guarantee are loaded when your type is loaded. The other is to interact with the loader explicitly.

The loader typically does its work implicitly on your behalf. Developers can interact with the loader explicitly via the **assembly loader**. The assembly loader is exposed to developers via the `LoadFrom` static method on the `System.Reflection.Assembly` class. This method accepts a CODEBASE string, which can be either a file system path or a **uniform resource locator (URL)** that identifies the module containing the assembly manifest. If the specified file cannot be found, the loader will throw a `System.FileNotFoundException` exception. If the specified file can be found but is not a CLR module containing an assembly manifest, the loader will throw a `System.BadImageFormatException` exception. Finally, if the

CODEBASE is a URL that uses a scheme other than `file:`, the caller must have `WebPermission` access rights or else a `System.SecurityException` exception is thrown. Additionally, assemblies at URLs with protocols other than `file:` are first downloaded to the download cache prior to being loaded.

Listing 2.2 shows a simple C# program that loads an assembly located at `file://C:/usr/bin/xyzzy.dll` and then creates an instance of the contained type named `AcmeCorp.LOB.Customer`. In this example, all that is provided by the caller is the physical location of the assembly. When a program uses the assembly loader in this fashion, the CLR ignores the four-part name of the assembly, including its version number.

Listing 2.2: *Loading an Assembly with an Explicit CODEBASE*

```
using System;
using System.Reflection;
public class Utilities {
  public static Object LoadCustomerType() {
    Assembly a = Assembly.LoadFrom(
                      "file://C:/usr/bin/xyzzy.dll");
    return a.CreateInstance("AcmeCorp.LOB.Customer");
  }
}
```

Although loading assemblies by location is somewhat interesting, most assemblies are loaded by name using the **assembly resolver**. The assembly resolver uses the four-part assembly name to determine which underlying file to load into memory using the assembly loader. As shown in Figure 2.9, this name-to-location resolution process takes into account a variety of factors, including the directory the application is hosted in, versioning policies, and other configuration details (all of which are discussed later in this chapter).

The assembly resolver is exposed to developers via the `Load` method of the `System.Reflection.Assembly` class. As shown in Listing 2.3, this method accepts a four-part assembly name (either as a string or as an `AssemblyName` reference) and superficially appears to be similar to the `LoadFrom` method exposed by the assembly loader. The similarity is only skin deep because the `Load` method first uses the assembly resolver to find

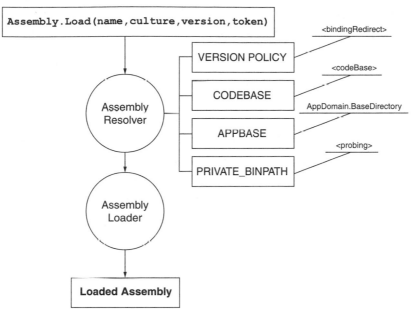

Figure 2.9: *Assembly Resolution and Loading*

a suitable file using a fairly complex series of operations. The first of these operations is to apply a version policy to determine exactly which version of the desired assembly should be loaded.

Listing 2.3: *Loading an Assembly Using the Assembly Resolver*

```
using System;
using System.Reflection;

public class Utilities {
  public static Object LoadCustomerType() {
    Assembly a = Assembly.Load(
      "xyzzy, Version=1.2.3.4, " +
      "Culture=neutral, PublicKeyToken=9a33f27632997fcc");
    return a.CreateInstance("AcmeCorp.LOB.Customer");
  }
}
```

The assembly resolver begins its work by applying any **version policies** that may be in effect. Version policies are used to redirect the assembly resolver to load an alternate version of the requested assembly. A version policy can map one or more versions of a given assembly to a different version; however, a version policy cannot redirect the resolver to an assembly whose name differs by any facet other than version number (i.e., an assembly named Acme.HealthCare cannot be redirected to an assembly named Acme.Mortuary). It is critical to note that version policies are applied only to assemblies that are fully specified by their four-part assembly name. If the assembly name is only partially specified (e.g., the public key token, version, or culture is missing), then no version policy will be applied. Also, no version policies are applied if the assembly resolver is bypassed by a direct call to Assembly.LoadFrom because you are specifying only a physical path and not an assembly name.

Version policies are specified via configuration files. These include a machine-wide configuration file and an application-specific configuration file. The **machine-wide** configuration file is always named machine.config and is located in the %SystemRoot%\Microsoft.Net\Framework\ V1.0.nnnn\CONFIG directory. The **application-specific** configuration file is always located at the APPBASE for the application. For CLR-based .EXE programs, the APPBASE is the base URI (or directory) for the location the main executable was loaded from. For ASP.NET applications, the APP-BASE is the root of the Web application's virtual directory. The name of the configuration file for CLR-based .EXE programs is the same as the executable name with an additional ".config" suffix. For example, if the launching CLR program is in C:\myapp\app.exe, the corresponding configuration file would be C:\myapp\app.exe.config. For ASP.NET applications, the configuration file is always named web.config.

Configuration files are based on the Extensible Markup Language (XML) and always have a root element named configuration. Configuration files are used by the assembly resolver, the remoting infrastructure, and by ASP.NET. Figure 2.10 shows the basic schema for the elements used to configure the assembly resolver. All relevant elements are under the assemblyBinding element in the urn:schemas-microsoft-com:asm. v1 namespace. There are application-wide settings to control probe paths and publisher version policy mode (both of which are described later in this chapter). Additionally, the dependentAssembly elements are used to specify version and location settings for each dependent assembly.

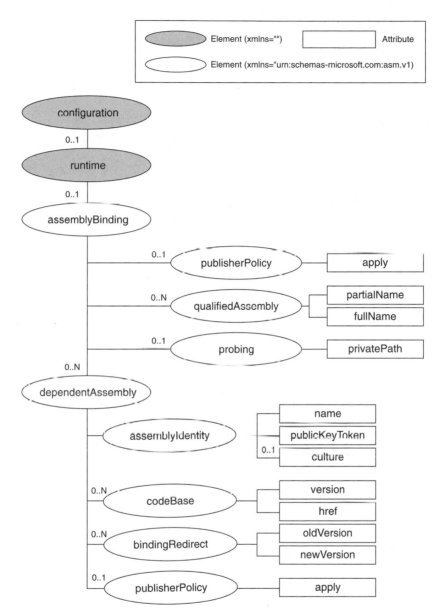

Figure 2.10: *Assembly Resolver Configuration File Format*

Listing 2.4 shows a simple configuration file containing two version policies for one assembly. The first policy redirects version 1.2.3.4 of the specified assembly (`Acme.HealthCare`) to version 1.3.0.0. The second policy redirects versions 1.0.0.0 through 1.2.3.399 of that assembly to version 1.2.3.7.

Listing 2.4: *Setting the Version Policy*

```xml
<?xml version="1.0" ?>

<configuration
    xmlns:asm="urn:schemas-microsoft-com:asm.v1"
>
  <runtime>
    <asm:assemblyBinding>
<!-- one dependentAssembly per unique assembly name -->
      <asm:dependentAssembly>
        <asm:assemblyIdentity
           name="Acme.HealthCare"
           publicKeyToken="38218fe715288aac" />
<!-- one bindingRedirect per redirection -->
        <asm:bindingRedirect oldVersion="1.2.3.4"
                     newVersion="1.3.0.0" />
        <asm:bindingRedirect oldVersion="1-1.2.3.399"
                     newVersion="1.2.3.7" />
      </asm:dependentAssembly>
    </asm:assemblyBinding>
  </runtime>
</configuration>
```

Version policy can be specified at three levels: per application, per component, and per machine. Each of these levels gets an opportunity to process the version number, with the results of one level acting as input to

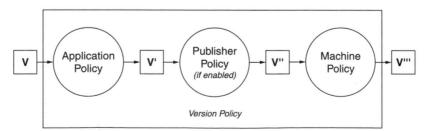

Figure 2.11: *Version Policy*

the level below it. This is illustrated in Figure 2.11. Note that if both the application's and the machine's configuration files have a version policy for a given assembly, the application's policy is run first, and the resultant version number is then run through the machine-wide policy to get the actual version number used to locate the assembly. In this example, if the machine-wide configuration file redirected version 1.3.0.0 of `Acme.` `HealthCare` to version 2.0.0.0, the assembly resolver would use version 2.0.0.0 when version 1.2.3.4 was requested because the application's version policy maps version 1.2.3.4 to 1.3.0.0.

In addition to application-specific and machine-wide configuration settings, a given assembly can also have a **publisher policy**. A publisher policy is a statement from the component developer indicating which versions of a given component are compatible with one another.

Publisher policies are stored as configuration files in the machine-wide global assembly cache. The structure of these files is identical to that of the application and machine configuration files. However, to be installed on the user's machine, the publisher policy configuration file must be wrapped in a surrounding assembly DLL as a custom resource. Assuming that the file `foo.config` contains the publisher's configuration policy, the following command line would invoke the assembly linker (`AL.EXE`) and create a suitable publisher policy assembly for `AcmeCorp.Code` version 2.0:

```
al.exe /link:foo.config
       /out:policy.2.0.AcmeCorp.Code.dll
       /keyf:pubpriv.snk
       /v:2.0.0.0
```

The name of the publisher policy file follows the form `policy.` `major.minor.assmname.dll`. Because of this naming convention, a given assembly can have only one publisher policy file per major.minor version. In this example, all requests for `AcmeCorp.Code` whose major.minor version is 2.0 will be routed through the policy file linked with `policy.2.0.AcmeCorp.Code.DLL`. If no such assembly exists in the **global assembly cache (GAC)**, then there is no publisher policy. As shown in Figure 2.11, publisher policies are applied after the application-specific version policy but before the machine-wide version policy stored in `machine.config`.

Given the fragility inherent in versioning component software, the CLR allows programmers to turn off publisher version policies on an application-wide basis. To do this, programmers use the `publisher-Policy` element in the application's configuration file. Listing 2.5 shows this element in a simple configuration file. When this element has the attribute `apply="no"`, the publisher policies will be ignored for this application. When this attribute is set to `apply="yes"` (or is not specified at all), the publisher policies will be used as just described. As shown in Figure 2.10, the `publisherPolicy` element can enable or disable publisher policy on an application-wide or an assembly-by-assembly basis.

Listing 2.5: *Setting the Application to Safe Mode*

```
<?xml version="1.0" ?>

<configuration xmlns:rt="urn:schemas-microsoft-com:asm.v1">
  <runtime>
    <rt:assemblyBinding>
      <rt:publisherPolicy apply="no" />
    </rt:assemblyBinding>
  </runtime>
</configuration>
```

Resolving Names to Locations

After the assembly resolver decides which version of the assembly to load, it must locate a suitable file to pass to the underlying assembly loader. The CLR looks first in the directory specified by the DEVPATH operating system (OS) environment variable. This environment variable is typically not set on the deployment machine. Rather, it is intended for developer use only and exists to allow delay-signed assemblies to be loaded from a shared file-system directory. Moreover, the DEVPATH environment variable is considered only if the following XML configuration file element is present in the `machine.config` file:

```
<configuration>
  <runtime>
    <developmentMode developerInstallation="true" />
  </runtime>
</configuration>
```

Because the DEVPATH environment variable is not intended for deployment, the remainder of the chapter will ignore its existence.

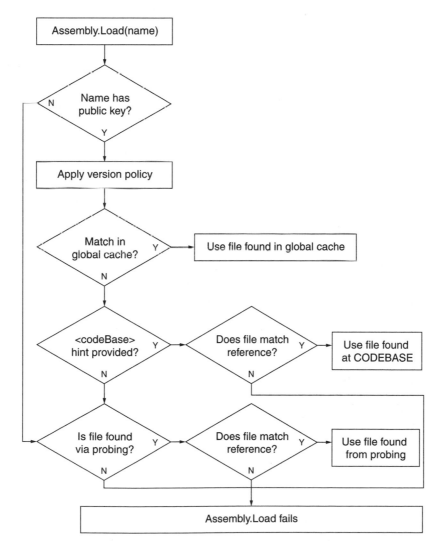

Figure 2.12: *Assembly Resolution*

Figure 2.12 shows the entire process the assembly resolver goes through in order to find an appropriate assembly file. In normal deployment scenarios, the first location that the assembly resolver uses to find an assembly is the global assembly cache (GAC). The GAC is a machine-wide code cache that contains assemblies that have been installed for machine-wide use. The GAC allows administrators to install assemblies once per machine for all applications to use. To avoid system corruption, the GAC accepts only assemblies that have valid digital signatures and public keys. Additionally, entries in the GAC can be deleted only by administrators, something that prevents non-admin users from deleting or moving critical system-level components.

To avoid ambiguity, the assembly resolver will look in the GAC only if the requested assembly name contains a public key. This prevents requests for generic names such as `utilities` from being satisfied by the wrong implementation. The public key can be provided either explicitly as part of an assembly reference or parameter to `Assembly.Load` or implicitly via the `qualifyAssembly` configuration file element.

The GAC is controlled by a system-level component (`FUSION.DLL`) that keeps a cache of DLLs under the `%WINNT%\Assembly` directory. `FUSION.DLL` manages this directory hierarchy for you and provides access to the stored files based on the four-part assembly name, as shown in Table 2.4. Although one can traverse the underlying directories, the scheme used by FUSION to store cached DLLs is an implementation detail that is guaranteed to change as the CLR evolves. Instead, you must interact with the GAC via the `GACUTIL.EXE` tool or some other facade over the FUSION

TABLE 2.4 Global Assembly Cache

Name	Version	Culture	Public Key Token	Mangled Path
yourcode	1.0.1.3	de	89abcde...	t3s\e4\yourcode.dll
yourcode	1.0.1.3	en	89abcde...	a1x\bb\yourcode.dll
yourcode	1.0.1.8	en	89abcde...	vv\a0\yourcode.dll
libzero	1.1.0.0	en	89abcde...	ig\u\libzero.dll

application programming interface (API). One such facade is SHFUSION. DLL, a Windows Explorer shell extension that provides a user-friendly interface to the GAC.

If the assembly resolver cannot find the requested assembly in the GAC, the assembly resolver then tries to use a **CODEBASE hint** to access the assembly. A CODEBASE hint simply maps an assembly name to a file name or URL where the module containing the assembly manifest is located. Like version policies, CODEBASE hints are located in both application- and machine-wide configuration files. Listing 2.6 shows an example configuration file that contains two CODEBASE hints. The first hint maps version 1.2.3.4 of the Acme.HealthCare assembly to the file C:\acmestuff\Acme.HealthCare.DLL. The second hint maps version 1.3.0.0 of the same assembly to the file located at http://www.acme.com/ bin/Acme.HealthCare.DLL.

Assuming that a CODEBASE hint is provided, the assembly resolver can simply load the corresponding assembly file, and the loading of the assembly proceeds as if the assembly were loaded by an explicit CODE-BASE a la Assembly.LoadFrom. However, if no CODEBASE hint is provided, the assembly resolver must begin a potentially expensive procedure for finding an assembly file that matches the request.

Listing 2.6: *Specifying the CODEBASE Using Configuration Files*

```
<?xml version="1.0" ?>

<configuration
    xmlns:asm="urn:schemas-microsoft-com:asm.v1"
>
  <runtime>
    <asm:assemblyBinding>
<!-- one dependentAssembly per unique assembly name -->
      <asm:dependentAssembly>
        <asm:assemblyIdentity
            name="Acme.HealthCare"
            publicKeyToken="38218fe715288aac" />
<!-- one codeBase per version -->
        <asm:codeBase
            version="1.2.3.4"
            href="file://C:/acmestuff/Acme.HealthCare.DLL"/>
        <asm:codeBase
            version="1.3.0.0"
```

```
                href="http://www.acme.com/Acme.HealthCare.DLL"/>
            </asm:dependentAssembly>
          </asm:assemblyBinding>
        </runtime>
      </configuration>
```

If the assembly resolver cannot locate the assembly using the GAC or a CODEBASE hint, it performs a search through a series of directories relative to the root directory of the application. This search is known as **probing**. Probing will search only in directories that are at or below the APPBASE directory (recall that the APPBASE directory is the directory that contains the application's configuration file). For example, given the directory hierarchy shown in Figure 2.13, only directories m, common, shared, and q are eligible for probing. That stated, the assembly resolver will probe only into subdirectories that are explicitly listed in the application's configuration file. Listing 2.7 shows a sample configuration file that sets the relative search path to the directories shared and common. All subdirectories of APPBASE that are not listed in the configuration file will be pruned from the search.

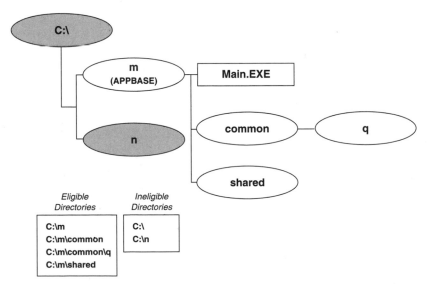

Figure 2.13: *APPBASE and the Relative Search Path*

Listing 2.7: *Setting the Relative Search Path*

```
<?xml version="1.0" ?>
<configuration
    xmlns:asm="urn:schemas-microsoft-com:asm.v1"
>
  <runtime>
    <asm:assemblyBinding>
      <asm:probing privatePath="shared;common"  />
    </asm:assemblyBinding>
  </runtime>
</configuration>
```

When probing for an assembly, the assembly resolver constructs CODEBASE URLs based on the simple name of the assembly, the relative search path just described, and the requested culture of the assembly (if present in the assembly reference). Figure 2.14 shows an example of the CODEBASE URLs that will be used to resolve an assembly reference with no culture specified. In this example, the simple name of the assembly is `yourcode` and the relative search path is the `shared` and `common` directories. The assembly resolver first looks for a file named `yourcode.dll` in the APPBASE directory. If there is no such file, the resolver then assumes that the assembly is in a directory with the same name and looks for a file with that name under the `yourcode` directory. If the file is still not found, this process is repeated for each of the entries in the relative search path until a file named `yourcode.dll` is found. If the file is found, then probing stops. Otherwise, the probe process is repeated, this time looking for the file named `yourcode.exe` in the same locations as before. Assuming that a file is found, the assembly resolver verifies that the file matches all properties of the assembly name specified in the assembly reference and then loads the assembly. If one of the properties of the file's assembly name does not match all of the (post-version policy) assembly reference's properties, the `Assembly.Load` call fails. Otherwise, the assembly is loaded and ready for use.

Probing is somewhat more complex when the assembly reference contains a culture identifier. As shown in Figure 2.15, the preceding algorithm is augmented by looking in subdirectories whose names match the

Assembly Reference

> **yourcode,** Culture=**neutral,...**

APPBASE

> **file://C:/myapp/**myapp.exe

Application Configuration File

```
<configuration xmlns:asm="...">
  <runtime>
    <asm:assemblyBinding>
      <asm:probing
        privatePath="shared;common"/>
    </asm:assemblyBinding>
  </runtime>
</configuration>
```

Potential CODEBASEs (in order)

```
file://C:/myapp/yourcode.dll
file://C:/myapp/yourcode/yourcode.dll
file://C:/myapp/shared/yourcode.dll
file://C:/myapp/shared/yourcode/yourcode.dll
file://C:/myapp/common/yourcode.dll
file://C:/myapp/common/yourcode/yourcode.dll
```

```
file://C:/myapp/yourcode.exe
file://C:/myapp/yourcode/yourcode.exe
file://C:/myapp/shared/yourcode.exe
file://C:/myapp/shared/yourcode/yourcode.exe
file://C:/myapp/common/yourcode.exe
file://C:/myapp/common/yourcode/yourcode.exe
```

Figure 2.14: *Culture-Neutral Probing*

requested culture. In general, applications should keep relative search paths small to avoid excessive load-time delays.

Versioning Hazards

The preceding discussion of how the assembly resolver determines which version of an assembly to load focuses primarily on the mechanism used by the CLR. What was not discussed is what policies a developer should use to determine when, how, and why to version an assembly. Given that the platform being described has not actually shipped at the time of this writing, it

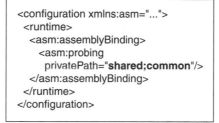

Assembly Reference

> **yourcode,** Culture=**en-US,...**

APPBASE

> **file://C:/myapp/**myapp.exe

Application Configuration File

```
<configuration xmlns:asm="...">
  <runtime>
    <asm:assemblyBinding>
      <asm:probing
        privatePath="shared;common"/>
    </asm:assemblyBinding>
  </runtime>
</configuration>
```

Potential CODEBASEs (in order)

```
file://C:/myapp/en-US/yourcode.dll
file://C:/myapp/en-US/yourcode/yourcode.dll
file://C:/myapp/shared/en-US/yourcode.dll
file://C:/myapp/shared/en-US/yourcode/yourcode.dll
file://C:/myapp/common/en-US/yourcode.dll
file://C:/myapp/common/en-US/yourcode/yourcode.dll
```

```
file://C:/myapp/en-US/yourcode.exe
file://C:/myapp/en-US/yourcode/yourcode.exe
file://C:/myapp/shared/en-US/yourcode.exe
file://C:/myapp/shared/en-US/yourcode/yourcode.exe
file://C:/myapp/common/en-US/yourcode.exe
file://C:/myapp/common/en-US/yourcode/yourcode.exe
```

Figure 2.15: *Culture-Dependent Probing*

is somewhat difficult to list a set of "best practices" that are known to be valid based on hard-won experiences. However, it is reasonable to look at the known state of the CLR and extrapolate a set of guidelines.

It is important to note that assemblies are versioned as a unit. Trying to replace a subset of the files in an assembly without changing the version number will certainly lead to unpredictability. To that end, the remainder of this section looks at versioning with respect to an assembly as a whole rather than versioning individual files in an assembly.

The question of when to change version numbers is an interesting one. Obviously, if the public contract of a type changes, the type's assembly must be given a new version number. Otherwise, programs that depend on one version of the type signature will get runtime errors when a type with a different signature is loaded. This means that if you add or remove a `public` or `protected` member of a public type, you must change the version number of the type's assembly. If you change the signature of a public or protected member of a public type (e.g., adding a method parameter, changing a field's type), you also need a new assembly version number. These are absolute rules. Violating them will result in unpredictability.

The more difficult question to answer relates to modifications that do not impact the public signature of the assembly's types. For example, changes to a member that is marked as `private` or `internal` are considered nonbreaking changes, at least as far as signature matching is concerned. Because no code outside of your assembly can rely upon `private` or `internal` members, having signature mismatches occur at runtime is a nonissue because it doesn't happen. Unfortunately, signature mismatches are only the tip of the iceberg.

There is a reasonable argument to be made for changing the version number for every build of an assembly, even if no publicly visible signatures have changed. This approach is supported by the fact that even a seemingly innocuous change to a single method body may have a subtle but very real rippling effect on the behavior of programs that use the assembly. If the developer gives each build of an assembly a unique version number, code that is tested against a particular build won't be surprised at deployment time.

The argument against giving each build of an assembly a unique version number is that "safe" fixes to the code won't be picked up by programs that are not rebuilt against the new version. This argument doesn't hold water in the face of publisher policy files. Developers who use unique version numbers for every build are expected to provide publisher policy files that state which versions of their assembly are backward-compatible. By default, this gives consumers of the down-level version an automatic upgrade to the newer (and hopefully faster or less buggy) assembly. For times when the assembly's developer guesses wrong, each application can use the `publisherPolicy` element in its configuration file to disable the automatic upgrade, in essence running the application in "safe mode."

As discussed earlier, the CLR assembly resolver supports side-by-side installation of multiple versions of an assembly via CODEBASE hints, private probe paths, and the GAC. This allows several versions of a given assembly to peacefully coexist in the file system. However, things become somewhat unpredictable if more than one of these assemblies is actually loaded into memory at any one time, either by independent programs or by a single program. Side-by-side execution is much harder to deal with than side-by-side installation.

The primary problem with supporting multiple versions in memory at once is that, to the runtime, the types contained in those assemblies are distinct. That is, if an assembly contains a type called `Customer`, then when two different versions of the assembly are loaded, there are two distinct types in memory, each with its own unique identity. This has several serious downsides. For one, each type has its own copy of any static fields. If the type needed to keep track of some shared state is independent of how many versions of the type had been loaded, it could not use the obvious solution of using a static field. Rather, developers would need to rewrite the code with versioning in mind and store the shared state in a location that is not version-sensitive. One approach would be to store the shared state in some runtime-provided place such as the ASP.NET application object. Another approach would be to define a separate type that contained only the shared state as static fields. Developers could deploy this type in a separate assembly that would never be versioned, thus ensuring that only one copy of the static fields would be in memory for a given application.

Another problem related to side-by-side execution arises when versioned types are passed as method parameters. If the caller and callee of a method have differing views on which version of an assembly will be loaded, the caller will pass a parameter whose type is unknown to the callee. Developers can avoid this problem by always defining parameter types using version-invariant types for all public (cross-assembly) methods. More importantly, these shared types need to be deployed in a separate assembly that itself will not be versioned.

The metadata for an assembly has three distinguished attributes that allows the developer to specify whether multiple versions of the assembly can be loaded at the same time. If none of these attributes is present, the assembly is assumed safe for side-by-side execution in all scenarios. The `nonsidebysideappdomain` attribute indicates that only one version of the assembly can be loaded per AppDomain. The `nonsidebyside-process` attribute indicates that only one version of the assembly can be loaded per process. Finally, the `nonsidebysidemachine` attribute indicates that only one version of the assembly can be loaded at a time for the entire machine. At the time of this writing, these metadata bits are ignored by the assembly resolver and loader. However, they do serve as a hint that hopefully will be enforced in future versions of the CLR.

Where Are We?

Modules and assemblies are the component building blocks of the CLR. Each CLR type resides in exactly one physical file (called a module), which contains the code and metadata that make that type real. To be deployed, a module must be associated with a logical assembly that gives the module's types a fully qualified name. The CLR loader works primarily in terms of assemblies, with modules (and types) being loaded only as they are needed. The CLR loader typically works in terms of location-independent assembly names that are resolved to physical file paths or URLs prior to loading. This not only allows more flexible deployment and versioning, but it also ensures that the component's origin cannot be spoofed through the use of public keys and digital signatures.

3

Type Basics

C HAPTER 2 DESCRIBED how CLR-based programs are built out of one or more molecules called assemblies. Furthermore, these assemblies are themselves built out of one or more atoms called modules. This chapter attempts to split the atom of the module into subatomic particles called types. The focus of this chapter is the CLR's common type system (CTS), which transcends specific programming languages. However, to make the CTS real, one typically uses a programming language. To that end, this chapter illustrates CTS concepts and mechanisms through the lens of C#. That said, the reader is encouraged not to get too enamoured with language syntax and instead focus on the core concepts of the CTS.

Type Fundamentals

Types are the building block of every CLR program. Once developers decide how to partition a project into one or more assemblies, most of their time is spent thinking about how their types will work and how their types will interrelate. Programming languages such as C# and VB.NET may have several constructs for expressing types (e.g., classes, structs, enums, etc.), but ultimately all of these constructs map down to a CLR type definition.

A **CLR type** is a named, reusable abstraction. The description of a CLR type resides in the metadata of a CLR module. That module will also contain any CIL or native code required to make the type work. CLR type

This chapter describes the common type system, which is much broader than most programming languages can handle. In addition to the CTS, the ECMA CLI submission carves out a subset of the CTS that all CLI-compliant languages are expected to support. This subset is called the Common Language Specification (CLS). Component writers are strongly encouraged to make their components' functionality accessible through CLS-compliant types and members. To that end, the CLI defines an attribute, `System.CLSCompliant`, that instructs compilers to enforce CLS compliance for all public members. The primary limitations of the CLS are the lack of support for unsigned integral types or pointers, and restrictions on how overloading may be used.

names have three parts: an assembly name, an optional namespace prefix, and a local name. One controls the assembly name by using the custom attributes described in Chapter 2. One controls the namespace prefix and the local name by using various programming language constructs. For example, the C# code shown in Listing 3.1 defines a type whose local name is `Customer` and whose namespace prefix is `AcmeCorp.LOB`. As discussed in Chapter 2, the namespace prefix often matches the name of the containing assembly, but this is simply a convention, not a hard requirement.

Listing 3.1: *Defining a Type in C#*

```
namespace AcmeCorp.LOB {
  public sealed class Customer {
// type name is AcmeCorp.LOB.Customer
  }
}
```

A CLR type definition consists of zero or more **members**. The members of a type control how the type can be used as well as how the type works. Each member of a type has its own **access modifier** (e.g., `public`, `internal`) that controls access to the member. The accessible members of a type are often referred to collectively as the **contract** of the type.

In addition to controlling access to a given member, developers can control whether an instance of the type is needed to access the member. Most kinds of members can be defined as either per instance or per type. A **per-instance member** requires an instance of the type in order to access it. A **per-type member** does not have this requirement. In C# and VB.NET, members default to per instance. One can change this to per type using the `static` keyword in C# or the `Shared` keyword in VB.NET.

There are three fundamental kinds of type members: fields, methods, and nested types. A **field** is a named unit of storage that is affiliated with the declaring type. A **method** is a named operation that can be invoked and executed. A **nested type** is simply a second type that is defined as part of the implementation of the declaring type. All other type members (e.g., properties, events) are simply methods that have been augmented with additional metadata.

The fields of a type control how memory is allocated. The CLR uses the field declarations of a type to determine how much storage to allocate for the type. The CLR will allocate memory for `static` fields once: when the type is first loaded. The CLR will allocate memory for non-`static` (instance) fields each time it allocates an instance of the type. The CLR initializes all `static` fields to a default value upon allocation. For numeric types, the default value is zero. For Booleans, the default value is false. For object references, the default value is null. The CLR will also initialize the fields of heap-allocated instances to the default values just described.

The CLR guarantees the initial state of `static` fields and fields in heap-allocated instances. The CLR treats local variables allocated on the stack differently. By adding an attribute to its metadata, a given method can indicate that its local variables should be auto-initialized to their default values. Languages such as VB.NET add this attribute, so the CLR auto-initializes local variables in Visual Basic as part of the method prolog. The C# compiler also adds this attribute; however, C# requires local variables to be explicitly initialized. To avoid introducing security holes, the CLR's verifier requires that this attribute be present on verifiable methods.

To see an example of fields in use, consider the C# code in Listing 3.2. The comments next to the field declarations indicate the initial values that the CLR will use when allocating the memory for the fields. In the case of customerCount, the storage will be allocated and initialized once prior to the type's first use. In the case of all of the other fields, the storage will be allocated and initialized each time a new instance of AcmeCorp.LOB.Customer is allocated on the heap. This is illustrated in Figure 3.1. Note that in this example, there are multiple copies of the balance field, but only one copy of the customerCount field. To access the customerCount field, simply qualify the field name with the declaring type name, as follows:

```
AcmeCorp.LOB.Customer.customerCount = 3;
int x = AcmeCorp.LOB.Customer.customerCount - 7;
```

Listing 3.2: *Fields in C#*

```
namespace AcmeCorp.LOB {
  public sealed class Customer {
    internal static int customerCount; // starts at 0

    internal bool isGoodCustomer;        // starts at false
    internal string lastName;            // starts at null
    internal double balance;             // starts at 0.0
    internal byte extra;                 // starts at 0
    internal char firstInitial;          // starts at '\0'
  }
}
```

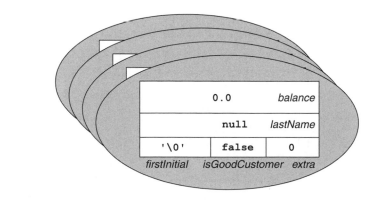

customerCount

0

Figure 3.1: *CLR Fields*

To access one of the instance fields, one needs a valid instance of the type:

```
AcmeCorp.LOB.Customer o = new AcmeCorp.LOB.Customer();
o.balance = 3;
if (!o.isGoodCustomer) {
  o.firstInitial = 'I';
  o.lastName = "Deadbeat";
}
```

Note that this example uses the C# new operator to allocate a new instance on the heap.

By default, the exact memory layout of a type is opaque. The CLR uses a virtualized layout scheme and will often reorder the fields to optimize memory access and usage, as in Figure 3.1. Note that the order of declaration was isGoodCustomer, lastName, balance, and extra, followed by firstInitial. If the CLR laid out the type's fields in order of declaration, it would have to insert a good deal of padding between fields in order to avoid unaligned access to individual fields—something that would kill performance. To avoid this, the CLR reorders the fields so that no packing is necessary. On the author's 32-bit IA-32 machine, that means that the following order is used: balance, lastName, firstInitial, and isGood-Customer, followed by extra. This layout results in no wasted padding as well as perfectly aligned data. Be aware, however, that the exact layout policy used by the CLR is undocumented, and one should not rely on a specific policy for all versions of the CLR.

It is sometimes desirable to constrain a field to a constant value that cannot change for the lifetime of the field. The CLR supports two ways of declaring fields whose value is constant. The first technique—used for fields whose constant value can be calculated at compile time—is the most efficient: The field's static value is only stored as a literal in the metadata of the type's module, it is not a true field at runtime. Rather, compilers are required to inline away any access to literal fields, in essence embedding the literal value into the instruction stream. To declare a literal field in C#, one must use the const keyword. This will also require an initialization expression whose value can be calculated at compile time. The following is an example of such a field declaration:

```
public sealed class Customer {
  public const int MAX_CUSTOMER_AGE = 128 * 365;
}
```

Any attempts to modify the field will be caught as compile-time errors.

The initial value of literal fields must be known at compile time. In the second technique, the CLR allows programmers to declare fields as immutable yet dynamically initializable by declaring a field `initonly`. Applying the `initonly` attribute to a field disallows modification of the field's value once the constructor has completed execution. To specify an `initonly` field in C#, one must use the `readonly` keyword. One can specify the initial value either by using an initialization expression or simply by assigning to the field inside the type's constructor method. In either case, the value used can take into account dynamic aspects of the program's execution state. The following shows the canonical example of an `initonly` field in C#:

```
public sealed class Customer {
  public readonly long created = System.DateTime.Now.Ticks;
}
```

Note that this code dynamically generates the initial value of the `created` field based on the current time. That stated, once the value of `created` is set, one cannot change it after the new instance's constructor has completed execution.

Developers use the fields of a type to specify the state of an object. They specify an object's behavior using methods. Methods are named operations that are affiliated with a type. One can declare a method to return a typed value or to return no value. In C# and C++, one indicates the latter by using the `void` keyword as the return type. In VB.NET, one declares methods that return no value by using the `Sub` keyword; one defines methods that return a typed value by using the `Function` keyword.

As with fields, one can restrict access to methods using access modifiers such as `private` or `public`. As with fields, one can designate methods as per instance or per type (`static`). One can access a `static` method without an instance of the type. A non-`static` method requires an instance in order to be invoked (however, languages such as C++ allow a null reference to be used to invoke non-virtual, non-static methods). Consider the following type declaration:

```
namespace AcmeCorp.LOB {
  public sealed class Customer {
    public static int GetCount() { return 0; }
    public static void ResetCount() { }

    public void ClearStatus() { }
    public byte GetExtraInfo() { return 0; }
  }
}
```

This type has four methods declared. Two of the methods (GetCount and ResetCount) are static and do not require an instance to invoke. One accesses these methods using the type name for qualification, as follows:

```
int c = AcmeCorp.LOB.Customer.GetCount();
AcmeCorp.LOB.Customer.ResetCount();
```

The other two methods (ClearStatus and GetExtraInfo) require a valid instance to invoke against:

```
AcmeCorp.LOB.Customer o
            = new AcmeCorp.LOB.Customer();
if (o.GetExtraInfo() == 42)
  o.ClearStatus();
```

Some programming languages (e.g., C++) allow programmers to invoke static methods using either an instance or the type name as a qualification. Other programming languages (e.g., C#) do not allow programmers to use the instance name when accessing static members. Consult the language reference for your language of choice.

In addition to returning a typed value, a method can also accept **parameters**. Method parameters act as additional local variables for the method body. One specifies the type and name of each parameter statically as part of the method declaration. The caller provides the value of each parameter dynamically at invocation time. By default, the method's parameters are independent copies of the values provided by the caller, and changes made to the parameter value inside the method body do not affect the caller. This parameter passing style is called **pass-by-value**. If only one copy of the parameter value is to be shared between the caller and callee (i.e., the method body), then one must explicitly declare the parameter as **pass-by-reference** using a programming language-specific construct. In VB.NET, one specifies the mode using either the `ByVal` or `ByRef` parameter modifier. In C#, the default is pass-by-value, and adding either the `ref` or the `out` parameter modifier changes the mode to pass-by-reference. Both keywords indicate pass-by-reference; the `out` keyword also indicates that the initial value of the parameter is undefined. This extra bit of information is useful both to the CLR verifier and to RPC-style marshaling engines.

Consider the C# type definition shown in Listing 3.3. In this example, the `Recalc` method accepts three parameters. The first parameter (`initialBalance`) is passed by value, and this means that the method body has its own private copy of the value. The other two parameters are declared as pass-by-reference, and this means that any changes the method body makes to the parameters will be reflected in the caller's version of the parameter. In the `CheckJohnSmith` method shown in this example, that means that the `Recalc` method can modify the two local variables `current` and `sol`. The local variable that was passed by value (`initial`), however, will not see any changes made in the `Recalc` method body.

Listing 3.3: *Method Parameters in C#*

```
namespace AcmeCorp.LOB {
  public sealed class Customer {
    public static void Recalc(double initialBalance,
                              ref double currentBalance,
                              out bool overdrawn)
    {
      initialBalance = initialBalance / 2; // scale down
      currentBalance -= 0.02;                 // surcharge
      overdrawn = currentBalance < initialBalance;
    }
    public static void CheckJohnSmith() {
      double initial = 1000.00;
      double current = 1000.00;
      bool sol;
      Recalc(initial, ref current, out sol);
```

```
        Debug.Assert(initial == 1000.00);
        Debug.Assert(current == 999.98);
        Debug.Assert(sol     == false);
    }
  }
}
```

In general, the number of parameters for a given method is fixed. To allow the usage characteristics of variable argument lists, the CLR allows the last parameter of a method to use the [System.ParamArray-Attribute] attribute. One can apply the ParamArrayAttribute only to the last parameter of a method, and one must declare the type of that parameter as an array type. As far as the CLR is concerned, the caller must provide the last parameter as the declared array type. That stated, the [System.ParamArrayAttribute] acts as a hint to compilers that the intended use is to support a variable number of arguments whose types match the element type of the array. In C#, the params keyword adds the [System.ParamArrayAttribute] attribute:

```
public sealed class Dialer {
  public static void DialEm(string message,
                            params string[] numbers) {
    for (int i = 0; i < numbers.Length; i++)
      Util.Dial(message, numbers[i]);
  }
  public static void CallFred() {
    DialEm("Hi Fred!", "310-555-1716", "781-555-9895");
  }
}
```

Notice that this example declares the DialEm method as having a ParamArray parameter, something that allows the caller (in this case, the CallFred method) to pass as many strings as it desires as if they were individual parameters. The callee (in this case, the DialEm method), however, sees that part of the parameter list as a single array.

The body of a method has unrestricted access to the declaring type's members. It also has unrestricted access to members of the declaring type's base type that are declared as protected or public. Most programming languages allow methods to access the members of the declaring type without explicit qualification, although explicit qualification is typically allowed. To qualify `static` member names, the type name can be used. To qualify instance member names, each language provides a keyword that corresponds to the instance used to invoke the method. In C# and C++, the keyword is `this`. In VB.NET, the keyword is the somewhat friendlier-sounding `Me`. In either case, `this` or `Me` is a valid expression whose type corresponds to the declaring type, thereby allowing programmers to pass `this` or `Me` as a parameter or assign it to a variable or field. Note, however, that `static` methods do not have a `this` or `Me` variable and cannot access non-`static` members without first acquiring a valid instance.

Many programming languages support the **overloading** of a method name to accept somewhat different lists of parameters. To support this feature, a CLR type can contain multiple method definitions that use the same name provided that the parameter list for each definition differs either in the count of the parameters or in the type of one or more of the parameters. The CLR allows you to overload based on return type; however, few languages support this and therefore it is prohibited by the CLS. The CLS does allow overloading based on pass-by-reference versus pass-by-value. However, you cannot overload based on the difference between the C# `ref` and `out` keywords because they are not part of the method signature proper. Rather, both `ref` and `out` simply indicate that the parameter is passed as a managed pointer (more on this in Chapter 10). The additional metadata attribute that distinguishes between `ref` and `out` is not part of the method signature but rather is an out-of-band hint regarding the intended usage of the parameter.

The CLR makes no attempt to prohibit overloads that may result in ambiguity. For example, if an overload is to be selected based on the type of a given parameter, it is possible that, via numeric promotion or type relationships (or both), multiple overloads might be legal. The CLR is happy to let you define such a type; that stated, not every compiler will use the same rules for selecting which overload to use for a given call site. Some compilers will use language-specific heuristics. Other compilers may simply give up and return a compile-time error. This is one reason (among many) why one should use overloading judiciously, especially when the language of the type's consumer cannot be known *a priori*.

The third and final kind of type member to look at is the nested type. A nested type is simply a type that is declared in the scope of another type. Nested types are typically used to build auxiliary helper objects (e.g., iterators, serializers) that support instances of the declaring type. Listing 3.4 shows an example of a nested type in C#.

Listing 3.4: *Nested Types in C#*

```
namespace AcmeCorp.LOB {
  public sealed class Customer {
    public sealed class Helper {
      private static int incAmount;
      public static void IncIt() {
// legal - methods in nested types can access private
// members of containing type
        nextid += incAmount;
      }
    }
    private static int nextid;
    public static void DoWork() {
// legal - IncIt is public member
      Helper.IncIt();
// illegal   incAmount is private
      Helper.incAmount++;
    }
  }
}
```

Nested types have two fundamental advantages over "top-level" types. For one thing, the name of the nested type is scoped by the surrounding type name, a practice that reduces namespace pollution. More importantly, one can protect access to a nested type using the same access modifiers used to protect fields and methods.

Unlike Java's inner classes, nested types in the CLR are always considered static members of the declaring type and are not affiliated with any particular instance. The name of the nested type is qualified by the surrounding type name. For purposes of CLR reflection, one uses a "+" to delimit the declaring type's name and the nested type's name. In the example shown in Listing 3.4, the CLR type name of the `Helper` type is `AcmeCorp.LOB.Customer+Helper`. That stated, each programming language has its own delimiter characters. In C++, the delimiter is "::". In VB.NET and C#, the delimiter is ".", and this means that in this C#-based example, the `Helper` type can be referenced using the `AcmeCorp.LOB.Customer.Helper` symbol (note the period between `Customer` and `Helper`).

Perhaps the most important benefit of nested types is the way their methods relate to the members of the declaring type. Because a nested type is considered part of the implementation of the declaring type, the methods of a nested type are given special privileges. A nested type's methods have unrestricted access to the private members of the declaring type. The converse is not the case; the declaring type has no special access to members of the nested type. Note that in this example, the `Helper.IncIt` method can freely access the private `nextid` field of the declaring type. In contrast, the `Customer.DoWork` method cannot access the private `incAmount` field of the nested type.

Types and Initialization

Before we conclude the discussion of type members, there are two methods that bear special discussion. Types are allowed to provide a distinguished method that is called when the type is first initialized. This type initializer is simply a static method with a well-known name (`.cctor`). A type can have at most one type initializer, and it must take no parameters and return no value. Type initializers cannot be called directly; rather, they are called automatically by the CLR as part of the type's initialization. Each programming language provides its own syntax for defining a type initializer. In VB.NET, you simply write a `Shared` (per type) subroutine named `New`. In C#, you must write a static method whose name is the same as the declaring type name but has no return type. The following shows a type initializer in C#:

```
namespace AcmeCorp.LOB {
  public sealed class Customer {
    internal static long t;
```

```
      static Customer() { // this is the type initializer!
        t = System.DateTime.Now.Ticks;
      }
    }
  }
```

This code is semantically equivalent to the following type definition, which uses a C# field initializer expression rather than an explicit type initializer:

```
namespace AcmeCorp.LOB {
  public sealed class Customer {
    internal static long t = System.DateTime.Now.Ticks;
  }
}
```

In both cases, the resultant CLR type will have a type initializer. In the former case, you can put arbitrary statements into the initializer. In the latter case, you can use only initializer expressions. In both cases, however, the resultant types will have identical .cctor methods, and the t field will be properly initialized prior to its access.

As a point of interest, it is legal for a single C# type to have both an explicit type initializer method and static field declarations with initializer expressions. When both are present, the resultant .cctor method will begin with the field initializers (in order of declaration), followed by the body of the explicit type initializer method. Consider the following C# type definition:

```
namespace AcmeCorp.LOB {
  public sealed class Customer {
    static Customer() {
      t1 = System.DateTime.Now.Ticks;
      Debug.Assert(t2 <= t3); // obvious
      Debug.Assert(t3 <= t1); // not so obvious
    }
    internal static long t1;
    internal static long t2 = System.DateTime.Now.Ticks;
    internal static long t3 = System.DateTime.Now.Ticks;
  }
}
```

Given this type definition, the fields will be initialized in the following order: t2, t3, t1.

The CLR is somewhat flexible with respect to when a type initializer will actually be run. Type initializers are always guaranteed to execute prior to the first access to a static field of the type. Beyond that guarantee, the CLR supports two policies. The default policy is to execute the type initializer at the first access to any member of the type, and not one moment earlier. A second policy (indicated by the beforefieldinit metadata attribute) gives the CLR more flexibility. Types marked beforefieldinit differ in two ways from those that are not so marked. For one thing, the CLR is free to aggressively call the type initializer before the first member access. Second, the CLR is free to postpone invocation of the type initializer until the first access to a static field. This means that calling a static method on a beforefieldinit type does not guarantee that the type initializer has run. It also means that instances can be created and used freely before the type initializer executes. That stated, the CLR guarantees that the type initializer will have executed before any method touches a static field.

The C# compiler sets the beforefieldinit attribute for all types that lack an explicit type initializer method. Types that do have an explicit type initializer method will not have this metadata attribute set. The presence of initializer expressions in static field declarations does not impact whether the C# compiler uses the beforefieldinit attribute.

The previous discussion looked at the distinguished method that the CLR invokes as part of type initialization. There is another distinguished method that the CLR will call automatically each time an instance of the type is allocated. This method is called a **constructor** and must have the distinguished name .ctor. Unlike the type initializer, a constructor can accept as many parameters as desired. Additionally, a type can provide multiple overloaded constructor methods using the same guidelines as method overloading. The constructor method that accepts no parameters is often called the **default constructor** of the type. To grant or deny access to individual members, constructor methods can use the same access modifiers used by fields and normal methods. This is in sharp contrast to the type initializer method, which is always private.

Each programming language provides its own syntax for writing constructors. In VB.NET, you write a (non-Shared) subroutine called New. In

C# and C++, you write a (non-static) method whose name is the same as the declaring type name and returns no value. The following is an example of a C# type with two constructors:

```
namespace AcmeCorp.LOB {
  public sealed class Customer {
    internal long t1;
    internal long t2 = System.DateTime.Now.Ticks;
    internal long t3 = System.DateTime.Now.Ticks;
    public Customer() {
      t1 = System.DateTime.Now.Ticks;
    }
    public Customer(long init) {
      t1 = init;
    }
  }
}
```

The C# compiler will inject any non-static field initialization expressions into the generated .ctor method before the explicit method body. In the case of the default constructor, the t2 and t3 initialization statements will precede the initialization of t1.

The C# compiler also supports **chaining** constructors by allowing one constructor to call another. The following type definition, which uses constructor chaining, is semantically identical to the previous example:

```
namespace AcmeCorp.LOB {
  public sealed class Customer {
    internal long t1;
    internal long t2 = System.DateTime.Now.Ticks;
    internal long t3 = System.DateTime.Now.Ticks;
    public Customer()
    : this(System.DateTime.Now.Ticks)  // calls ctor below
    {
    }
    public Customer(long init) {
      t1 = init;
    }
  }
}
```

Note that the syntax for chaining constructors is language-specific. Consult the language reference for languages other than C#.

Types and Interfaces

So far, the discussion of type has been largely structural, focusing on how a CLR type is held together. Issues of type semantics have largely been ignored. It is now time to look at how types convey semantics, starting with type categorization.

It is often desirable to partition types into categories based on common assumptions made by two or more types. Such categorization can serve as additional documentation for a type because only the types that explicitly declare affiliation with the category are known to share the assumptions implicit in that category. In the CLR, these categories of types are referred to as **interfaces**. Interfaces are type categories that are integrated into the type system. Because categories represented by interfaces are themselves types, one can declare fields (and variables and method parameters) simply to require category affiliation rather than hard-code the actual concrete type to be used. This looser requirement enables substitution of implementation, which is the cornerstone of polymorphism.

Structurally, an interface is just another type to the CLR. Interfaces have type names. Interfaces can have members, with the restriction that an interface cannot have instance fields nor instance methods with implementation. Structurally, all that really distinguishes an interface from any other type is the presence or absence of the `interface` attribute on the type's metadata. However, the semantics of the use of interfaces in the CLR are highly specialized.

Interfaces are abstract types that form categories or families of types. It is legal to declare variables, fields, and parameters of interface type. That stated, it is not legal to instantiate new objects based solely on an interface type. Rather, variables, fields, and parameters of interface type must refer to instances of concrete types that have explicitly declared compatibility with the interface.

The following example illustrates why interfaces are important.

```
public sealed class AmericanPerson {}
public sealed class CanadianPerson {}
public sealed class Turnip {}

class Quack {
  void OperateAndTransfuseBlood(Object patient) {
    // what if patient is a Turnip?
  }
}
```

In this example, the Quack.OperateAndTransfuseBlood method accepts a single parameter of type System.Object. The type System. Object is the universal type in the CLR; this means that one can pass instances of any type as the parameter value. In this example, that means that one can legally pass instances of AmericanPerson, CanadianPerson, and Turnip to the method. However, given the method name, one might assume that there is little the method could do if a Turnip were to be passed. Because the parameter type does not discriminate against Turnips, this error will not be discovered until runtime.

The following example shows how interfaces solve this problem.

```
public interface IPatient {}
public sealed class AmericanPerson : IPatient {}
public sealed class CanadianPerson : IPatient {}
public sealed class Turnip {}

class Doctor {
  void OperateAndTransfuseBlood(IPatient patient) {
    // Turnips not allowed!
  }
}
```

In this example, there is a category of types called IPatient. That category is declared as an interface. Types that are compatible with IPatient explicitly declare this compatibility as part of their type definition. Both AmericanPerson and CanadianPerson do exactly this. The OperateAnd-TransfuseBlood method now declares its parameter to disallow types that are not compatible with IPatient. Because the Turnip type did not declare compatibility with IPatient, attempts to pass Turnip objects to this method will fail at compile time. This solution is preferable to simply providing two explicit overloads of the method—one for `AmericanPerson` and one for `CanadianPerson`—because this approach lets one define new types that one can pass to the `Doctor.OperateAndTransfuseBlood` method without having to explicitly define new overloads.

It is legal for a type to declare compatibility with more than one interface. When a concrete type (e.g., a class) declares compatibility with multiple interfaces, it is stating that instances of the type can be used in multiple contexts. For example, in Listing 3.5 the type `AmericanPerson` declares compatibility with both `IPatient` and `IBillee`, indicating its willingness to participate as either a patient or a billee. In this example, `CanadianPerson` declares compatibility only with `IPatient` and requires an instance of a second type (either `CanadianGovernment` or `American-Person`) if a billee is also required.

Listing 3.5: *Supporting Multiple Interfaces*

```
public interface IPatient { }
public interface IBillee { }
public sealed class AmericanPerson : IPatient, IBillee {}
public sealed class CanadianPerson : IPatient {}
public sealed class CanadianGovernment : IBillee {}

class Doctor {
// American patient acceptable for both parameters
  void OperateAndTransfuseBlood(IPatient patient,
                                IBillee moneySrc)
  {
  }
}
```

One can view interfaces as partitioning the set of all possible objects into subsets. Which subsets an object belongs to depends on which interfaces the object's type has declared compatibility with. Figure 3.2 shows the types defined in Listing 3.5 as viewed from this perspective. Along these lines, it is also possible for an interface type to declare compatibility with one or more other interfaces. In doing so, the new interface is stating that all types that declare compatibility with the new interface are required to be compatible with the additional interfaces. Most languages (e.g., C#, VB.NET) will make this assertion implicitly when you declare compatibility with the new interface.

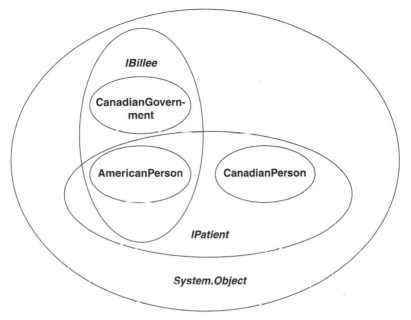

Figure 3.2: *Interfaces as Subsets*

Consider the example shown in Listing 3.6. In this example, the interface ISelfFundedPatient has declared compatibility with both IPatient and IBillee. That means that types that declare compatibility with ISelfFundedPatient (such as WealthyPerson) must be compatible with IPatient and IBillee. This is not to say, however, that all types that are compatible with both IPatient and IBillee are in turn compatible with ISelfFundedPatient. In the example shown here, instances of type InsuredPerson are explicitly not allowed as parameters to the Operate-AndTransfuseBlueBlood method. This is illustrated in Figure 3.3.

Listing 3.6: *Multiple Interface Inheritance*

```
public interface IPatient { }
public interface IBillee { }
public interface ISelfFundedPatient : IPatient, IBillee {}
public sealed class InsuredPerson : IPatient, IBillee {}
public sealed class WealthyPerson : ISelfFundedPatient {}

class Doctor {
// accepts any kind of patient, provided that
// a billee is supplied
```

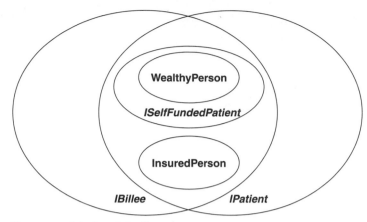

Figure 3.3: *Interface Inheritance*

```
void OperateAndTransfuseBlood(IPatient p,
                              IBillee b,
                              string color) {

}

// accepts only wealthy patients
void OperateAndTransfuseBlueBlood(ISelfFundedPatient sfp){
  OperateAndTransfuseBlood(sfp, sfp, "blue");
}
}
```

Interfaces can also impose explicit requirements on types that claim compatibility. Specifically, an interface can contain **abstract method declarations**. These declarations act as requirements for all types that claim to support the interface. If a concrete type claims to be compatible with interface I, that concrete type must provide method implementations for each abstract method declared in interface I.

To see how an interface can force types to implement methods, consider the following interface definition in C#:

```
public interface IPatient {
  void AddLimb();
  void RemoveLimb();
}
```

All concrete types that claim compatibility with IPatient must now provide implementations of the AddLimb and RemoveLimb methods that match the signatures declared in IPatient.

The following is a concrete type that implements the IPatient interface just defined:

```
public sealed class AmericanPerson : IPatient {
  internal int limbCount = 4;
  public void AddLimb() { ++limbCount; }
  public void RemoveLimb() { --limbCount; }
}
```

In this example, the IPatient interface's methods are part of the concrete type's public contract. The CLR also allows the concrete type to declare the methods as private provided that one uses some mechanism to indicate that the methods are used to satisfy the requirements of the interface. For example, the following implementation hides the Remove-Limb method from its public contract:

```
public sealed class CanadianPerson : IPatient {
  internal int limbCount = 4;
  public void AddLimb() { ++limbCount; }
  void IPatient.RemoveLimb() { --limbCount; }
}
```

In this example, only the AddLimb method is accessible through references of type CanadianPerson. To access the RemoveLimb method, one must use a reference of type IPatient, which can access both methods.

When invoking a method through an interface-based reference, the CLR determines at runtime which method to actually call based on the concrete type of the referenced object. This **dynamic method dispatch** is a necessary feature to enable polymorphism and is discussed in great detail in Chapter 6.

Types and Base Types

In addition to declaring compatibility with multiple interfaces, a type can also specify at most one **base type**. A base type cannot be an interface, and, strictly speaking, the set of supported interfaces are not considered base types of the declaring type. Moreover, interfaces themselves have no base type. Rather, at most an interface has a set of supported interfaces just like those of a concrete type.

Non-interface types that do not specify a base type get `System.Object` as their base type. Base types sometimes trigger different runtime semantics from the CLR (e.g., reference vs. value type, marshal by reference, delegates). Base types can also be used to package common members into a single type that multiple types can then leverage. When defining a type, you can control whether the type can or will be used as a base type. Declaring a type as `sealed` prohibits the use of the type as a base type. Declaring a type as abstract, on the other hand, disallows direct instantiation of the type and makes it useful only as a base type. Interfaces are always implicitly `abstract`. If a type is neither `abstract` nor `sealed`, then programmers can use it as a base type or to instantiate new objects. Types that are not `abstract` are often referred to as **concrete** types.

The non-`private` members of a base type implicitly become part of the contract of the derived type modulo cross-assembly accessibility. The derived type's methods can access non-`private` members of the base type as if they were explicitly declared in the derived type. It is possible (either by accident or deliberate design) for a member name in the derived type to collide with a non-`private` member name in the base. When this occurs, the derived type has both members. If the member is static, one can use the type name to disambiguate. If the member is non-`static`, then one can use language-specific keywords such as `this` or `base` to select either the derived member or the base member, respectively. For example, consider the following pair of types defined in C#:

```
public abstract class Mammal {
  public double age;
  public static int count;
}
public sealed class Human : Mammal {
  public double age;
  public static int count;

  public void Work(int count) {
    ++age;              // Human.age
    ++this.age;         // Human.age
```

```
    ++base.age;       // Mammal.age
    ++count;          // count parameter
    ++Human.count;    // Human.count
    ++Mammal.count;   // Mammal.count
  }
}
```

In this example, both the base and the derived types have age and count fields. To select the derived age field, one uses the this keyword. To select the base age field, one uses the base keyword. In the case of statics, one uses the explicit type name. Things get much more interesting when one looks at the type from the outside. Consider the following usage:

```
Human h = new Human();
Mammal m = h; // legal, Human is compatible with Mammal
h.age = 100;  // accesses Human.age
m.age = 200;  // accesses Mammal.age
```

In this example, both h and m refer to the same object. However, because the type of each variable is different, the two variables see different public contracts. In the case of h, the Human's definition of age hides the definition in the base, so the Human's age field is affected. If, however, the m variable is used instead, it does not take into account the public contract of any derived types. Rather, all it knows about is Mammal, and it will access the Mammal's age field.

Note that in the example just shown, the C# compiler will emit a warning indicating that the derived fields hide the visibility of the base fields. You can suppress this warning by adding the new keyword to the derived field definitions as follows:

```
new public double age;
new public static int count;
```

Note that the presence (or absence) of the new keyword in no way affects the metadata or the executable code. As a point of interest, VB.NET uses the more demonstrative Shadows keyword for the same purpose rather than overloading the meaning of the new keyword, as is done in C#.

The previous discussion of name collisions illustrated what happens when one reuses a field name in a derived type. The policy for dealing with collisions when method names are reused is somewhat different because method names may already be reused due to overloading.

The CLR supports two basic policies to use when the base and derived types have a method of the same name: hide-by-name and hide-by-signature. Every CLR method declaration indicates which policy to use via the presence or absence of the `hidebysig` metadata attribute on the derived type's method. When one declares a method using **hide-by-signature**, only the base method with the same name and the same signature will be hidden. Any other same-named methods in the base will remain a visible part of the derived type's contract. In contrast, when one declares a method using **hide-by-name**, the derived method hides all methods in the base type that have the same name, no matter what their signature may be. Types defined in C++ use hide-by-name by default because that is the way the C++ language was originally defined. Types defined in C#, in contrast, always use hide-by-signature. Types defined in VB.NET can use either policy, based on whether the method uses the `Overloads` (hide-by-signature) or `Shadows` (hide-by-name) keyword.

Figure 3.4 shows an example in C# of two types that overload both a field name and a method name. Note that because C# uses hide-by-signature, the `f` method that accepts an `int` does not hide the base's `f`

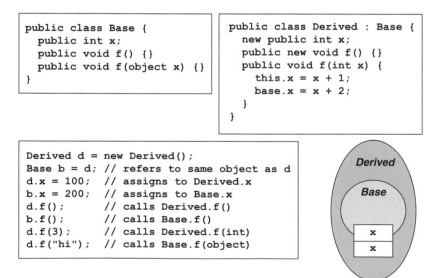

```
public class Base {
   public int x;
   public void f() {}
   public void f(object x) {}
}
```

```
public class Derived : Base {
   new public int x;
   public new void f() {}
   public void f(int x) {
      this.x = x + 1;
      base.x = x + 2;
   }
}
```

```
Derived d = new Derived();
Base b = d; // refers to same object as d
d.x = 100;   // assigns to Derived.x
b.x = 200;   // assigns to Base.x
d.f();       // calls Derived.f()
b.f();       // calls Base.f()
d.f(3);      // calls Derived.f(int)
d.f("hi");   // calls Base.f(object)
```

Figure 3.4: *Member Overloading and Shadowing*

method that accepts an `object`. This is illustrated when the example calls the `f` method with a string argument. If the derived type had used hide-by-name, the base's `f` methods would not be visible, and this would mean that the derived contract would have no `f` method that could accept a string parameter. However, because the derived type was defined in C#, the method is marked `hidebysig`, and that allows the other methods in the base to seep through to the derived type's public contract.

It is important to note that with overloading, the exact method to be invoked is determined at compile time. No runtime tests are performed to determine which overload to choose. The CLR does support dynamic binding to method code at runtime, a topic covered in Chapter 6.

One last topic to address with respect to base types is related to constructors. When the CLR allocates a new object, it calls the constructor method from the most-derived type. It is the job of the derived type's constructor to explicitly call the base type's constructor. This means that at all times, the actual type of the object is the most-derived type, even when the base type's constructor is executing.

The behavior just described is similar to the way Java works but extremely different from the way C++ works. In C++, an object is constructed "from the inside out"—that is, from base to derived type. Additionally, the type affiliation of a C++ object during the base type's constructor is that of the base type and not the derived type. That means that any virtual methods that may be invoked during the base type's constructor will not dispatch to a derived type's implementation. For a CLR-based type, this is not the case. Instead, if a base type constructor causes a virtual method call to be invoked, the most-derived type's method will be dispatched even though the derived type's constructor has probably not completed execution.

To avoid this problem, you are strongly encouraged to avoid virtual method calls in a constructor of a non-`sealed` type. This includes eschewing seemingly innocuous things such as passing your `this` or `Me` reference to a `WriteLine` method.

The C# language adds its own twist to how derived and base construction works, as shown in Figure 3.5. In the face of instance field declarations with initializer expressions, the compiler-generated `.ctor` will first call all

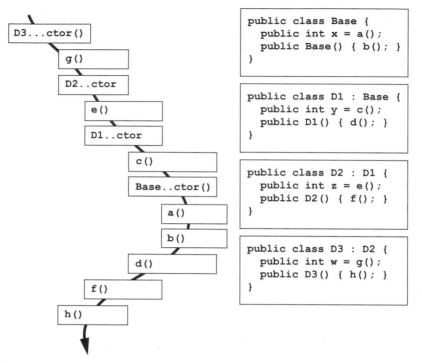

Figure 3.5: *Derivation and Construction*

field initializers in order of declaration. Once the derived type's field initializers have been called, the derived constructor calls the base type constructor, using the programmer-provided parameters if the base construct was used. Once the base type's constructor has completed execution, the derived constructor resumes execution at the body of the constructor (i.e., the part of the constructor in braces). This means that when the base type's constructor executes, the derived type's constructor body has not even begun to execute.

In general, designing a type to be used as a base type is considerably more difficult than defining a type that will simply be used to instantiate objects. For that reason, it is good practice to mark all types as sealed unless you are willing to ensure that your type is safe to use as a base. In a similar vein, it is easier to ensure that a type is safe as a base type if you are in control of all types that may use it as a base type. You can restrict a type's use as a base type by marking all of its constructors as internal. This technique makes all constructors inaccessible to types outside the assembly, thereby prohibiting them from using the type as a base type. However, types within the same assembly can safely use the type as a base without restriction.

Where Are We?

Types are the fundamental building blocks of a CLR program and make up the lion's share of a module's metadata. Each programming language maps its local constructs onto CLR types in language-specific ways. CLR types consist primarily of fields and methods; however, developers can call out the intended usage of a method in the metadata through the use of properties and events. To support object-oriented programming languages, developers can factor CLR types into hierarchies using both interfaces and base types. Developers spend most of their time defining new types in terms of existing types.

4

Programming with Type

CHAPTER 3 DESCRIBED the CLR's common type system (CTS). The focus of that chapter was largely on the static definition of types, assuming that the use of type in running programs would be implicit. In this chapter, we will focus on explicit programming techniques that deeply integrate type into applications and supporting infrastructure.

Types at Runtime

Types by themselves are rarely all that useful. What makes types interesting is the ability they give programmers to have instances of types to interact with. An **instance** of a type is either an object or a value, depending on how the type is defined. Instances of the primitive types are values. Instances of most user-defined types are objects, although one can define types that yield values, as Chapter 5 will illustrate in great detail.

Every object and every value is an instance of exactly one type. The affiliation between an instance and a type is often implicit. For example, declaring a variable or field of type System.Int32 results in a block of memory whose affiliation with its type exists only by virtue of the executable code that manipulates it. The CLR (and CLR-based compilers) will allow operations only on those values that are affiliated with the type definition for System.Int32. No additional overhead is needed to enforce this affiliation because the compiler will do the enforcement at compile time and the CLR's verifier will ensure that the affiliation is maintained after the code is loaded.

Each object is also affiliated with a type. However, because objects are always accessed via object references, it is possible that the actual type of the referenced object may not match the declared type of the reference. This will always be the case when an object reference is of an `abstract` type. Clearly, some mechanism is needed to explicitly affiliate the object with its type to deal with this situation. Enter the CLR **object header**.

Every object in the CLR begins with a fixed-size object header, as shown in Figure 4.1. The object header is not directly accessible programmatically, but it nonetheless exists. The exact format of this header is undocumented, and the following description is based on empirical analysis of version 1.0 of the CLR on IA-32 architectures. Other implementations of the CLI are likely to diverge somewhat from this format.

The object header has two fields. The first field of the object header is the **sync block** index. One uses this field to lazily associate additional resources (e.g., locks, COM objects) with the object. The second field of the object header is a **handle** to an opaque data structure that represents the object's type. Although the location of this handle is undocumented, there

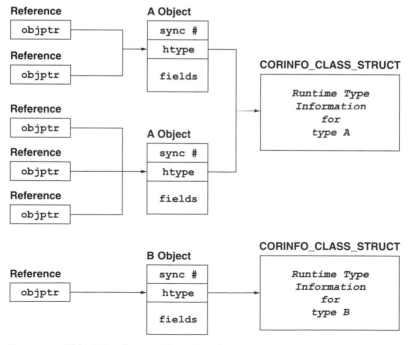

Figure 4.1: *Object Headers and Type Handles*

is explicit support for it via the `System.RuntimeTypeHandle` type. As a point of interest, in the current implementation of the CLR, an object reference always points to the type handle field of the object's header. The first user-defined field is always `sizeof(void*)` bytes beyond where the object reference points to.

Every instance of a given type will have the same type handle value in its object header. The **type handle** is simply a pointer to an undocumented, opaque data structure that contains a complete description of the type, including a pointer to the in-memory representation of the type's metadata. The contents of this data structure are optimized in a manner that makes various performance-critical operations (e.g., virtual method dispatching, object allocation) as fast as possible. The first application of this data structure to look at is **dynamic type coercion.**

When converting from one type of object reference to another, one must consider the relationship between the two types. If the type of the initial reference is known to be compatible with the type of the new reference, all the CLR needs to make the conversion is a simple IA-32 `mov` instruction. This is always the case when one is assigning from a reference of a derived type to a reference of a direct or indirect base type or of a known compatible interface **(up-casting).** If, on the other hand, the type of the initial reference is not known to be compatible with the type of the new reference, then the CLR must perform a runtime test to ascertain whether or not the object's type is compatible with the desired type. Such tests are always necessary when one is assigning from a base type or interface reference to a reference of a more-derived type **(down-casting)** or of an orthogonal type **(side-casting).**

To support down-casts and side-casts, CIL defines two opcodes: `isinst` and `castclass`. Both opcodes take two arguments: an object reference and a metadata token representing the type of reference desired. Both opcodes generate code that examines the object's type handle to determine whether or not the object's type is compatible with the requested type. The two opcodes differ in how they report the result of the test. If the test succeeds, both opcodes simply leave the object reference on the evaluation stack. If the test fails, the two opcodes behave differently. If the requested type is not supported, the `castclass` opcode throws an exception of type

System.InvalidCastException. In contrast, the isinst opcode simply puts a null reference onto the evaluation stack if the test fails. Because of the relatively high cost of exceptions, one should use constructs that result in the castclass opcode only when the cast is always expected to succeed. Similarly, you should use constructs that result in the isinst opcode when either result is expected. As a point of interest, the JIT compiler will translate the CIL isinst and castclass instructions into calls to the internal, undocumented functions JIT_IsInstanceOf and JIT_ChkCast, respectively. The remainder of this discussion, however, will attribute the behavior of these undocumented functions to the documented CIL instructions described earlier.

Both isinst and castclass take advantage of the data structure referenced by a RuntimeTypeHandle. Although it's not documented, this data structure (internally called a CORINFO_CLASS_STRUCT) contains several critical pieces of information. As shown in Figure 4.2, each type has an **interface table**. This table contains one entry for each interface that the type is compatible with. Each entry in a type's interface table contains the type handle for the supported interface. Coercions to interface types will be matched using this table. To support coercions to direct or indirect base types, the data structure also contains a pointer to the in-memory representation of the type's metadata, which includes a pointer to the metadata for the type's base type. Conversions to direct or indirect base types will be matched using this part of the data structure. In both cases, the test for type compatibility is simply a linear search through the interface table, followed by a linear traversal through the linked list of metadata structures. This means that for types that support large numbers of interfaces or have a highly layered base type hierarchy (or both), runtime tests for type compatibility will be slower than for simpler types that support fewer interfaces or have a flatter type hierarchy (or both).

Each programming language exposes the isinst and castclass opcodes in its own way. In C#, the isinst opcode is exposed via the as and is keywords. The as keyword is a binary operator that takes a variable and a type name. The C# compiler will then emit the proper isinst

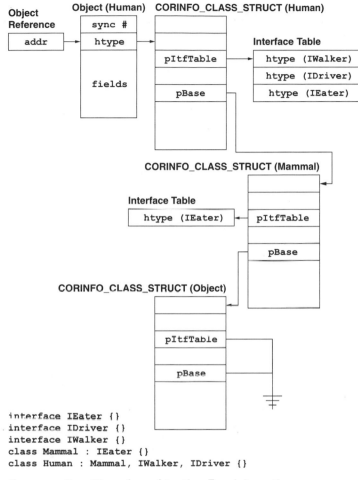

interface IEater {}
interface IDriver {}
interface IWalker {}
class Mammal : IEater {}
class Human : Mammal, IWalker, IDriver {}

Figure 4.2: *Type Hierarchy and Runtime Type Information*

instruction, and the reference that is returned becomes the result of the operator. Consider the following example:

```
static void Operate(IPatient p) {
  IBillee b = p as IBillee; // here is the isinst
  if (b == null)
    AskForFederalFunds();
}
```

C#'s is operator works similarly, except that the resultant reference is converted to a Boolean based on whether or not it is null. Here is the same code written using the is operator:

```
static void Operate(IPatient p) {
  bool isBillee = p is IBillee; // here is the isinst
  if (!isBillee)
    AskForFederalFunds();
}
```

This code is semantically equivalent to the previous example. The difference is that the IBillee reference is not available in the second example.

C# exposes the castclass opcode via its cast operator. A C# cast uses the same syntax as a C cast. Consider the following example:

```
static void Operate(IPatient p) {
  try {
    IBillee b = (IBillee)p; // here is the castclass
  }
  catch (System.InvalidCastException ex) {
    AskForFederalFunds();
  }
}
```

Note that in this example an exception handler is used to deal with the potential failure. Again, given the relative expense of exceptions, if the coercion cannot be guaranteed to succeed a priori, a construct that uses the isinst opcode would be more appropriate.

Although the type handle and the data structure it references are largely opaque to programmers working with the CLR, most of the information that is stored in this data structure (and the type's subordinate metadata) is made accessible to programmers via the System.Type type. System.Type provides an easy-to-use facade over the underlying optimized type information. You can get a System.Type object from a type handle by using the GetTypeFromHandle static method of System.Type. You can recover the type handle via the TypeHandle property of System.Type.

Each programming language provides its own mechanism for converting a symbolic type name to a System.Type object. In C#, one uses the typeof operator. The typeof operator takes a symbolic type name and results in a reference to the type's System.Type object. The following demonstrates the typeof operator:

```
using System;

public sealed class Util {
  public static void UseType() {
// get the type object
    Type type = typeof(AcmeCorp.LOB.Customer);
// get the underlying type handle
    RuntimeTypeHandle htype = type.TypeHandle;
// recover the type object from the handle
    Type t2 = Type.GetTypeFromHandle(htype);
// t2 and type now refer to the same System.Type object
  }
}
```

The CLR guarantees that exactly one System.Type object will exist in memory for a given type. That means that in this example, type and t2 are guaranteed to refer to the same System.Type object.

The previous example assumes that the name of the desired type is available at the time of compilation. Additionally, the requested type's assembly will become a static dependency of this module and assembly. To support loading types dynamically without a static dependency, you first need to load the type's assembly dynamically using Assembly.Load or Assembly.LoadFrom. After the assembly is loaded, you can then call the Assembly object's GetType method to extract the desired type. The following code is semantically equivalent to the previous example:

```
using System;
using System.Reflection;
public sealed class Util {
  public static void UseType() {
// load the assembly
    Assembly assm = Assembly.LoadFrom("C:\\acme.dll");
// get the type object
    Type type = assm.GetType("AcmeCorp.LOB.Customer");
// get the underlying type handle
    RuntimeTypeHandle htype = type.TypeHandle;
// recover the type object from the handle
    Type t2 = Type.GetTypeFromHandle(htype);
// t2 and type now refer to the same System.Type object
  }
}
```

This UseType method differs from the previous example in that this version explicitly loads the assembly containing the type rather than assuming that the assembly dependencies will be resolved automatically.

The previous two examples show how to get a System.Type object based on the name of the type. One can also get the System.Type object for any object or value in memory. To do this, one calls the System.Object.Get-Type method. Recall that System.Object is the universal type and that all types are compatible with System.Object. One of the methods of System.Object is GetType. When called on a value, the GetType method simply returns the type object that is implicitly affiliated with the value. When called on an object reference, the GetType method uses the System.RuntimeTypeHandle stored in the object header and calls GetType-FromHandle.

Calling GetType on an object or value allows you to discover aspects of an object or value's type at runtime. The simplest application of Get-Type is to discover whether two object references point to instances of the same type:

```
using System;

public sealed class Util {
  public static bool IsSameType(object o1, object o2) {
    Type t1 = o1.GetType(); // get type of o1
    Type t2 = o2.GetType(); // get type of o2
    return t1 == t2;        // are they the same type?
  }
}
```

This test will return true only when o1 and o2 refer to instances of exactly the same type. System.Type also supports type compatibility tests via its IsSubclassOf and IsAssignableFrom methods. The following code tests whether one object is an instance of a subclass of another object's type:

```
using System;

public sealed class Util {
  public static bool IsRelatedType(object o1, object o2) {
    Type t1 = o1.GetType();      // get type of o1
```

```
      Type t2 = o2.GetType();        // get type of o2
      return t2.IsSubclassOf(t1)
            || t1.IsSubclassOf(t2);
   }
 }
```

Note that in this example, the test will return true only if one of the objects is an instance of a type that is a direct or indirect base type of the other object's type. That stated, the `System.Type.IsSubclassOf` method will return false if `t1` and `t2` refer to the same type. Additionally, `System.Type.IsSubclassOf` will return false if either `t1` or `t2` refers to interface types. That cannot happen in this example because the `System.Object.GetType` method is guaranteed never to return a reference to an interface type.

The `System.Type.IsSubclassOf` method is rarely useful. A much more useful variation on this method is `System.Type.IsAssignableFrom`. The `System.Type.IsAssignableFrom` method tests for type compatibility. If the two types are the same, the result is true. If the specified type derives from the current type, then the result is true. If the current type is an interface, then the result is true if the specified type is compatible with the current type. Consider the following example:

```
using System;

public sealed class Util {
  public static bool IsCompatible(object o1, object o2) {
    Type t1 = o1.GetType();         // get type of o1
    Type t2 = o2.GetType();         // get type of o2
    return t2.IsAssignableFrom(t1)
          || t1.IsAssignableFrom(t2);
  }
}
```

In this example, the `IsCompatible` method works similarly to the `IsRelatedType` method shown earlier. The difference is that in this example, if `o1` and `o2` refer to objects of the same type, the result will now be true. It is also possible to enumerate the base types or interfaces (or both) of a given type. To enumerate a type's interfaces, one calls the `System.Type.GetInterfaces` method, which returns an array of `Type` objects, one per supported interface. To enumerate a type's base types, one recursively chases the System.Type.BaseType property. The following code prints the list of every type a given object is compatible with:

```
using System;
public sealed class Util
{
  public static void DumpTypes(object o) {
// get the object's type
    Type type = o.GetType();
// walk the list of direct and indirect base types
    for (Type c = type; c != null; c = c.BaseType)
      Console.WriteLine(c.AssemblyQualifiedName);
// walk the list of explicit and implicit interfaces
    Type[] itfs = type.GetInterfaces();
    for (int i = 0; i < itfs.Length; i++)
      Console.WriteLine(itfs[i].AssemblyQualifiedName);
  }
}
```

This example uses the AssemblyQualifiedName property to get the fully qualified name of the type. If one wanted a more human-friendly version, one could use the FullName property to get the namespace-qualified name or use the Name property to return the local part of the name without the namespace prefix. This example also demonstrates another way in which the CLR treats base types and interfaces differently.

Programming with Metadata

The previous section ended with an example that displayed a list of types a given object was compatible with. That example is just the tip of the iceberg of what is possible when type definitions are made machine-readable. This facility is often called **reflection**, a term made popular by Java.

Reflection makes all aspects of a type's definition available to programs, both at development time and at runtime. Although reflection is useful for building highly dynamic systems, it is far more applicable as a development-time tool. The primary application for reflection is for code generation. Code generation is typically thought of as a development-time activity, and reflection is useful in this capacity. However, even systems that use reflection at runtime can gain performance benefits from dynamically generating code rather than using interpretive-style designs.

The CLR provides ample facilities for generating code on-the-fly. The `System.Reflection.Emit` library allows CLR-based programs to emit types, modules, and assemblies. The `IMetaDataEmit` interface provides the same functionality to C++/COM programs. Finally, the `System.Code-DOM` provides facilities for constructing higher-level C# or VB.NET programs in memory and then compiling them down to modules and assemblies prior to execution. This chapter will focus primarily on the reading of type definitions, which is the purview of the `System.Reflection` namespace.

Figure 4.3 shows the reflection object model. Note that this object model reflects the fact that types belong to a module, which in turn belongs to an assembly. Additionally, this object model also reflects the fact that types contain members such as fields and methods.

The primary type in the `System.Reflection` namespace is the `MemberInfo` type. As discussed in the previous chapter, a type contains members. A runtime description of each of these members is available programmatically via the `System.Type.GetMembers` method. Each member description is an instance of a type that is derived from the `System.Reflection.MemberInfo` type. As shown in Figure 4.4, the `MemberInfo` type acts as the generic base type for most of the more specific reflection types.

The `MemberInfo` type has four significant properties. The `Name` property returns the name of the member as a string. The `MemberType` returns a `System.Reflection.MemberTypes` value indicating whether the member is a field, a method, or another kind of member. The `ReflectedType` property returns the `System.Type` that the `MemberInfo` object is affiliated with. In the face of inheritance, this may or may not be the same as the type that actually declared the member. To access that type, one should use the `DeclaringType` property.

The following program enumerates all the members of a given type. Note that the array returned by the `GetMembers` method will consist of fields, methods, and nested types all interleaved. The order the members are returned in will match the order in which they are stored in the module's metadata.

```
using System;
using System.Reflection;

public sealed class Util {
  public static void DumpMembers(Type type) {
// get the type's members
    MemberInfo[] members = type.GetMembers();
// walk the list of members
    for (int i = 0; i < members.Length; i++)
      Console.WriteLine("{0} {1}",
                        members[i].MemberType,
                        members[i].Name);
  }
}
```

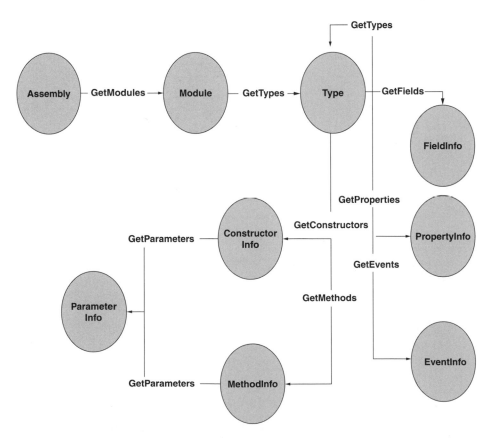

Figure 4.3: *Reflection Object Model*

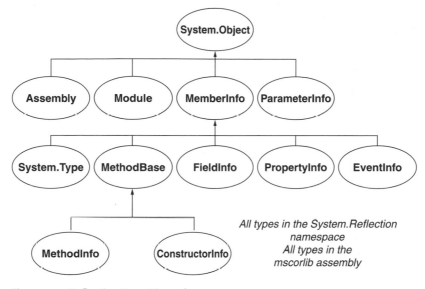

Figure 4.4: *Reflection Type Hierarchy*

This implementation will display only those members that are part of the public contract of the type. Additionally, this implementation skips any static members of the type. To change either or both of these characteristics, one must provide a System.Reflection.BindingFlags parameter that indicates which members are to be returned.

System.Reflection.BindingFlags is an enumeration type that is used throughout the reflection type hierarchy. Most methods that allow you to access the members of a type accept an optional BindingFlags parameter to tailor which members will be considered. The Static and Instance flags control whether static or instance members (or both) are to be considered. The Public and NonPublic flags control whether public or nonpublic instance members are to be considered. However, one can discover the private members of base types only by calling GetMembers on the base type and not on a derived type. Finally, even when the NonPublic and Static flags are specified, static members of base types will not be considered. To include these members for consideration, one must specify the FlattenHierarchy flag.

The following variation on the previous example will display all members of the type independent of access level or static/instance status:

```
using System;
using System.Reflection;

public sealed class Util {
  public static void DumpMembers(Type type) {
// get the type's members
    BindingFlags f = BindingFlags.Static
                   | BindingFlags.Instance
                   | BindingFlags.Public
                   | BindingFlags.NonPublic
                   | BindingFlags.FlattenHierarchy;
    MemberInfo[] members = type.GetMembers(f);
// walk the list of members
    for (int i = 0; i < members.Length; i++)
      Console.WriteLine("{0} {1}",
                        members[i].MemberType,
                        members[i].Name);
  }
}
```

In this example, the only members that will not be displayed are the private members of base types, which are never exposed via reflection.

The GetMembers method returns every member of a type modulo binding flag settings. It is possible to look up individual members by name using the System.Type.GetMember method. This method takes an additional parameter indicating the desired member's name and, like the Get-Members method, will return an array of MemberInfo objects, one per member. By default, only members whose name matches the requested name exactly will be considered. One can perform a case-insensitive search by specifying the BindingFlags.IgnoreCase flag. Finally, the System.Type.GetMember method allows the caller to indicate which kinds of members are to be considered. The caller can provide a Member-Types flag indicating the desired member kinds. The following example will display all of the methods named DoIt independent of case:

```
public sealed class Utils {
  public static void DumpMembers(Type type) {
// we want all members - period!
    BindingFlags bf = BindingFlags.Static
                    | BindingFlags.Instance
                    | BindingFlags.Public
```

```
                           | BindingFlags.NonPublic
                           | BindingFlags.IgnoreCase
                           | BindingFlags.FlattenHierarchy;
    // but we only want methods
        MemberTypes mt = MemberTypes.Method;

    // and their name must be "doit"
        string n = "doit";

    // get the desired members of the type
        MemberInfo[] members = type.GetMember(n, mt, bf);
    // walk the list of members
        for (int i = 0; i < members.Length; i++)
          Console.WriteLine("{0} {1}",
                                members[i].MemberType,
                                members[i].Name);


    }
  }
```

Note that when one uses the `BindingFlags.IgnoreCase` flag, one can specify the requested member name using any case.

The previous examples did very little with the member descriptions other than display the member's name. To do anything interesting with a member, one typically needs to use the more specific types. For example, the member descriptions for fields also support the `FieldInfo` type. The `FieldInfo` type has properties that indicate which access modifier was used to declare the field. The `IsStatic` property of `FieldInfo` indicates whether the field is an instance or a static field. The `IsInitOnly` and `IsLiteral` properties of `FieldInfo` indicate whether the field's value corresponds to a runtime or compile-time constant expression. Finally, the `FieldType` property of `FieldInfo` indicates the declared type of the field.

Either the generic `GetMembers` method or the more specific `GetFields` method fetches the fields of a type. The following example generates a VB subroutine that sets all of a type's public fields to their default values.

```
    public sealed class Utils {
      public static void GenFieldSetter(Type type)
      {
        Console.WriteLine("Public Sub SetEm(obj as {0})",
                          type.FullName);
```

```
// consider all public/instance fields
   FieldInfo[] fields = type.GetFields();
   for (int i = 0; i < fields.Length; i++)
   {
// skip initonly fields
      if (fields[i].IsInitOnly) continue;
      Type ft = fields[i].FieldType;
// skip nonprimitive value types
      if (ft.IsValueType && !ft.IsPrimitive) continue;

// ok, now generate the easy part of the statement
      Console.Write("  obj.{0} = ", fields[i].Name);

// figure out the type-specific literal to use
      if (!ft.IsValueType)
        Console.WriteLine("Nothing");
      else if (ft == typeof(bool))
        Console.WriteLine("False");
      else
        Console.WriteLine("0");
   }
   Console.WriteLine("End Sub");
  }
}
```

Now suppose that this routine is run against the following C# type:

```
public sealed class XYZ {
  public int x;
  public bool y;
  public char c;
  public string s;
  public object o;
  public double n;
}
```

The routine would generate the following VB.NET source code:

```
Public Sub SetEm(obj as XYZ)
  obj.x = 0
  obj.y = False
  obj.c = 0
  obj.s = Nothing
```

```
      obj.o = Nothing
      obj.n = 0
   End Sub
```

No matter how wonderful Visual Studio's IntelliSense feature may be, this routine can generate VB code faster than any human on the planet. Additionally, the generated code will perform much faster than would the corresponding reflection-based code. Furthermore, by isolating the machine-generated code from the human-generated code, as the types involved change or the pattern of code to be generated changes, one can regenerate this code, providing the same flexibility as reflection.

The `System.Reflection.FieldInfo` type is fairly simple and easy to grasp. The descriptions of methods are somewhat more complex due to the increased number of facets that are inherent in methods. Because constructors are largely the same as normal methods, the `System.Reflection.MethodInfo` and `System.Reflection.ConstructorInfo` types share a common base: `System.Reflection.MethodBase`. Because normal methods and constructors can both have parameters, `MethodBase` exposes the ability to enumerate parameter definitions. Because normal methods and constructors also have access modifiers and can be static or instance, `MethodBase` exposes these properties. Because only normal methods can return a typed value, this aspect of a method is visible only via the more specific `MethodInfo` type. Similarly, because only constructors can be used to initialize objects, the ability to create new instances of the type is visible only on the more specific `ConstructorInfo` type.

One can access the type initializer for a type via the `System.Type.TypeInitializer` property. One cannot use the `ConstructorInfo` returned by this property to create new instances. To access a type's (instance) constructors, one must use the `System.Type.GetConstructors` or `System.Type.GetConstructor` routine. One can access the non-constructor methods of a type via the `System.Type.GetMethods` or `System.Type.GetMethod` routine.

To make the `MethodInfo` type concrete, an example is in order. The following code demonstrates the use of `MethodInfo` by generating the C# method definitions needed to support a given interface.

```csharp
public sealed class Utils {
  public static void GenItfMethods(Type type)  {
// this works only for interfaces!
    if (!type.IsInterface) return;

// consider all methods
    MethodInfo[] methods = type.GetMethods();
    for (int i = 0; i < methods.Length; i++)
    {
// spit out the easy part
      MethodInfo meth = methods[i];
      Type retval = meth.ReturnType;
      if (retval == typeof(void))
        Console.Write("  public void {0}(", meth.Name);
      else
        Console.Write("  public {0} {1}(", retval.FullName,
                      meth.Name);

// walk the list of parameters
      bool needComma = false;
      ParameterInfo [] parameters = meth.GetParameters();
      foreach (ParameterInfo param in parameters)
      {
// add a comma if needed
        if (needComma)
          Console.Write(", ");
        else
          needComma = true;

        Type pt = param.ParameterType;
// cope with C#'s ref and out keywords
        if (pt.IsByRef)
        {
          if (!param.IsOut)
            Console.Write("ref ");
          else
            Console.Write("out ");

          pt = pt.GetElementType();
        }
// spit out the parameter type and name
        Console.Write("{0} {1}", pt.FullName, param.Name);
      }
```

```
    // generate a boilerplate method body
        Console.WriteLine(")");
        Console.WriteLine("  {");
        Console.WriteLine("  // TODO: put your code here");
        Console.Write("    throw new System.");
        Console.WriteLine("NotImplementedException();");
        Console.WriteLine("  }");
        Console.WriteLine();
    }
  }
}
```

Suppose you provide this method with a description of the following interface:

```
public interface ILoveLucy {
  void f();
  void g(int x, ref double y);
  double h(int[] x, out bool y);
}
```

The routine will generate the following C# method bodies:

```
public System.Double h(System.Int32[] x,
                  out System.Boolean y)
{
// TODO: put your code here
  throw new System.NotImplementedException();
}

public void g(System.Int32 x, ref System.Double y)
{
// TODO: put your code here
  throw new System.NotImplementedException();
}

public void f()
{
// TODO: put your code here
  throw new System.NotImplementedException();
}
```

Note that this simple implementation does not bother to translate the names of the primitive types (e.g., `System.Int32`) into their language-specific keywords (e.g., `int`). At the risk of sounding trite, that rather simple exercise is left to the reader.

Looking up particular methods or constructors is complicated by the presence of overloading. When looking up methods and constructors, the caller can specify an array of `System.Type` objects that will be used to match a specific overload's signature. For example, the following code looks up the `g` method defined in the `ILoveLucy` interface just described:

```
Type[] argTypes = {
  typeof(int),
  Type.GetType("System.Double&")
};
Type itf = typeof(ILoveLucy);
MethodInfo method = itf.GetMethod("g", argTypes);
```

Note that to specify that a parameter is passed by reference, one uses the `System.Type.GetType` method, passing the desired type name followed by an ampersand. This is the CLR convention for specifying a managed pointer type, as is used in pass-by-reference scenarios.

Special Methods

The motivation for having rich metadata is to more accurately retain and convey the intentions of the programmer. For example, programmers often define a pair of methods that correspond to a named value. Typically, one of the methods *gets* the value, and the other method *sets* the value. A CLR type can contain additional metadata that indicates which methods are intended to be used in this fashion. This additional metadata is formally called a **property**.

A CLR property is a member of a type that specifies one or two methods that correspond to a named value that is affiliated with the type. Like a field, a property has a name and a type. However, unlike a field, a property has no allocated storage. Rather, a property is simply a named reference to other methods in the same type. No more, no less.

The properties of a type are accessible via the `System.Type.GetProp-erties` and `System.Type.GetProperty` methods, both of which return a `System.Reflection.PropertyInfo` that describes the property. You can determine the name and type of the property via the `PropertyInfo.Name` and `PropertyInfo.PropertyType` members, respectively. The more interesting members are the `GetGetMethod` and `GetSetMethod` methods. As shown in Figure 4.5, each of these methods returns a `MethodInfo` that describes the **getter** or **setter** method of the property, respectively. These two methods can accept a Boolean that controls whether or not nonpublic methods will be returned. Because either the getter or the setter is optional, either of these methods may return null.

To reduce the surface area of a type that uses properties, the methods that correspond to a property are typically marked with the `specialname` metadata attribute, which informs compilers and tools to hide the property's individual methods from normal use. Alternatively, many programming languages allow properties to be read or written to using the same syntax as field access.

The following C# code uses a type `Invoice` that has a property named `Balance` of type `System.Decimal`:

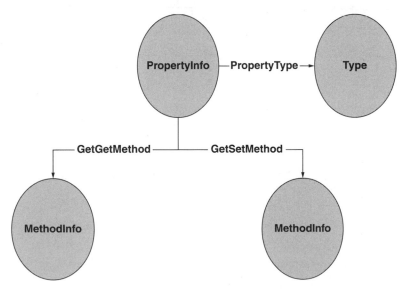

Figure 4.5: *CLR Properties*

```
public sealed class Utils {
  public static void Adjust(Invoice inv) {
    decimal amount = inv.Balance; // calls "getter" method
    amount *= 1.0825;
    inv.Balance = amount;          // calls "setter" method
  }
}
```

Despite the fieldlike syntax, this code will trigger method invocations against the methods that correspond to the Balance property's getter and setter methods. The fact that Balance is not a field becomes apparent when one tries to pass it by reference to another method:

```
public sealed class Utils {
  public void TaxIt(ref decimal amount) {
    amount = amount * 1.0825;
  }
  public static void Adjust(Invoice inv) {
// illegal - inv.Balance has no storage!
    TaxIt(ref inv.Balance);
  }
```

This is just one example of how syntactic constructs created by programming languages can sometimes obfuscate semantics.

On the topic of obfuscation, each programming language creates its own syntax for defining properties as members of a type. In C#, the syntax is a hybrid of field and method declaration syntax. Consider the following C# type definition:

```
public sealed class Invoice {
// property definitions start out looking like a field
  public decimal Balance
  {
// C# property definitions contain
// one or two method definitions

    get {
      return currentBalance;
    }
    set {
      if (value < 0)
```

```
            throw new System.ArgumentOutOfRangeException();
        currentBalance = value;
    }
  }
  internal decimal currentBalance;
}
```

Note that in this property definition, two methods are being declared. The C# compiler will infer the names and signatures of the methods based on the name and type of the property as follows:

```
public decimal get_Balance()
public void set_Balance(decimal value)
```

The generated type will also contain the additional metadata that binds the two methods together as a property called `Balance`, whose type is `System.Decimal`. Consistent with the discussion so far, each of the methods will be marked `specialname` to suppress its appearance in Visual Studio's IntelliSense.

In the same spirit as properties, the CLR provides explicit support for designating methods that are used to register or revoke event handlers. A **CLR event** is a named member of a type that refers to other methods in the same type. One of the referenced methods is used to register an event handler. The other method is used to revoke the registration. A given event can have multiple event handlers, provided that they have distinct names. Like a property, an event is affiliated with a type. The type of an event must be derived from `System.Delegate`, which is described in detail in Chapter 6.

The events of a type are accessible via the `System.Type.GetEvents` and `System.Type.GetEvent` methods, both of which return a `System.Reflection.EventInfo` that describes the event. An `EventInfo` object has properties that indicate the name and type of the event. The most interesting members are the `GetAddMethod` and `GetRemoveMethod` methods. As shown in Figure 4.6, each of these methods returns a `MethodInfo` that describes the register and revoke methods of the event, respectively. These two methods can accept a Boolean that controls whether or not non-public methods will be returned.

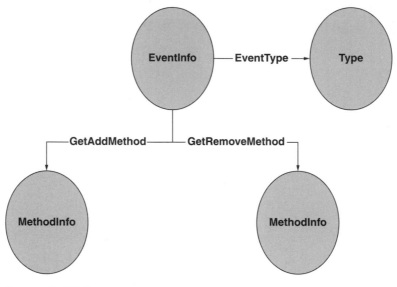

Figure 4.6: *CLR Events*

Like the methods of a property, an event's methods are marked with the `specialname` metadata attribute to suppress their direct use. Most programming languages invent their own syntax for registering or revoking event handlers. In VB.NET, you simply add the `WithEvents` modifier to a field declaration. In C#, the `+=` and `-=` operators are overloaded to invoke the register or revoke the method of an event, respectively.

The following C# code uses a type `Invoice` that has an event named `OnSubmit` of type `System.EventHandler`:

```
using System;

public sealed class Utils {
 public static void FinishIt(Invoice inv, EventHandler eh){
  inv.OnSubmit += eh; // call "add" method
  inv.CompleteWork(); // do work that may fire event
  inv.OnSubmit -= eh; // call "remove" method
 }
}
```

Despite the overly cute syntax, the C# compiler will emit calls to the underlying `add` and `remove` methods that are designated in the metadata for the `OnSubmit` event.

As with properties, each programming language creates its own syntax for defining events as members of a type. In C#, the syntax looks strikingly similar to the syntax used by property definitions. Consider the following C# type definition:

```
using System;

public sealed class Invoice {
// event definitions start out looking like a property
  public event EventHandler OnSubmit
  {
// event definitions contain one or two method definitions
    add {
      eh = (EventHandler)Delegate.Combine(eh, value);
    }
    remove {
      ch = (EventHandler)Delegate.Remove(eh, value);
    }
  }
  internal EventHandler eh;
}
```

C# also provides an abbreviated syntax for declaring events. The following class definition is equivalent to the previous example:

```
using System;

public sealed class Invoice {
  public event EventHandler OnSubmit;
}
```

In either of these examples, the C# compiler will emit two method definitions whose signatures are as follows:

```
public void add_OnSubmit(EventHandler value);
public void remove_OnSubmit(EventHandler value);
```

Note that the first example uses the System.Delegate.Combine and System.Delegate.Remove methods, which are explained in Chapter 6.

One last member kind to investigate is indexed properties. If the methods of a property accept parameters other than the standard value parameter of the setter method, the property is called an **indexed property**. Indexed properties are a throwback to classic versions of Visual Basic. Indexed properties are fully supported in VB.NET. Indexed properties are only partially supported in C#.

C# supports only one indexed property per type. That property is called an **indexer** and must be marked as the "default" member of the type using the [System.Reflection.DefaultMemberAttribute]. Indexers are similar to any other property. They can have a get or a set method (or both). C# treats indexers as distinct from other properties in two ways. For one thing, indexers accept one or more parameters and in fact can be overloaded. Second, unlike arbitrary properties, indexers defined in C# cannot be static.

Many programming languages expose indexers using array syntax. For example, the following C# code uses a type called InvoiceLines that has an indexer of type decimal. The indexer's parameter is a string that corresponds to a simple part number:

```
public sealed class Utils {
  public static void Adjust(InvoiceLines iq) {
    iq["widget"] = 3;            // calls set method
    decimal cs = iq["gizmo"];    // calls get method
    iq["doodad"] = cs * 2;       // calls set method
  }
}
```

As shown in this example, indexers allow variables to be treated as associative arrays.

Each programming language invents its own syntax for defining an indexer. The following is an example of an indexer defined in C#:

```
using System;

public sealed class InvoiceLines {
  internal decimal cWidgets;
  internal decimal cGizmos;
  internal decimal cDooDads;
```

```
    // here is the indexer...
      public decimal this[string partID] {

    // public decimal get_Item(string partID)
        get {
          switch (partID) {
            case "widget":
              return cWidgets;
            case "gizmo":
              return cGizmos;
            case "doodad":
              return cDooDads;
            default:
              throw new InvalidArgumentException("partID");
          }
        }

    // public void set_Item(string partID, decimal value)
        set {
          switch (partID) {
            case "widget":
              cWidgets - value;
            case "gizmo":
              cGizmos = value;
            case "doodad":
              cDooDads = value;
            default:
              throw new InvalidArgumentException("partID");
          }
        }
      }
    }
```

As implied by the comments in this example, the underlying property name will be Item. This name is chosen by the C# compiler, and, in general, the choice of name does not matter. However, some languages (e.g., VB.NET) allow a type's indexer to be accessed explicitly by name. In those languages, the choice of indexer name is significant. To control the name of the indexer, one can use the [System.Runtime.CompilerServices. IndexerName] attribute. For example, to cause the indexer just defined to use the name Quantities, one would declare the indexer as follows:

```
[
  System.Runtime.CompilerServices.IndexerName("Quantities")
]
public decimal this[string partID] {
// remainder as before...
```

Given this modification, a VB.NET programmer can now use the type as follows:

```
Public Sub Adjust(iq as InvoiceLines)
  iq("widget") = 3
  iq.Quantities("widget") = 3 ' same as previous line!
End Sub
```

At this point, it is important to note that properties, indexers, and events are all simply additional metadata hints that convey the intended use of one or more methods. Their use is strictly optional.

Metadata and Extensibility

This chapter has alluded to metadata attributes rather liberally up to this point without providing a formal definition. Most constructs in CLR metadata have a 32-bit **attribute** field that is used to fine-tune the definition of the type, field, or method the attribute is associated with. The interpretation and format of these attributes is fixed and is defined in the CLI specification submitted to ECMA. Some of the metadata attributes discussed so far include `initonly` (field), `beforefieldinit` (type), and `hidebysig` (method). One can make these fixed attributes visible via reflection as well as using the unmanaged metadata interface `IMetaDataImport`.

Compilers are responsible for setting these attributes based on programming language-specific polices. This chapter has described some of the policies used by various compilers, including the C# compiler (`CSC.EXE`).

Sometimes a programming language designer will elect to expose a metadata attribute as a **modifier** keyword (e.g., C#'s `readonly` field modifier). However, to avoid the proliferation of keywords, another mechanism is often used. That mechanism is a **custom attribute**.

Custom attributes allow language designers to support arbitrary metadata attributes without introducing new keywords into the programming language. When used to support the CLI's predefined attributes, the custom attribute is called a **pseudo-custom attribute** because it is converted into a standard fixed attribute when the compiler emits the CLR metadata. For example, the CLI predefines a flag in the type metadata to indicate whether or not instances of the type support object serialization. Although this attribute is simply a bit in the metadata, it is controlled using the System.SerializableAttribute pseudo-custom attribute.

The more interesting application of custom attributes is that they allow anyone to extend the CLR metadata format. If there is some aspect of a field or method that you feel is not captured in the existing CLR metadata format, you can define your own custom attribute that expresses that aspect. Your custom attribute can then be inspected using reflection or other mechanisms discussed later in this book.

Custom attributes themselves are strongly typed. A custom attribute is an instance of a type that derives directly or indirectly from System.Attribute. Consider the following C# class definitions:

```
public sealed class TestedAttribute : System.Attribute
{
}
public sealed class DocumentedAttribute : System.Attribute
{
}
```

Because these types have System.Attribute as their base type, they can now be used to augment the definition of a field, a method, a type, or any other metadata construct.

Each programming language must provide a mechanism for applying arbitrary attributes to the declaration of a type, field, method, or other CLR construct. The syntax used to apply custom attributes varies from language to language. In C++ and C#, one can precede a definition with a pair of brackets (e.g., [TestedAttribute]) containing the custom attributes. VB.NET instead uses angle brackets (e.g., < TestedAttribute >).

No matter which language one uses, the attribute name must correspond to a type whose direct or indirect base type is System.Attribute.

The following C# type definition applies one or both of our custom attributes to each of its methods:

```
public sealed class MyCode {
   [ TestedAttribute ]
   [ DocumentedAttribute ]
   static void f() {}

   [ Tested ]
   static void g() {}

   [ Tested, Documented ]
   static void h() {}
}
```

Note that in each of these methods, the attribute declarations precede the target of the attribute. Also note that in C#, if an attribute's name ends in `Attribute`, one can omit the `Attribute` suffix. Finally, note that when multiple attributes are applied, they can appear either in independent [ ] blocks or as a comma-delimited list inside a single [ ] block.

Occasionally, the target of the custom attribute may be ambiguous. For example, when a custom attribute precedes a method declaration, it is also preceding the type name of the return value. In this case, which is the target of the attribute? To resolve this ambiguity, each language provides a mechanism for making the target explicit. Consider the following C# code:

```
[assembly: Red ]
[module: Green ]
[class: Blue ]
[ Yellow ]
public sealed class Widget
{
   [return: Cyan ]
   [method: Magenta ]
   [ Black ]
   public int Splat() {}
}
```

In this example, the `Red` attribute applies to the declaring assembly. The `Green` attribute applies to the declaring module. The `Blue` and `Yellow` attributes apply to the type Widget. The Magenta and Black attributes apply to the Widget.Splat method. The Cyan attribute applies to the Widget.Splat method's return type.

Custom attributes are stored as passive BLOBs in the CLR metadata. These BLOBs represent serialized constructor calls to the attribute type. The presence (or absence) of a custom attribute does not affect the CLR's treatment of the type. Rather, custom attributes lie dormant, waiting for a program to read them using reflection or other metadata interfaces.

The System.Reflection.ICustomAttributeProvider interface models attributable elements in the reflection object model. The ICustomAttributeProvider interface is supported by MemberInfo, ParameterInfo, Assembly, and Module, and that covers most elements in the reflection object model.

As shown in Listing 4.1, the ICustomAttributeProvider interface supports two methods for discovering attributes: IsDefined and GetCustomAttributes. The IsDefined method takes the System.Type describing the attribute you are querying for and returns a Boolean indicating whether or not the member has an attribute of the specified type. The inherited parameter controls whether or not attributes applied in the base type are to be considered. The IsDefined method is relatively cheap, as no new objects need to be initialized to determine the presence of an attribute. A simple yes or no answer is all that is returned.

Listing 4.1: *System.Reflection.ICustomAttributeProvider*

```
namespace System.Reflection {
// supported by MemberInfo, ParameterInfo,
//              Assembly and Module
  public interface ICustomAttributeProvider {
// test for presence or absence of attribute of type
// attType
    bool IsDefined(System.Type attType, bool inherited);

// return all attributes that are compatible with attType
    object[] GetCustomAttributes(System.Type attType,
                                 bool inherited);
// return all attributes irrespective of type
    object[] GetCustomAttributes(bool inherited);
  }
}
```

Listing 4.2 shows `IsDefined` at work. This example checks each of the methods of a type to see whether either the `TestedAttribute` or the `Doc-umentedAttribute` attribute has been applied. For simple attributes such as these, `IsDefined` is all one needs because all one cares about is the presence or absence of the attribute.

Listing 4.2: *Detecting a Custom Attribute*

```
using System;
using System.Reflection;

public sealed class Utils {
  static void DisplayMethodStatus(Type type) {
    foreach (MethodInfo m in type.GetMethods()) {
      Console.Write("{0}: ", m.Name);

// check the doc'ed attribute
      if (m.IsDefined(typeof(DocumentedAttribute),true))
        Console.Write("Documented");
      else
        Console.Write("Undocumented");

// check the tested attribute
      if (m.IsDefined(typeof(TestedAttribute),true))
        Console.WriteLine(" - OK");
      else
        Console.WriteLine(" - Broken");
    }
  }
}
```

Custom attributes can also accept parameters as part of their declaration. The public constructor methods of the attribute type dictate the type and number of parameters that are allowed. For example, consider the following update to the `TestedAttribute` type just defined:

```
public sealed class TestedAttribute : System.Attribute
{
  public TestedAttribute() {}
  public TestedAttribute(string tester) {}
  public TestedAttribute(string tester,
                         double confidence) {}
}
```

Given this new version, one could use the custom attribute as follows:

```
public sealed class MyCode {
  [ Tested ]
  static void f() {}

  [ Tested("Don Box") ]
  static void g() {}

  [ Tested("Chris Sells", 100) ]
  static void h() {}
}
```

The parameters were allowed simply because the attribute type had compatible constructor methods. The CLR restricts the types of attribute parameters to primitives, strings, and System.Type references.

The previous example showed the custom attribute parameters being passed by position based on a constructor signature. It is also legal to pass parameters to a custom attribute by name. Passing attribute parameters by name requires that the underlying attribute type have a public property or field whose name matches the parameter name specified. Consider this updated version of the DocumentedAttribute type defined earlier:

```
public sealed class DocumentedAttribute : System.Attribute
{
  public DocumentedAttribute() {  }
  public DocumentedAttribute(string w) { Writer = w; }
  public string Writer;
  public int   WordCount;
  public bool  Reviewed;
}
```

This attribute can be applied in the following ways:

```
public sealed class MyCode {
  [ Documented("Don Box", WordCount = 42) ]
  static void f() {}

  [ Documented(WordCount = 42, Reviewed = false) ]
  static void g() {}
```

```
    [ Documented(Writer = "Don Box", Reviewed = true) ]
    static void h() {}
}
```

The positional parameter applied to the f method is allowed because the attribute type has a compatible constructor method that accepts a lone string parameter. The named parameters are allowed because the attribute type has public fields or properties of the same name.

The parameters passed to a custom attribute are serialized into the metadata for the attribute when the compiler emits the module. To allow the parameter values to be recovered at runtime via reflection, custom attributes typically store their parameters as instance fields for later inspection. To read these fields, you must use the ICustomAttributeProvider. GetCustomAttributes method to acquire a reference to the attribute object in memory.

The GetCustomAttributes method returns an array of attribute objects to allow interrogation of an attribute's fields and properties. Calling GetCustomAttributes causes the serialized attribute constructors to execute as the attribute objects are instantiated from the metadata prior to your code seeing them.

The GetCustomAttributes method is overloaded to accept an optional System.Type object, which indicates what type of attribute is desired. If no System.Type is specified, GetCustomAttributes will return all of the custom attributes regardless of type. In either case, the method returns a (potentially empty) array of System.Object references.

The routine in Listing 4.3 demonstrates how one can inspect a custom attribute's fields at runtime. This example accesses the Documented-Attribute object that is affiliated with each method and displays the various fields of that attribute.

Listing 4.3: *Inspecting Custom Attribute Parameters*

```
using System;
using System.Reflection;

public sealed class Utils {
  static void DisplayMethodStatus2(Type type) {

    Type attType = typeof(DocumentedAttribute);
```

```
    foreach (MethodInfo m in type.GetMethods()) {
      Console.Write("{0}: ", m.Name);

// check the doc'ed attribute
      if (!m.IsDefined(attType,true)) {
        Console.WriteLine("Undocumented");
        continue;
      }
      object[] atts = m.GetCustomAttributes(attType, true);
      DocumentedAttribute att = (DocumentedAttribute)atts[0];
      Console.WriteLine("{0}: {1} words [{2}]",
                        att.Writer,
                        att.WordCount,
                        (att.Reviewed ? "ok" : "hold" ));
    }
  }
}
```

Finally, it is often desirable to restrict where and how a custom attribute may be applied. To allow a custom attribute type to control its usage, the CLR defines the `System.AttributeUsageAttribute` attribute. This custom attribute is to be applied to a custom attribute's type definition and supports three properties. The `ValidOn` property indicates which constructs (e.g., fields, methods) the attribute can be applied to. The `Inherited` property indicates whether or not the attribute's presence should be visible to derived types. The `AllowMultiple` property specifies whether one can apply the attribute multiple times to the same target. For simple attributes, this usage makes no sense. For custom attributes that correspond to lists or sets (think security roles), `AllowMultiple=true` would allow one to apply the attribute once for each member of the list.

Consider this last variation on the `DocumentedAttribute` type used throughout this discussion:

```
using System;

[
  AttributeUsage(AttributeTargets.Method,
                 Inherited = false,
                 AllowMultiple = true)
]
```

```
public sealed class DocumentedAttribute : System.Attribute
{
  public DocumentedAttribute() {   }
  public DocumentedAttribute(string w) { Writer = w; }
  public string Writer;
  public int    WordCount;
  public bool   Reviewed;
}
```

This new definition indicates that one can apply the DocumentedAttribute only to methods. Attempts to apply it to a field or type will fail. The fact that the AllowMultiple parameter is true allows the following usage:

```
public sealed class MyCode {
  [ Documented("Don Box", WordCount = 193) ]
  [ Documented("Chris Sells", WordCount = 1722) ]
  [ Documented("John Smith", Reviewed = true) ]
  static void f() {}
}
```

In this usage, the f method will have three instances of the attribute applied. When one calls GetCustomAttributes on the corresponding MethodInfo object, the resultant array will contain three elements, one per attribute declaration.

Where Are We?

Types are the fundamental unit of currency in CLR metadata. Unlike classic C++ and Visual Basic types, CLR types are made visible to running programs and are an integral part of the runtime execution of all CLR-based programs. Type definitions are easily emitted and read programmatically, and one can extend the format for a type definition's metadata in a clean, strongly typed manner using custom attributes. The extensibility and expressiveness afforded by broadly accessible custom attributes are arguably the most profound features of the CLR. To paraphrase a famous COM guy, Charlie Kindel, custom attributes are more powerful than you think.

■ 5 ■
Instances

T HE BASIC PROGRAMMING model of the CLR is based on types, objects, and values. Chapters 3 and 4 focused primarily on types and danced lightly around the idea of objects and values. This chapter will clarify how all three of these concepts relate and are used in CLR-based programs. Again, the concepts illustrated in this chapter transcend programming languages and apply to everyone using the CLR.

Objects and Values Compared

The type system of the CLR distinguishes between types that correspond to simple values and types that correspond to more traditional "objects." The former are called **value types**; the latter are called **reference types**. Value types support a limited subset of what a reference type supports. In particular, instances of value types do not carry the storage overhead of full-blown objects. This makes value types useful in scenarios where the costs of an object would otherwise be prohibitive. It is important to note that both reference types and value types can have members such as fields and methods, and this means that statements such as the following are legal:

```
string s = 53.ToString();
```

Here, 53 is an instance of a type (System.Int32) that has a method called ToString.

The term *object* is overloaded in the literature as well as in the CLR documentation. For consistency, we will define an object as an instance of a CLR type on the garbage-collected (GC) heap. Objects support all the methods and interfaces declared by their type. To implement polymorphism, objects always begin with the two-field object header described in Chapter 4. Value types (such as `System.Int32` or `System.Boolean`) are also CLR types, but instances of a value type are not objects because they do not begin with an object header, nor are they allocated as distinct entities on the GC heap. This makes instances of value types somewhat less expensive than instances of reference types. Like reference types, value types can have fields and methods. This applies to primitives as well as user-defined value types.

Reference types and value types are distinguished by base type. All value types have `System.ValueType` as a base type. `System.ValueType` acts as a signal to the CLR that instances of the type must be dealt with differently. Figure 5.1 shows one view of the CLR type system. Note that the primitive types such as `System.Int32` are descendants of `System.Value-Type`, as are all user-defined structures and enumerations. All other types are reference types.

Programming languages typically have a set of built-in or primitive types. It is the job of the compiler to map these built-in types to CLR types. The CLR provides a fairly rich set of standard numeric types as well as `Boolean` and string types. Figure 5.2 shows the VB.NET and C# built-in types and the CLR types they correspond to. Note that all numeric types and `Boolean` types are value types. Also note that `System.String` is a reference type. That stated, in the CLR, `System.String` objects are **immutable** and cannot be changed after they are created. This makes `System.String` act much more like a value type than a reference type, as will be further explored later in this chapter.

For a variety of reasons, one cannot use value types as base types. To that end, all value types are marked as `sealed` in the type's metadata and cannot declare abstract methods. Additionally, because instances of value types are not allocated as distinct entities on the heap, value types cannot have finalizers. These are restrictions imposed by the CLR. The C# programming language imposes one additional restriction, which is that value

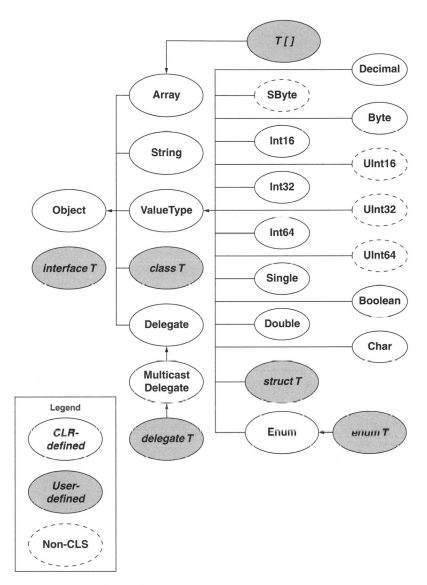

Figure 5.1: *The CLR Type System*

types cannot have default constructors. In the absence of a default constructor, the CLR simply sets all of the fields of the value type to their default values when constructing an instance of a value type. Finally, because instances of value types do not have an object header, method invocation against a value type does not use virtual method dispatch. This helps performance but loses some flexibility.

CLR	C#	VB.NET	Size (bits)	Ref/Val
Object	object	Object	N/A	Reference
String	string	String	N/A	
Boolean	bool	Boolean	8	Value
Char	char	Char	16	
Single	float	Single	32	
Double	double	Double	64	
Decimal	decimal	Decimal	128	
SByte	sbyte	N/A	8	
Byte	byte	Byte		
Int16	short	Short	16	
UInt16	ushort	N/A		
Int32	int	Integer	32	
UInt32	uint	N/A		
Int64	long	Long	64	
UInt64	ulong	N/A		

Figure 5.2: *C# and VB.NET Built-in Types*

There are two ways to define new value types. One way is to define a type whose base type is System.ValueType. The other way is to define a type whose base type is System.Enum. A C# struct definition is strikingly similar to a C# class definition except for the choice of keyword. There are a few subtle differences, however. For one thing, you cannot specify an explicit base type for a C# struct; rather, System.ValueType is always implied. Neither can you explicitly declare a C# struct as abstract or sealed; rather, the compiler implicitly adds sealed. Consider the following simple C# struct definition:

```
public struct Size {
  public int height;
  public int width;
  public void Scale(double factor) {
    height *= factor;
    width *= factor;
  }
  public int Area { get { return height * width; } }
}
```

Note that like a C# class definition, a C# struct can have methods and fields. A C# struct can also support arbitrary interfaces. Ultimately, a C# struct definition is equivalent to defining a new C# class that derives from `System.ValueType`. For example, the previous `struct` is conceptually equivalent to the following class definition:

```
public sealed class Size : System.ValueType {
  public int height;
  public int width;
  public void Scale(double factor) {
    height *= factor;
    width *= factor;
  }
  public int Area { get { return height * width; } }
}
```

However, the C# compiler will not allow `ValueType` to be used as a base. Rather, one must use the `struct` construct to achieve the same end.

C# `structs` are useful for defining types that act like user-defined primitives but contain arbitrary composite fields. It is also possible to define specializations of the integral types that do not add any new fields but rather simply restrict the value space of the specified integral type. These restricted integral types are called **enumeration types**.

Enumeration types are CLR value types whose immediate base type is `System.Enum` rather than `System.ValueType`. Enumeration types must specify a second type that will be used for the data representation of the enumeration. This second type must be one of the CLR's built-in integral types (excluding `System.Char`). An enumeration type can contain members; however, the only members that are supported are literal fields. The literal fields of an enumeration type must match the enumeration's underlying representation type and act as the set of legal values that can be used for instances of the enumeration.

One can create new enumeration types using C# enum definitions. A C# enum looks similar to a C or C++ enum. A C# enum definition contains a comma-delimited list of unique names:

```
public enum Breath {
  None, Sweet, Garlicky, Oniony,
  Rancid, Horrid, Sewerlike
}
```

The compiler will assign each of these names a numeric value. If no explicit values are provided (as is the case in this example), then the compiler will assign the values 0, 1, 2, and so on, in order of declaration. Conceptually, this enum is equivalent to the following C# class definition:

```
public sealed class Breath : System.Enum {
  public const int None      = 0;
  public const int Sweet     = 1;
  public const int Garlicky  = 2;
  public const int Oniony    = 3;
  public const int Rancid    = 4;
  public const int Horrid    = 5;
  public const int Sewerlike = 6;
}
```

However, as with ValueType, the C# compiler prohibits the explicit use of System.Enum as a base type and requires that one instead use the enum construct. Also, unlike C, C# does not consider numeric types to be type-compatible with enumerations. Rather, to treat an enum like an int (or vice versa), one must first explicitly cast to the desired type. In contrast, C++ allows implicit conversion from an enumerated type to a numeric type.

If no explicit underlying type is specified as part of the enum definition, the C# compiler will assume that the underlying type is System.Int32. One can override this default using the following syntax:

```
[ System.Flags ]
public enum Organs : byte {
  None   = 0x00,
  Heart  = 0x01,
  Lung   = 0x02
  Liver  = 0x04,
  Kidney = 0x08
}
```

This example declares the underlying type of each of the literal values to be System.Byte.

Although the member names of an enumeration must be unique, there is no such uniqueness requirement for the integral values of each member. In fact, it is common to use enumeration types to represent bitmasks. To make this usage explicit, an enumeration can have the `[System.Flags]` attribute. This attribute signals the intended usage to developers. This attribute also affects the underlying `ToString` implementation so that the stringified version of the value will be a comma-delimited list of member names rather than just a number.

Variables, Parameters, and Fields

Reference types always yield instances that are allocated on the heap. In contrast, value types yield instances that are allocated relevant to the context in which the variable is declared. If a local variable is of a value type, the CLR allocates the memory for the instance on the stack. If a field in a class is a member of a value type, then the CLR allocates the memory for the instance as part of the layout of the object or type in which the field is declared. The rules for dealing with value and reference types are consistent for variables, fields, and parameters. To that end, this chapter will use the term *variable* to refer to all three concepts and will use the term *local variable* when discussing variables by themselves.

As their name implies, **reference type variables** contain object references and not instances of the type they are declared as. A reference type variable simply contains the address of the object it refers to. This means that two reference type variables may refer to the same object. It also means that it is possible for an object reference to not refer to an object at all. Before one can use a reference type variable, one must first initialize it to point to a valid object. Attempts to access a member through an object reference that does not refer to a valid object will result in a runtime error. The default value for a reference type field is null, which is a well-known address that refers to no object. Any attempts to use a null reference will result in a `System.NullReferenceException`. As a point of interest, one can safely assume that any object reference one uses will always point to a valid object or null because the use of an uninitialized reference would be caught by either the compiler or the CLR's verifier. Moreover, the CLR will not deallocate the object while you have a live variable or field that refers to it.

To do any meaningful work, reference type variables require an object. In contrast, **value type variables** are the instances themselves, not references.

This means that a value type variable is useful immediately upon declaration. Listing 5.1 shows an example of two types that are identical except that one is a reference type and the other is a value type. Note that the variable v can be used immediately because the instance has already been allocated as part of the variable declaration. In contrast, the variable r cannot be used until it refers to a valid object on the heap. Figure 5.3 shows how the two variables are allocated in memory.

Listing 5.1: *Using Value and Reference Types*

```
public struct Size {
  public int height;
  public int weight;
}
public sealed class CSize {
  public int height;
  public int weight;
}
static App {
  static void Main() {
    Size v;              // v is an instance of Size
    v.height = 100;   // legal
    CSize r;             // r is a reference
    r.height = 100;   // illegal, r is dangling
    r = new CSize(); // r refers to an instance of CSize
    r.height = 100;   // legal, r no longer dangling
  }
}
```

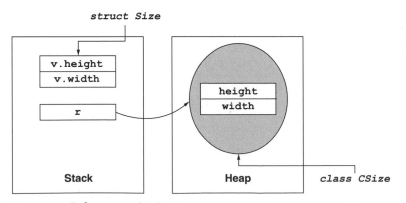

Figure 5.3: *Reference and Value Types*

It is interesting to note that the C# language allows you to use the new operator for both reference and value types. When used with a reference type, the C# new operator is translated to a CIL newobj instruction, which triggers an allocation on the heap followed by a call to the type's constructor. When one uses a value type, the CLR translates the C# new operator to a CIL initobj instruction, which simply initializes the instance in place using the default values for each field. In this respect, using new with a value type is similar to using C++'s placement operator new to invoke a constructor without allocating memory.

Assignment works differently for value and reference types. For reference types, assignment simply duplicates the reference to the original instance, resulting in two variables that refer to the same instance in memory. For value types, assignment overwrites one instance with the contents of another, with the two instances remaining completely unrelated after the assignment is done. Compare the code in Listing 5.2 (illustrated by Figure 5.4) to that in Listing 5.3 (illustrated by Figure 5.5). Note that in the reference type case, the assignment is only duplicating the reference and that changes through one variable are visible through the other. In contrast, the assignment of the value type yields a second independent instance. In the value type example, v1 and v2 name two distinct instances of type Size. In the reference type example, r1 and r2 are simply two names for the one instance of type CSize.

Listing 5.2: *Using Reference Types*

```
static App {
  static void Main() {
    CSize r1 = new CSize();// r1 refers to instance of CSize
    CSize r2 = r1;          // r2 points to same object as r1
    r1.height = 100;
    r2.height = 200;
    bool truth = r2.height == r1.height;
    bool moreTruth = r1.height == 200;
  }
}
```

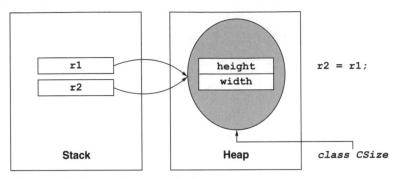

Figure 5.4: *Reference Types and Assignment*

Listing 5.3: *Using Value Types*

```
static App {
  static void Main() {
    Size v1 = new Size();    // v1 is an instance of Size
    Size v2 = v1;            // v2 is a 2nd instance of Size
    v1.height = 100;
    v2.height = 200;
    bool truth = v2.height != v1.height;
  }
}
```

Passing parameters to a method is a variation on assignment that bears special consideration. When one passes parameters to a method, the method's declaration determines whether the parameters will be passed by reference or by value. Passing parameters by value (the default) results in the method or callee getting its own private copy of the parameter values. As shown in Figure 5.6, if the parameter is a value type, the method

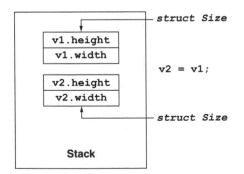

Figure 5.5: *Values and Assignment*

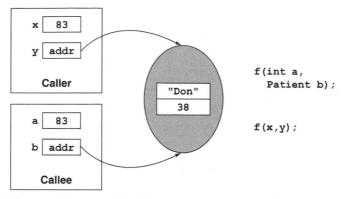

Figure 5.6: *Pass-by-Value Parameters*

gets its own private copy of the instance. If the parameter is a reference type, it is the reference (not the instance) that is passed by value. The object the reference points to is not copied. Rather, both the caller and the callee wind up with private references to a shared object.

Passing parameters by reference (indicated in C# using the ref or out modifier) results in the method or callee getting a managed pointer back to the caller's variables. As shown in Figure 5.7, any changes the method makes to the value type or the reference type will be visible to the caller. Moreover, if the method overwrites an object reference parameter to redirect it to another object in memory, this change also affects the caller's variable.

In the example shown in Figure 5.7, any assignments that the callee's method body may perform on the a or b parameter will affect the caller.

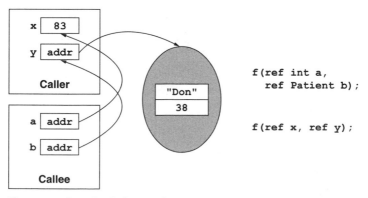

Figure 5.7: *Pass-by-Reference Parameters*

Specifically, this means that setting the b parameter to null will also set the caller's y variable to null. In contrast, in the example shown in Figure 5.6, the callee's method body may freely assign a and b to the parameters without affecting the caller in any way. However, the object referenced by the b parameter is shared with the caller, and the caller will see any changes made through b. This is true in both examples.

Equivalence Versus Identity

The CLR (like many other technologies) distinguishes between object equivalence and identity. This is especially important for reference types such as classes. In general, two objects are **equivalent** if they are instances of the same type and if each of the fields in one object matches the values of the fields in the other object. That does not mean that they are "the same object" but only that the two objects have the same values. In contrast, two objects are **identical** if they share an address in memory. Practically speaking, two references are identical if they refer to the same object.

Comparing object references for identity is trivial, requiring only a comparison of memory addresses, independent of type. One can perform this test via the `System.Object.ReferenceEquals` static method. This method simply compares the addresses contained in two object references independent of the types of objects involved.

Unlike identity comparison, comparing for equivalence is type-specific, and for that reason, `System.Object` provides an `Equals` virtual method to compare any two objects for equivalence, as shown in Listing 5.4. As shown in Figure 5.8 and Listing 5.5, the `Equals` method returns true provided that the two objects have equivalent values. `System.Object.ReferenceEquals` returns true only when the references refer to the same object.

Listing 5.4: *System.Object*

```
namespace System {
  public class Object {
// identity test
    public static bool ReferenceEquals(Object a, Object b);
// equivalence test
    public virtual   bool   Equals(Object rhs);
```

```
// equivalence test (false positives allowed)
   public virtual    int    GetHashCode();

   protected           Object MemberwiseClone();
   protected virtual void   Finalize();

// ToString and GetType omitted for clarity
  }
}
```

Listing 5.5: *Testing for Identity and Equivalence*

```
class Util {
  static void Main() {
    Object o1 = new Person();
    Object o2 = new Person();
    Debug.Assert(Object.ReferenceEquals(o1, o2) == false);
    bool whoKnows = o1.Equals(o2);  // cannot predict...
    o1 = o2;
    Debug.Assert(Object.ReferenceEquals(o1, o2) == true);
    Debug.Assert(o1.Equals(o2) == true);
  }
}
```

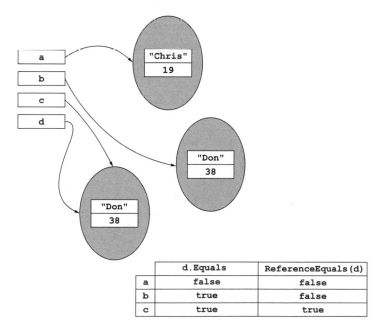

	d.Equals	ReferenceEquals(d)
a	false	false
b	true	false
c	true	true

Figure 5.8: *Object Equivalence versus Identity*

Implementations of Object.Equals need to ensure that the operation is reflexive, symmetric, and transitive. That is, given an instance of any type, the following assertion must always be true:

```
public sealed class Utils {
  public static void AssertReflexive(object o) {
    if (o != null)
      Debug.Assert(o.Equals(o));
  }
}
```

Similarly, Equals implementations must be **symmetric**:

```
public sealed class Utils {
  public static void AssertSymmetric(object o1, object o2){
    if (o1 != null && o2 != null)
      Debug.Assert(o1.Equals(o2) == o2.Equals(o1));
  }
}
```

Finally, Equals implementations must be **transitive** with respect to equality:

```
public sealed class Utils {
  public static void AssertTransitive(object o1,
                                      object o2,
                                      object o3) {
    if (o1 != null && o2 != null && o3 != null)
      if (o1.Equals(o2) && o2.Equals(o3))
        Debug.Assert(o1.Equals(o3));
  }
}
```

In most cases, the naive implementation of Equals will adhere to these three requirements.

Each type can implement its own version of the System.Object. Equals method, as shown in Listing 5.6. The default implementation of Object.Equals for reference types simply tests for identity, and this means that it returns true if and only if the two objects are actually the same object. Because value types typically do not have meaningful identity, the default implementation of `Object.Equals` for value types simply does a memberwise comparison by calling `Object.Equals` for all instance fields. The CLR is smart enough to optimize these calls away in many cases, such as when all of a type's fields are primitives, in which case the CLR can do a type-ignorant memory comparison.

Listing 5.6: *Implementing System.Object.Equals*

```
public sealed class Person {
  string name;
  double age;
  public override bool Equals(Object rhs) {
// always equal to self
    if (rhs == this) return true;
// other object must be a Person
    Person other = rhs as Person;
    if (other == null) return false;
// compare name and age
    return other.name == name && other.age == age;
  }
  public override int GetHashCode() {
// this assumes Person.name never changes!
    return name.GetHashCode();
  }
}
```

Types that override `Object.Equals` must also override `Object.Get-HashCode`. Programs can use the `Object.GetHashCode` method to determine whether two objects might be equivalent. If two objects return different hash codes, then they are guaranteed to not be equivalent. If two objects return the same hash codes, then they may or may not be equivalent. The only way to tell for sure is to then call the `Object.Equals` method. Implementations of `Object.GetHashCode` are typically much cheaper than `Object.Equals` because a definitive answer is not required.

It is difficult to look at identity and equivalence tests without considering program language specifics. In C++ and C#, the standard comparison operators are `==` and `!=`. When applied to primitives, these operators simply emit the CIL instructions to compare the two values directly. When applied to object references, these operators emit the CIL instruction that is the moral equivalent of calling System.Object.ReferenceEquals. However, both C++ and C# support operator overloading, and this means that a specific type may elect to map the == (and !=) operator to arbitrary code. One notable type that does just this is System.String. The System.String type overloads these operators to call the Equals method, and this results in the more intuitive equivalence comparison when used with strings. In general, types that override the Equals method should strongly consider overloading the == and != operators, especially if the type is (or behaves like) a value type.

GetHashCode and Equals are really designed for objects that act like values. In particular, they are designed for objects whose underlying values are immutable (such as System.String). Unfortunately, the contracts for GetHashCode and Equals have several inconsistencies when applied to objects whose equivalence can change over time. In general, implementing GetHashCode when there is no immutable (e.g., read only) field is exceedingly difficult.

For types that act like values, it is often useful to impose an ordering relationship on the instances of the type. To support this idea in a uniform way, the CLR provides a standard interface: System.IComparable. Types that implement the System.IComparable interface are indicating that their instances may be ordered. As shown here, IComparable has exactly one method, CompareTo:

```
namespace System {
  public interface IComparable {
    int CompareTo(Object rhs);
  }
}
```

The CompareTo method returns an int and can have three possible results. CompareTo must return a negative number if the object's value is less than that of the specified argument. CompareTo must return a positive number if the object's value is greater than that of the specified argument. If the object's value is equivalent to that of the specified argument, then CompareTo must return zero.

The IComparable interface is related to the System.Object.Equals method. Types that implement IComparable must provide an implementation of Object.Equals that is consistent with their IComparable. CompareTo implementation. Specifically, the following constraints must always be met:

```
using System;
public class Utils {
  static void Test(IComparable o1, object o2) {
// assert CompareTo == 0 implies Equals
    if (o1.CompareTo(obj2) == 0)
      Debug.Assert(o1.Equals(o2));

// assert Equals implies CompareTo == 0
    if (o1.Equals(o2))
      Debug.Assert(o1.CompareTo(o2) == 0);
  }
}
```

Similarly, types that override the System.Object.Equals method should also consider implementing IComparable. All of the primitive types and System.String are ordered and implement IComparable. Classes you write can be ordered provided that you implement IComparable in a way that makes sense for your type. Listing 5.7 shows a type that implements IComparable to support ordering of its instances.

Listing 5.7: *Implementing System.IComparable*

```
public sealed class Person : System.IComparable {
  internal int age;
  public int CompareTo(object rhs) {
    if (this == rhs) return 0; // same
    Person other = (Person)rhs;
    if (other.age > this.age)
      return -1;
    else if (other.age < this.age)
      return 1;
    else
      return 0;
  }
}
```

One could easily rewrite the compound `if-else` statement in the `CompareTo` method as follows:

```
return this.age - other.age;
```

That's because if `this.age` is greater than `other.age`, the method will return a positive number. If the two values are equivalent, the method will return zero. Otherwise, the method will return a negative number.

Cloning

Assigning one reference variable to another simply creates a second reference to the same object. To make a second copy of an object, one needs some mechanism to create a new instance of the same class and initialize it based on the state of the original object. The `Object.MemberwiseClone` method does exactly that; however, it is not a public method. Rather, objects that wish to support **cloning** typically implement the `System.ICloneable` interface, which has one method, `Clone`:

```
namespace System {
  public interface ICloneable {
    Object Clone();
  }
}
```

The `MemberwiseClone` method performs what is called a **shallow copy**, which means that it simply copies each field's value from the source object to the clone. If the field is an object reference, only the reference, and not the referenced object, is copied. The following class implements `ICloneable` using shallow copies:

```
public sealed class Marriage : System.ICloneable {
  internal Person g;
  internal Person b;

  public Object Clone() {
    return this.MemberwiseClone();
  }
}
```

Figure 5.9 shows the results of the shallow copy.

A **deep copy** is one that recursively copies all objects that its fields refer to, as shown in Figure 5.10. Deep copying is often what people expect; however, it is not the default behavior, nor is it a good idea to implement in the general case. In addition to causing additional memory movement and resource consumption, deep copies can be problematic when a graph of objects has cycles because a naive recursion would wind up in an infinite loop. However, for simple object graphs, it is at least implementable, as shown in Listing 5.8.

Listing 5.8: *Implementing System.ICloneable*

```
public sealed class Marriage : System.ICloneable {
   internal Person g;
   internal Person b;
   public Object Clone() {
// shallow copy first
      Marriage result = (Marriage)this.MemberwiseClone();
// deep copy each field
      result.g = (Person)(this.g.Clone());
      result.b = (Person)(this.b.Clone());
      return result;
   }
}
```

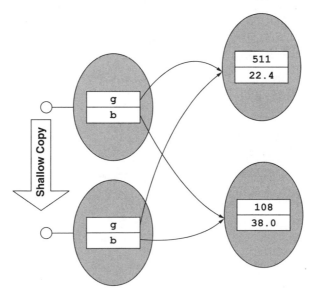

Figure 5.9: *Shallow Copy*

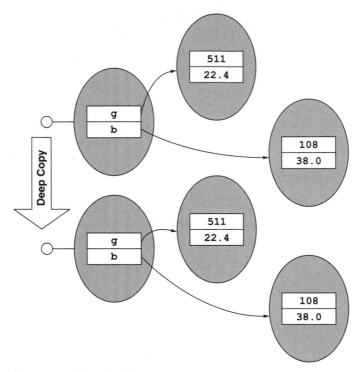

Figure 5.10: *Deep Copy*

It is interesting to note that the `Clone` implementation in Listing 5.8 could have been written without a call to `MemberwiseClone`. An alternative implementation could have simply used the `new` operator to instantiate the second object and then manually populate the fields. Moreover, a private constructor could have been defined to allow the two parts (instantiation and initialization) to happen in one step. Listing 5.9 shows just such an implementation.

Listing 5.9: *Implementing System.ICloneable Using the New Keyword*

```
public sealed class Marriage : System.ICloneable {
  internal Person g;
  internal Person b;

  private Marriage(Person g, Person b) {
    this.g = (Person)g.Clone();
    this.b = (Person)b.Clone();
  }
  public Object Clone() {
    return new Marriage(g, b);
  }
}
```

Boxing

As shown in Figure 5.1, all types are compatible with System.Object. However, because System.Object is a polymorphic type, instances in memory require an object header to support dynamic method dispatching. Value types do not have this header, nor are they necessarily allocated on the heap. The CLR allows one to use a value type (which ultimately is just memory) in contexts that use object references, such as collections or generic functions that accept System.Object as a method parameter. To support this, the CLR allows one to "clone" instances of value types onto the heap in a format that is compatible with System.Object. This procedure is known as **boxing** and occurs whenever an instance of a value type is assigned to an object reference variable, parameter, or field.

For example, consider the code in Listing 5.10. Note that when the instance of Size is assigned to an object reference variable (itf in this case), the CLR allocates a heap-based object that implements all of the interfaces that the underlying value type declared compatibility with. This boxed object is an independent copy, and changes to it do not propagate back to the original value type instance. However, it is possible to copy the boxed object back into a value type instance simply by using a down-cast operator, as shown in Listing 5.10. Figure 5.11 shows the process of boxing and unboxing, both visually and in code.

Listing 5.10: *Boxing in Action*

```
public interface IAdjustor {
  void Adjust();
}
public struct Size : IAdjustor {
  public void Adjust() { height+=2; weight+=3; }
  public int height;
  public int weight;
}
static App {
  static void Main() {
    Size s = new Size();
    bool truth = s.height == 0 && s.weight == 0;
    s.Adjust();
    truth = s.height == 2 && s.weight == 3;
    IAdjustor itf = s; // box
```

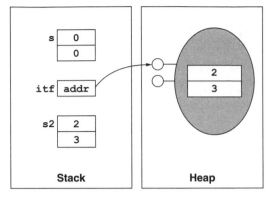

```
// create value type
size s = new Size ();
// box and use
IAdjustor itf = s;
itf.Adjust();
// unbox into s2
Size s2 = (Size)itf;
```

Figure 5.11: *Boxing and Unboxing*

```
    itf.Adjust();        // operate on boxed copy
    truth = s.height == 2 && s.weight == 3;
    s = (Size)itf;       // unbox
    truth = s.height == 4 && s.weight == 6;
  }
}
```

Arrays

The CLR supports two kinds of composite types: one kind whose members are accessed by a locally unique name, and another whose members are unnamed but instead are accessed by position. The classes and structs described so far are examples of the former. **Arrays** are an example of the latter.

Arrays are instances of a reference type. That reference type is **synthesized** by the CLR based on the element type and rank of the array. All array types extend the built-in type System.Array, which is shown in Listing 5.11. This implies that all of the methods of System.Array are implicitly available to any type of array. That also means that one can write a method that accepts any type of array by declaring a parameter of type System.Array. In essence, System.Array identifies the subset of objects that are actually arrays.

Listing 5.11: *System.Array (Excerpt 1)*

```
namespace System {
  public class Array {
// size/shape properties
    int Length { get; }
    int Rank    { get; }
    int GetLength(int dimension);
// getters
    Object GetValue(int i);
    Object GetValue(int i, int j);
    Object GetValue(int i, int j, int k);
    Object GetValue(int [] indices);
// setters
    void SetValue(Object value, int i);
    void SetValue(Object value, int i, int j);
    void SetValue(Object value, int i, int j, int k);
    void SetValue(Object value, int [] indices);
  }
}
```

Array types have their own type-compatibility rules based on the element type and the **shape** of the array. The shape of the array consists of the number of dimensions (also known as **rank**) as well as the capacity of each dimension. For determining type compatibility, two arrays whose element types and rank are identical are **type-compatible**. If the two arrays' element types are reference types, then additional compatibility can be assumed.

An array whose element type is a reference type (T) is type-compatible with all same-rank arrays having element type V provided that T is type-compatible with V. What this means is that all single-dimensional arrays (whose element types are reference types) are type-compatible with the type System.Object[] because all possible element types are themselves type-compatible with System.Object. Figure 5.12 illustrates this concept.

Most programming languages have some sort of array type. It is the job of the compiler to map the language-level array syntax down to a CLR array type. In the CLR, an array is an instance of a reference type and has methods, properties, and interfaces. Because arrays are reference types, an array can be passed efficiently wherever a System.Object is expected.

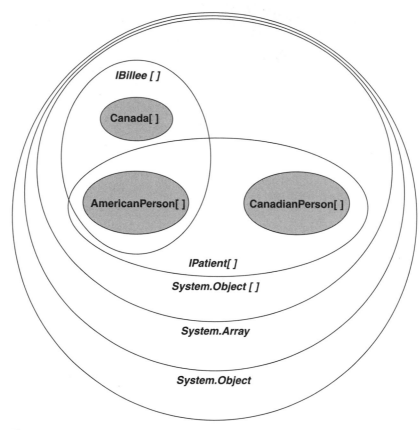

Figure 5.12: *Arrays and Type Compatibility*

Independent of the language in use, the total number of elements in the array is always available using the Length property.

Each programming language provides its own syntax for declaring array variables, initializing arrays, and accessing array elements. The following C# program fragment creates and uses a single-dimensional array of integers:

```
// declare reference to array of Int32
int[] rgn;
// allocate array of 9 elements
rgn = new int[9];
// touch all elements (index 0 through 8)
for (int i = 0; i < rgn.Length; ++i)
  rgn[i] = (i + 1) * 2;
```

Because arrays are reference types, the rgn variable in this example is a reference. The memory for the array elements is allocated on the heap.

The C# programming language supports a variety of syntaxes for initializing arrays. The following three techniques yield identical results:

```
// verbose
int[] a = new int[4];
for (int i = 0; i < a.Length; ++i)
  a[i] = (i + 1) * 2;

// compact
int[] b = new int[] { 2, 4, 6, 8 };

// ultra-compact
int[] c = { 2, 4, 6, 8 };
```

The compact variation has the advantage that the right-hand side of the initialization statement is a valid C# expression and can be used anywhere an int[] is expected.

An array consists of zero or more elements. These elements are accessed by position and must be a uniform type. For arrays of value types, each element will be an instance of exactly the same type (e.g., System.Int32). For arrays of reference types, each element may refer to an instance of a class that supports at least the element type, but the element may in fact refer to an instance of a derived type.

In single-dimensional arrays, the array elements are preceded by a length field that indicates the capacity of the array. One sets this field when one creates the array, and one cannot change it for the lifetime of the array. When one first instantiates an array, the CLR sets its elements to their default values. Once one instantiates the array, one can treat the elements of the array just like any other field of a type except that one addresses them by index rather than by name. Figure 5.13 shows an array of value types after each element has been assigned to. For arrays of reference types, each element is initially null and must be overwritten with a valid object reference to be useful. Figure 5.14 shows an array of reference types after each element has been assigned to.

Although the contents of an array can change after it has been created, the actual shape or capacity of the array is immutable and set at

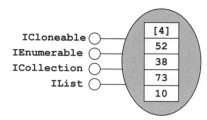

Figure 5.13: *Single-Dimensional Array of Value Types*

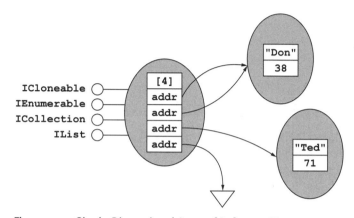

Figure 5.14: *Single-Dimensional Array of Reference Types*

array-creation time. The CLR provides higher-level collection classes (e.g., `System.Collections.ArrayList`) for dynamically sized collections. It is interesting to note that the array's capacity is not part of its type. For example, consider the following C# variable declaration:

```
int[] rgn = new int[100];
```

Note that the variable's type does not indicate the capacity of the array; that decision is postponed until the `new` operator is used. This is possible because the type of an array is based only on its element type and the number of dimensions (also known as rank) and not on its actual size.

Arrays in the CLR can be multidimensional. The preferred format for a multidimensional array is a **rectangular**, or C-style, array. A rectangular array has all of its elements stored in a contiguous block, as shown in Figure 5.15. Multidimensional arrays carry not only the capacity of each dimension but also the index used for the lower bound of each dimension.

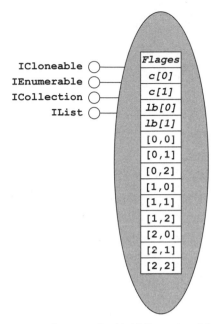

Figure 5.15: *Rectangular Multidimensional Array*

Despite the presence of a lower bound in the array, the CLR does not support arrays with nonzero lower bounds.

Each "row" in a rectangular array must have the same capacity, and hence we use the term *rectangular*. Listing 5.12 shows a simple rectangular array program. Note the use of commas to delimit the index of each dimension. Also note the use of the GetLength method to determine the length of each dimension. For rectangular arrays, the Length property returns the total number of elements in all dimensions (i.e., for an M-by-N two-dimensional array, Length returns M * N). Additionally, rectangular arrays have a variety of initialization syntaxes in C#, the most compact of which is shown here:

```
int[,] matrix = { { 1, 2, 3, 4  },
                  { 2, 4, 6, 8  },
                  { 3, 6, 9, 12 } };
```

Listing 5.12: *Creating and Using a Multidimensional Array*

```
// declare reference to 2D array of Int32
int[,] matrix;
// allocate array of 3x4 elements
matrix = new int[3,4];
```

```
// touch all elements in order
for (int i = 0; i < matrix.GetLength(0); ++i)
  for (int j = 0; j < matrix.GetLength(1); ++j)
    matrix[i,j] = (i + 1) * (j + 1);
```

Your programming language will likely have its own idiosyncratic ways of doing the same thing. As always, consult the appropriate programming language reference.

Another form of multidimensional array is a **jagged** array, or Java-style array. A jagged array is really just an "array of arrays" and rarely if ever are its elements stored in a contiguous block, as shown in Figure 5.16. Each "row" in a jagged array may have a different capacity, and hence we use the term *jagged*. Listing 5.13 shows a simple jagged array program. Note the alternate syntax for indexing each dimension. Also note that the use of the Length property now works as expected because the "root" array is actually a one-dimensional array whose elements are themselves references to arrays. Although jagged arrays are quite flexible, they lend themselves to a different set of optimizations from a rectangular array. Also, VB.NET has a difficult (but not impossible) time handling jagged arrays.

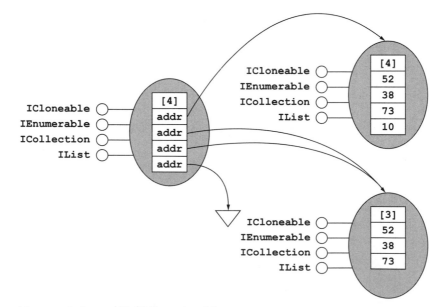

Figure 5.16: *Jagged Multidimensional Array*

Listing 5.13: *Creating and Using a Jagged Array*

```
// declare reference to jagged array of Int32
int[][] matrix;
// allocate array of 3 elements
matrix = new int[3][];
// allocate 3 subarrays of 4 elements
matrix[0] = new int[4];
matrix[1] = new int[4];
matrix[2] = new int[4];
// touch all elements in order
for (int i = 0; i < matrix.Length; ++i)
  for (int j = 0; j < matrix[i].Length; ++j)
    matrix[i][j] = (i + 1) * (j + 1);
```

Arrays support a common set of operations. Beyond the basic accessor methods shown in Listing 5.11, arrays support bulk copy operations, which are shown in Listing 5.14. In particular, the Copy method supports copying a range of elements from one array into another. Listing 5.15 shows these methods in action.

Listing 5.14: *System.Array (Excerpt 2)*

```
namespace System {
  public class Array {
// copy descriptor + elements
    Object Clone();
// copy elements
    static void Copy(Array source,
                     Array dest,
                     int nElems);
    static void Copy(Array source,
                     int sourceOffset,
                     Array dest,
                     int sourceOffset,
                     int nElems);
// clear (zero or null) elements
    static void Clear(Array source,
                      int initialIndex,
                      int nElems);
  }
}
```

Listing 5.15: *Using System.Array*

```
void Main() {
  int[] left = { 1, 2, 3, 4, 5, 6 };
  Array.Clear(left, 3, 2);
// left == { 1, 2, 3, 0, 0, 6 }
  Array.Copy(left, 0, left, 3, 2);
// left == { 1, 2, 3, 1, 2, 6 }
}
```

The System.Array type has several methods that apply only when the array's elements support IComparable. Listing 5.16 shows these methods. Technically, Array.IndexOf and Array.LastIndexOf require the elements only to implement Equals in a meaningful way. Listing 5.17 shows both the IndexOf and BinarySearch in action. Although the BinarySearch method requires the array to be already sorted, it performs in O(log(n)) time, which is considerably better than the O(n) time taken by IndexOf.

Listing 5.16: *System.Array (Excerpt 3)*

```
namespace System {
  public class Array {
// linear search using Object.Equals (-1 if not found)
    static int  IndexOf(Array array, Object value);
    static int  LastIndexOf(Array array, Object value);
// sort elements in place using IComparable
    static void Sort(Array array);
// reverse elements in place
    static void Reverse(Array array);
// binary search a sorted array
// (negative index of next highest value if not found)
    static int  BinarySearch(Array array, Object value);
  }
}
```

Listing 5.17: *Using System.Array (Revisited)*

```
void Main() {
  int[] values = { 0, 2, 4, 6, 8, 10, 12 };
  int index = Array.IndexOf(values, 6); // returns 3
  index = Array.BinarySearch(values, 6); // returns 3
  index = Array.IndexOf(values, 7); // returns -1
  index = Array.BinarySearch(values, 7); // returns -4
}
```

Object Life Cycle

This chapter has focused on how objects and values are allocated and referenced. There has been no mention of how or when programmers reclaim the underlying memory an object resides in over the lifetime of a running program. This is a feature. One of the primary benefits of the CLR's managed execution mode is that memory reclamation is no longer the purview of the programmer. Rather, the CLR is responsible for all memory allocation (and deallocation). The policies and mechanisms used by the CLR for managing memory are the subject of the remainder of this chapter.

The CLR is aware of all object references in the system. Based on this global knowledge, the runtime can detect when an object is no longer referenced. The runtime distinguishes between root references and nonroot references. A **root reference** is typically either a live local variable or a static field of a class. A **nonroot reference** is typically an instance field in an object. The existence of a root reference is sufficient to keep the referenced object in memory. An object that has no root references is potentially no longer in use. To be exact, an object is guaranteed to remain in memory only for as long as one can reach it by traversing an object graph starting with a root reference. Objects that cannot be reached directly or indirectly via a root reference are susceptible to automatic memory reclamation, also known as **garbage collection** (GC).

Figure 5.17 shows a simple object graph and both root and nonroot references. Note that the set of roots is dynamic based on the execution of the program. In this example, the reachability graph shown is the one that is valid during the execution of the highlighted ReadLine call. Note that lexical scope is unimportant. Rather, the CLR uses liveness information created by the JIT compiler to determine which local variables are live for any given instruction pointer value. This is why temp2 is not considered a Live root in Figure 5.17.

It is sometimes desirable to hold a reference to an object that does not prevent the object from being garbage-collected. For example, keeping a lookup table of named objects in a static collection would normally prevent the named objects from ever being garbage-collected:

```
using System;
using System.Collections;
public class FancyObjects {
  private string name;
  private FancyObjects(string name) { this.name = name; }

// private static cache of well-known objects
  static IDictionary table = new Hashtable();

// public accessor function
  public static FancyObject Get(string name) {
    lock (typeof(FancyObjects)) {
// check cache
      FancyObject result = (FancyObject)table[name];
// create and cache if not there already
      if (result == null) {
        result = new FancyObject(name);
        table[name] = result;
      }
      return result;
    }
  }
}
```

This class ensures that, at most, one instance of a given named object will reside in memory at one time. However, because the CLR never removes the references held by the Hashtable object from the collection, none of these objects will ever be garbage-collected because the Hashtable itself remains reachable for the lifetime of this class. Ideally, the cache represented by the Hashtable would hold only "advisory" references that, by themselves, would not be sufficient to keep the target object alive. This is the role of the System.WeakReference type.

The System.WeakReference type adds a level of indirection between an object reference and the target object. When the garbage collector is chasing down roots to determine which objects are reachable, the intermediate WeakReference stops further traversal by the garbage collector. If the target object is not reachable via some other path, the CLR will reclaim the object's memory. Equally important, the CLR sets the reference inside the WeakReference object to null to ensure that the object cannot be accessed after it has been collected. The CLR makes this internal reference

```
public sealed class Person {
  Person spouse;
  static Person dave;
  static Person() {
    dave = new Person() ;
    dave.spouse = new Person() ;
    dave.spouse.spouse = dave;
  }
  public static void f() {
    Person temp1 = new Person() ;
    Person temp2 = new Person() ;
    System.Console.ReadLine() ;
    Console.WriteLine(temp1) ;
  }
}
```

Legend: all spouse fields are non-roots; **dave** and **temp1** are Live roots; temp2 is a dead variable.

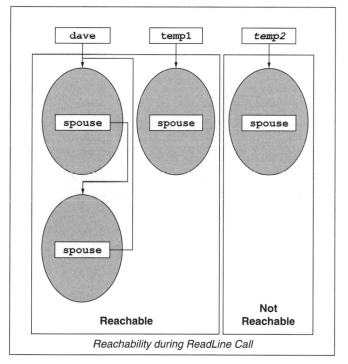

Reachability during ReadLine Call

Figure 5.17: *Root and Nonroot References*

available via the `WeakReference.Target` property, which will simply return `null` if the target has been collected.

To grasp how weak references are used, consider this modified version of the `Get` method just presented:

```
public static FancyObject Get(string name) {
   lock (typeof(FancyObjects)) {
// check cache for weak reference
      WeakReference weak = (WeakReference)table[name];
// try to dereference weak ref
      FancyObject result = null;
      if (weak != null)
        result = (FancyObject)weak.Target;

// create and cache if not there already or has been GCed
      if (result == null) {
         result = new FancyObject(name);
// cache weak reference only!
         table[name] = new WeakReference(result);
      }
      return result;
   }
}
```

Note that the `Hashtable` holds only weak references. This means that an entry in the cache is not sufficient to prevent the target object from being collected. Also note that when one performs a lookup on the cache, one must take care to ensure that the target object has not been collected since the time it was cached. One does this by checking the `Target` property for `null`.

The CLR performs garbage collection only when certain resource thresholds are exceeded. When this happens, the CLR takes over the CPU to track down objects that are reachable via a root reference. After identifying all of these objects, the garbage collector reclaims all remaining memory on the heap for subsequent allocations. As part of memory reclamation, the garbage collector will relocate the surviving objects in memory to avoid heap fragmentation and to tune the process's working set by keeping live objects in fewer pages of virtual memory.

The CLR exposes the garbage collector programmatically via the `System.GC` class. The most interesting method is `Collect`, which instructs the CLR to collect garbage immediately. Listing 5.18 shows this method in use. Note that in this example, one can reclaim the object referenced by r2 at the first call to System.GC.Collect inasmuch as the CLR can detect that the referenced object is no longer needed, despite the fact that it is still within lexical scope in C#. By the time the second call to System.GC.Collect executes, one can also reclaim the objects originally referenced by r1 and r3 because r1 is explicitly set to null and r3 is no longer a live variable. You can trick the garbage collector into keeping an object reference "alive" by inserting a call to System.GC.KeepAlive. This static method does nothing other than trick the CLR into thinking that the reference passed as the parameter is actually needed, thereby keeping the referenced object from being reclaimed.

Listing 5.18: *Liveness and Garbage Collection*

```
class UseEm {
  static Object r1; // r1 is a root!
  static void Main() {
    r1 = new Object();
    Object r2 = new Object();
    Object r3 = new Object();
    System.GC.Collect(); // what can be reclaimed here?
    r1 = null;
    r3.ToString();
    System.GC.Collect(); // what can be reclaimed here?
  }
}
```

The Collect method takes an optional parameter that controls how vast the search for unreferenced objects should be. The CLR uses a generational algorithm that recognizes that the longer an object is referenced, the less likely it is to become available for collection. The Collect method allows you to specify how "old" an object to consider. Be aware, however, that frequent calls to GC.Collect can have a negative impact on performance.

Finalization

In general, there is no need for your object to know when it is being garbage-collected. All subordinate objects that your object references will themselves be automatically reclaimed as part of normal GC operation.

The preferred mechanism for triggering the execution of cleanup code is to use a termination handler. **Termination handlers** protect a range of instructions inside a method by guaranteeing that a "handler" block will execute prior to leaving the protected range of instructions. This mechanism is exposed to C# programmers via the `try-finally` construct discussed in Chapter 6.

Despite the existence of the termination handler mechanism, old habits often die hard, and programmers who cut their teeth on C++ are accustomed to tying cleanup code to object lifetime. To allow these old dogs to avoid learning new tricks, the CLR supports a mechanism known as **object finalization**. However, because object finalization happens asynchronously, it is fundamentally different from the C++-style destructor that many programmers (the author included) grew to depend on in the previous millennium. Please be aware, however, that new designs that target the CLR should avoid making extensive use of finalization because it is fraught with complexity as well as performance penalties.

Objects that wish to be notified when they are about to be returned to the heap can override the `Object.Finalize` method. When the GC tries to reclaim an object that has a finalizer, the reclamation is postponed until the finalizer can be called. Rather than reclaim the memory, the GC enqueues the object requiring finalization onto the finalization queue. A dedicated GC thread will eventually call the object's finalizer, and after the finalizer has completed execution, the object's memory is finally available for reclamation. This means that objects with finalizers take at least two separate rounds of garbage collection before they are finally collected.

Your object can perform any application-specific logic in response to this notification. Be aware, however, that the CLR may call the `Object.Finalize` method long after the garbage collector identifies your object as unreachable and that this method will execute on one of the CLR's internal threads. A considerable amount of time can elapse between the point at which the garbage collector identifies your object as unreachable and the point when its finalizer is called. If you use your finalizer to release a scarce resource, in many cases it will run far later than is tolerable, and this limits the utility of finalization.

Classes that override the default `Finalize` method need to call their base type's version of the method to ensure that any base class functionality is not bypassed. In C#, you cannot implement the `Finalize` method directly. Rather, you must implement a **destructor**, which causes the compiler to emit your destructor code inside a `Finalize` method followed by a call to your base type's `Finalize`. Listing 5.19 shows a simple C# class that contains a destructor. Note that the comments show the compiler-generated `Finalize` method.

Listing 5.19: *Implementing System.Object.Finalize in C#*

```
public sealed class Transaction {
  int lowLevelTX;
  public Transaction() {
    lowLevelTX = raw.BeginTransaction();
  }
  public void Commit() {
    raw.CommitTransaction(lowLevelTX);
    lowLevelTX = 0;
  }
// Finalizer
  ~Transaction() {
    if (lowLevelTX != 0)
      raw.AbortTransaction(lowLevelTX);
  }
/*
  ~Transaction is equivalent to this:
  protected override void Finalize() {
    if (lowLevelTX != 0)
      raw.AbortTransaction(lowLevelTX);
    base.Finalize();
  }
*/
}
```

Because GC is asynchronous, it is a bad idea to rely on a finalizer to clean up scarce resources. To that end, there is a standard idiom in CLR programming of providing an explicit `Dispose` method that clients can call when they are finished using your object. In fact, the `System.IDisposable` interface standardizes this idiom. Here is the definition of `System.IDisposable`:

```
namespace System {
  public interface IDisposable {
    void Dispose();
  }
}
```

Classes that implement this interface are indicating that they require explicit cleanup. It is ultimately the client programmer's responsibility to invoke the `IDisposable.Dispose` method as soon as the referenced object is no longer needed. Because your `Dispose` method is likely to perform the same work as your `Finalize` method, it is standard practice to suppress the redundant finalization call inside your `Dispose` method by calling `System.GC.SuppressFinalize`, as shown in Listing 5.20.

Listing 5.20: *Implementing Dispose*

```
public sealed class Transaction : IDisposable {
  int lowLevelTX;
  public int id { get { return lowLevelTX; } }
  public Transaction() {
    lowLevelTX = raw.BeginTransaction();
  }
  public void Commit() {
    raw.CommitTransaction(lowLevelTX);
    lowLevelTX = 0;
  }
  private void cleanUp() {
    if (lowLevelTX != 0)
      raw.AbortTransaction(lowLevelTX);
  }
  public void Dispose() {
    System.GC.SuppressFinalize(this);
    cleanUp();
    // call base.Dispose(); if necessary
  }
// Finalizer
  ~Transaction() {
    cleanUp();
  }
}
```

Listing 5.21 shows a client that explicitly invokes the Dispose method on an object after it has finished using it. To ensure that the user of the object always calls the Dispose method even in the face of exceptions, the C# programming language provides a construct that wraps the declaration of an IDisposable-compatible variable with a termination handler that implicitly calls Dispose for you. This construct is the C# using statement.

Listing 5.21: *References and Deterministic Finalization*

```
class App {
  static void Main() {
    Transaction tx = new Transaction();
    Console.WriteLine(tx.id);
    tx.Dispose(); // transaction synchronously aborted
  }
}
```

Figure 5.18 shows the syntax for the using statement. The using statement allows the programmer to declare one or more variables whose IDisposable.Dispose method will be called automatically. The syntax for the resource acquisition clause is similar to that for a local variable declaration statement. One can declare more than one variable, but the types of each of the variables must be the same. Listing 5.22 shows a simple usage of the using statement. Note that in this example, because the using statement is used with IDisposable-compliant objects, the compiler emits code that ensures that the Dispose method is invoked even in the face of unhandled exceptions or other method termination (e.g., a return statement).

Resource acquisition/local variable declarations

```
using (T obj1 = new T(), obj2 = new T()) {
  // obj1 and obj2 are local variables
} // obj2.Dispose/obj1.Dispose called here
```

Figure 5.18: *The C# using Statement*

Listing 5.22: *C#'s using Statement*

```
class App {
  static void Main() {
    using (Transaction tx = new Transaction()) {
      Console.WriteLine(tx.id);
    } // IDisposable.Dispose called automatically here

// the following code is functionally identical to
// the previous using statement

    Transaction tx = new Transaction();
    try {
      Console.WriteLine(tx.id);
    }
    finally {
      if (tx != null) ((IDisposable)tx).Dispose();
    }
  }
}
```

Where Are We?

Objects are polymorphic entities that the CLR always allocates on the heap. Values are simply formatted memory that is allocated as part of a declaring context or scope. Both objects and values can support the concept of equivalence and ordering, but only objects can truly support the concept of identity. Although it is possible to force values to act like objects (or objects to act like values), the programming model is much easier to live with when one uses the right kind of instance for the task at hand.

■ 6 ■
Methods

T HE PREVIOUS CHAPTERS have constructed a world in which types, objects, and values are dynamically brought into existence and can be referenced, created, and, in some cases, destroyed. However, the most interesting thing one can do with a type, object, or value, is invoke a method because that is the primary way that the three entities can interact.

Methods and JIT Compilation

The CLR executes only native machine code. If a method body consists of CIL, it must be translated to native machine code prior to invocation. As discussed briefly in Chapter 1, there are two options for converting CIL to native machine code. The default scenario is to postpone the translation until sometime after the component is loaded into memory. This approach is called **just-in-time (JIT) compilation**, or JIT-compiling for short. An alternative scenario is to generate a native image when the component is first installed on the deployment machine. This approach is called **precompiling**. The CLR provides a deployment tool (NGEN.EXE) and an underlying library (MSCORPE.DLL) to generate native images at deployment time.

When NGEN.EXE and MSCORPE.DLL generate a native image, it is stored on disk in a machine-wide code cache so that the loader can find it. When the loader tries to load a CIL-based version of an assembly, it also looks in the cache for the corresponding native image and will use the native machine code if possible. If no suitable native image is found, the CLR will use the CIL-based version that it initially loaded.

Although generating native images at deployment time sounds attractive, it is not without its downsides. One reason not to cache native images on disk has to do with code size. As a rule, native IA-32 machine code is larger than the corresponding CIL. For a typical component, the application in its steady state is likely to use only a small number of methods. When the CLR generates a native image, the new DLL will contain the native code for every method, including methods that may never be called or, at best, are called only occasionally, such as initialization or termination code or error-handling code. The inclusion of every method implementation causes the overall in-memory code size to grow needlessly. Worse, the placement of individual method bodies does not take into account the dynamics of the running program. Because one cannot change the method locations in the NGEN.EXE-generated image after the code is generated, each of the handful of needed methods may wind up occupying a different virtual memory page. This fragmentation has a negative impact on the working set size of the application.

A second issue related to caching native images has to do with cross-component contracts. For the CLR to generate native code, all types that are used by a method must be visible to the translator, because the native code must contain nonvirtualized offsets a la classic C, C++, COM, and Win32 contracts. This cross-component dependency can be problematic when a method relies on types in another component because any changes whatsoever to the other component will invalidate the cached native code. For that reason, every module is assigned a **module version identifier (MVID)** when it is compiled. The MVID is simply a unique identifier that is guaranteed to be unique for a particular compilation of a module.

When the CLR generates and caches a native image, the MVID of every module used to generate the native image (including those from external assemblies) is stored with the native code. When the CLR loader tries to load a cached native image, it first checks the MVIDs of the components used during the CIL-to-native generation process to verify that none of them has been recompiled. If a recompilation has taken place, the CLR ignores the cached native image and falls back to the version of the component that contains CIL.

If a native image cannot be found in the cache (or is stale because of recompilation of dependencies), the CLR loads a CIL-based version of the component. In this scenario, the CLR JIT-compiles methods just before they are first executed. When a method is JIT-compiled, the CLR must load any types that the method uses as parameters or local variables. The CLR may or may not need to JIT-compile any subordinate methods that are to be called by this method at that time. To understand how JIT compilation works, let's examine a small amount of grunge code. Recall from the discussion of casting in Chapter 4 that the CLR allocates an in-memory data structure for each type that it initializes. Under version 1.0 of the CLR, this data structure is internally called a `CORINFO_CLASS_STRUCT` and is referenced by the `RuntimeTypeHandle` stored in every object. On an IA-32 processor, a `CORINFO_CLASS_STRUCT` has 40 bytes of header information followed by the method table. The method table is a length-prefixed array of memory addresses, one entry per method. Unlike those in C++ and COM, a CLR method table contains entries for both instance and static methods.

The CLR routes all method calls through the method table of the method's declaring type. For example, given the following simple class, the call from `Bob.f` to `Bob.c` will always go through `Bob`'s method table.

```
class Bob {
  static int x;
  static void a() { x += 2; }
  static void b() { x += 3; }
  static void c() { x += 4; }
  static void f()
  { c(); b(); a(); }
}
```

In fact, the native IA-32 code for `Bob.f` would look like this:

```
; set up stack frame
push ebp
mov  ebp,esp

; invoke Bob.c through method table
  call dword ptr ds:[37565Ch]

; invoke Bob.b through method table
  call dword ptr ds:[375658h]
```

```
; invoke Bob.a through method table
  call dword ptr ds:[375654h]

; clean up stack and return
pop  ebp
ret
```

The addresses used in the IA-32 `call` instructions correspond to the method table entries for `Bob.c`, `Bob.b`, and `Bob.a`, respectively.

Every entry in a type's method table points to a unique stub routine. Initially, each stub routine contains a call to the CLR's JIT compiler (which is exposed via the internal `PreStubWorker` routine). After the JIT compiler produces the native machine code, the JIT compiler overwrites the stub routine, inserting a `jmp` instruction that jumps to the freshly JIT-compiled code. This means that the second and subsequent calls to the method will not incur any overhead other than the single `jmp` instruction that sits between the call site and the method body. This technique is extremely similar to the delay-load feature added to Visual C++ 6.0. This feature was completely explained by Matt Peitrek and Jeff Richter in two articles in the December 1998 issue of *Microsoft Systems Journal*.

Figure 6.1 shows our simple C# class as it is being JIT-compiled. Specifically, this figure shows a snapshot of `Bob`'s method table during a call to `Bob.f` after f has called `Bob.c` but before f has called b or a. Note that because the `Bob.c` method has already been called, the stub for c is a `jmp` instruction that simply passes control to the native code for `Bob.c`. In contrast, `Bob.a` and `Bob.b` have yet to be called, so the stub routines for a and b contain the generic `call` statement that passes control to the JIT compiler.

Technically, Figure 6.1 doesn't tell the whole story. Specifically, each method stub initially contains both a `call` statement and the address of the specific method's CIL. The method stub calls into a small amount of prolog code that extracts the address of the method's CIL from the code stream and then passes that address to `PreStubWorker` (the JIT compiler). Figure 6.2 shows this process in detail.

That single `jmp` instruction may have performance wonks concerned. However, the level of indirection provided by the extra `jmp` instruction allows the CLR to tune the working set of an application on-the-fly. If the CLR determines that a given method will no longer be needed, it can

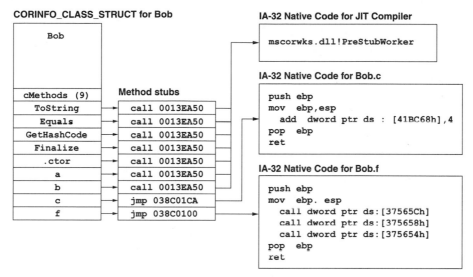

CORINFO_CLASS_STRUCT for Bob

Bob

cMethods (9)
ToString
Equals
GetHashCode
Finalize
.ctor
a
b
c
f

Method stubs

call 0013EA50
call 0013EA50
call 0013EA50
call 0013EA50
call 0013EA50
call 0013EA50
call 0013EA50
jmp 038C01CA
jmp 038C0100

IA-32 Native Code for JIT Compiler

```
mscorwks.dll!PreStubWorker
```

IA-32 Native Code for Bob.c

```
push ebp
mov  ebp,esp
  add  dword ptr ds : [41BC68h],4
pop  ebp
ret
```

IA-32 Native Code for Bob.f

```
push ebp
mov  ebp. esp
  call dword ptr ds:[37565Ch]
  call dword ptr ds:[375658h]
  call dword ptr ds:[375654h]
pop  ebp
ret
```

Figure 6.1: *JIT Compilation and Method Tables*

"pitch" the native method body and reset the jmp instruction to point to the JIT routine. Conceivably, native method bodies could even be relocated in memory to put frequently accessed methods in the same (or adjacent) virtual memory pages. Because all invocations go through the jmp instruction, making this change requires the CLR to rewrite only one memory location, no matter how many call sites refer to the relocated method.

Method Invocation and Type

Based on the discussion of JIT compilation and invocation, it is apparent that type is involved in method invocation. Specifically, the CLR uses the method table for a type to locate the address of the target method. Consider the following simple type definition:

```
public class Bob {
  public void f() { }
  static public void UseBob(int n, Bob b) {
    b.f();
  }
}
```

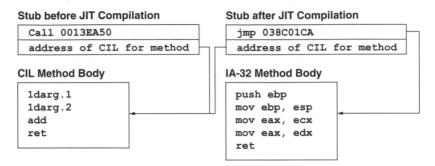

Figure 6.2: *Method Stub before and after JIT Compilation*

Ignoring method prolog and epilog, the JIT compiler would generate the following IA-32 native code for the `UseBob` method:

```
mov ecx, esi
call dword ptr ds:[352108h]
```

The first instruction moves the target object reference into the `ecx` register. This is because the JIT compiler typically uses the `__fastcall` stack discipline, and that causes the first two parameters to be passed in the `ecx` and `edx` registers, if possible. The second instruction calls the target method indirectly. The indirection uses a specific slot in the method table for `Bob`—in this case, `dword ptr [352108h]`.

Note that in the IA-32 `call` statement just shown, the exact address of `Bob`'s method table slot is baked into the JIT-compiled method. That means that even in the presence of a derived type (shown in the following code snippet), the `UseIt` method always dispatches to `Bob.f`, even if the derived type has a method whose name and signature match exactly.

```
public class Steve : Bob {
  public void f() { }
  static public Exploit(Steve s) {
    Bob.UseIt(s); // call UseIt but pass a Steve
  }
}
```

To cause the JIT compiler to consider the concrete type of the object, one needs to declare the method as `virtual`.

A **virtual method** is an instance method whose implementation can be replaced or overridden by a derived type. Virtual methods are identified by the presence of the `virtual` metadata attribute. At development time, when a compiler encounters a call to a `virtual` method in source code, it emits a `callvirt` CIL opcode rather than the traditional `call` opcode. The corresponding native code for a `callvirt` instruction is different than that for a `call` instruction. As described in the previous section, a CIL `call` instruction statically binds the native IA-32 `call` instruction to the method table of a particular type. In contrast, a CIL `callvirt` instruction results in an extra IA-32 instruction that determines which method table to use based on the target object's `RuntimeTypeHandle`. This allows the concrete type of the target object to determine which method will be invoked. Because the CLR needs the concrete type of an object to determine which method table to use, the virtual method mechanism is not available for `static` methods. Additionally, if a `callvirt` instruction is executed against a `null` reference, a `System.NullReferenceException` will be thrown.

The CLR allocates entries in the method table differently for virtual methods than for nonvirtual methods. Specifically, the method table has two contiguous regions. The first region is used for virtual methods. The second region is used for nonvirtual methods. The first region will contain one entry for each method that has been declared `virtual`, both in the current type and in all base types and interfaces. The second region will contain one entry for each non-`virtual` method that is declared in the current type. This separation allows a derived type's method table to replace a base type's method table for virtual method dispatch, because the indices used for a particular virtual method will be the same up and down the inheritance hierarchy.

The CLR dispatches calls to virtual methods by accessing the method table referenced by the target object's type handle. This allows the object's concrete type to determine exactly which code will execute. Had the `Bob.f` method in the previous example been declared `virtual`, the `Bob.UseIt` method would look like this:

```
move ecx, esi
move eax, dword ptr [ecx]
call dword ptr [eax + 38h]
```

The first mov instruction simply stores the target object reference in the IA-32 ecx register. This instruction is required for both virtual and nonvirtual calls because the CLR's calling convention requires that the this pointer be stored in ecx prior to invocation. The second mov instruction is unique to virtual method dispatching. This instruction stores the object's type handle in the IA-32 eax register. The type handle is then used by the IA-32 call instruction to locate the actual address of the target method. Figure 6.3 shows what this call looks like in memory.

Note that in the IA-32 call instruction just described, the CLR indexes the type's method table based on a fixed methodoffset. For a particular virtual method, this offset may be different for different executions of the program; however, it will be constant for the lifetime of a running program. Like field offsets, **method table offsets** are calculated at type load time. Each virtual method's metadata attributes control the offsets chosen. Table 6.1 shows the metadata attributes that influence the method table. The attribute that has the greatest influence on method offsets is newslot.

The CLR assigns each virtual method a **slot** in the method table that will contain a pointer to the method's code. The CLR assumes that virtual methods that are declared as newslot are unrelated to any methods declared in the base type. The CLR assigns virtual methods declared as newslot a new methodoffset that is at least 1 greater than the highest methodoffset used by the base type. Because System.Object, the ultimate base type of all concrete types, has four virtual methods, the first four slots in every method table correspond to these four methods.

If a virtual method does not have the newslot metadata attribute set, the CLR assumes that this method is a replacement for a virtual method in the base type. In this case, the CLR will look in the base type's metadata for a virtual method whose name and signature match the derived method. If it finds a match, then that method's methodoffset will be reused, and the corresponding slot in the derived type's method table will point to the derived replacement method. Because calls through references of the base type use this index, calls to the derived type will be dispatched to the derived type's method and not the base's method; the fact that the call may be issued through a base-type reference is immaterial.

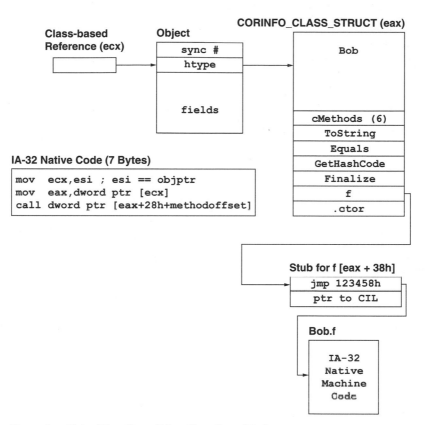

Figure 6.3: *Virtual Functions Using Class-Based References*

TABLE 6.1 Metadata Attributes and Virtual Methods

Metadata Attribute	Present (1)	Absent (0)
`virtual`	Method table index in virtual range	Method table index in nonvirtual range
`newslot`	Allocate a new virtual method table index	Reuse index from base type method if possible
`abstract*`	Require replacement in derived type	Allow replacement in derived type
`final*`	Prohibit replacement in derived type	Allow replacement in derived type

*`final` and `abstract` are mutually exclusive.

A virtual method that is not marked with the `newslot` metadata attribute is assumed to be a replacement for a virtual method of the base type. However, if the CLR finds no matching method in the base, then it treats the method as if it were declared as `newslot`.

It is possible to mandate or prohibit replacement of a virtual method using the `abstract` and `final` attributes, respectively. The `abstract` attribute mandates replacement of a virtual method by a derived type. Abstract methods are only declarations and do not have method implementations because their replacement by a derived type is mandatory. By inference, types that contain one or more `abstract` methods must themselves be marked `abstract` because the type specification is incomplete until a replacement for the abstract method is made available. All instance methods declared by an interface are required to be marked as `abstract`, and most programming languages do this for you implicitly.

When one replaces a virtual method in a base type, one can suppress further replacement by any downstream derived types. One does this by setting the `final` metadata attribute. Applying the `final` attribute to a method tells the CLR to disallow replacement of the method for all derived types. Obviously, one cannot combine the `final` attribute with the `newslot abstract` attribute, which mandates method replacement by the derived type.

Each programming language provides its own syntax for specifying the `virtual`, `abstract`, `newslot`, and `final` metadata attributes. Table 6.2 shows the keywords used by C#. As mentioned previously, marking a method as `new` in C# does not affect the generated code or metadata; rather, the keyword simply suppresses a compiler warning.

When a derived type provides an implementation overriding a base type's method, all invocations of that method will dispatch to the derived type's code. Consider the type hierarchy shown in Listing 6.1, which does not use virtual methods. Note that when a program calls the base type's `DoIt` method, the method ignores the existence of the `DoItForReal` method in the derived type and simply calls the base type's version. Because the `DoItForReal` method was not declared as `virtual` in the base type, the method code for `Base.DoIt` is statically bound to call `Base.DoItForReal`, independent of what any derived type may indicate. However, had the `DoItForReal` method been declared as virtual in the base

TABLE 6.2 Metadata Attribute Combinations

Metadata Attribute				C# Syntax	Meaning
virtual	final*	abstract*	newslot		
1	0	0	0	override	Replace virtual method from base and allow replacment in derived
1	0	0	1	virtual	Introduce new virtual method and allow replacement in derived
1	0	1	0	override abstract	Require replacement of existing virtual method from base
1	0	1	1	abstract	Introduce new virtual method and require replacement in derived
1	1	0	0	override sealed	Replace virtual method from base and prohibit further replacement

*final and abstract are mutually exclusive.

type, as shown in Listing 6.2, Base.DoIt method would always invoke the DoItForReal method via the virtual function mechanism, allowing the derived type to replace the base type's method by overriding it.

Listing 6.1: *Nonvirtual Method Dispatching*

```
public class Base {
  protected void DoItForReal() { a(); }
  public void DoIt() { this.DoItForReal(); }
}
public class Derived : Base {
  protected new void DoItForReal() { b(); }
}
void Main() {
  Base r1 = new Derived();
  r1.DoIt(); // calls a();
}
```

Listing 6.2: *Virtual Method Dispatching*

```
public class Base {
  protected virtual void DoItForReal() { a(); }
  public void DoIt() { this.DoItForReal(); }
}
public class Derived : Base {
  protected override void DoItForReal() { b(); }
}
void Main() {
  Base r1 = new Derived();
  r1.DoIt(); // calls b();
}
```

By default, when you override a virtual method, there is nothing to stop new types that derive from your type from replacing your implementation of the method with their own. If you want to prevent this, you can mark your override as being final. Final methods replace a virtual or abstract method in their base but prevent further replacement by more-derived types. In C#, you can mark a method as final by combining the sealed keyword with the override keyword. Listing 6.3 shows an example of this technique.

Listing 6.3: *Final Methods*

```
public class Base : ICommon {
  public virtual void DoIt() { a(); }
}
public class Derived : Base
// the sealed keyword marks this method as final
  public override sealed void DoIt() { b(); }
}
public class ReallyDerived : Derived {
// illegal - DoIt is final in Derived!
  public override void DoIt() { c(); }
}
```

In the previous examples of overriding methods, the method implementation of the most-derived type completely replaces the implementation in the base type. If the derived type wanted to augment rather than replace the base method implementation, then the derived type's method would need to explicitly invoke the base method using a language-specific qualifier (base in C#, MyBase in VB.NET). Listing 6.4 shows such an implementation. Whether or not the derived type should actually dispatch to the base type—as well as whether it should do this dispatching before or after its own work—has been one of the primary arguments against using virtual method replacement as a reuse technique, because it is rarely possible to know which approach to use without incestuous knowledge of the inner workings of the base type.

Listing 6.4: *The Virtual Method Dilemma*

```
public class Base {
  protected virtual void DoItForReal() { a(); }
  public void DoIt() { this.DoItForReal(); }
}
public class Derived1 : Base {
  protected override void DoItForReal() {
    base.DoItForReal();
    b(); // postprocess method call
  }
}
public class Derived2 : Base {
  protected override void DoItForReal() {
    b(); // preprocess method call
    base.DoItForReal();
  }
}
```

Interfaces, Virtual Methods, and Abstract Methods

The CLR deals with objects and interface types differently than its predecessors (C++ and COM). In C++ and COM, a given concrete type has one method table per base type or supported interface. In contrast, a given concrete type in the CLR has exactly one method table. By inference, a CLR-based object has exactly one type handle. This is in stark contrast to C++ and COM, where an object would routinely have one vptr per base type or interface. For this reason, the CLR's castclass does not result in a second pointer value in the same way as C++'s dynamic_cast or COM's Query-Interface.

Each CLR type has a single method table independent of its type hierarchy. The initial slots in the method table will correspond to virtual methods declared by the base type. These slots are then followed by entries that correspond to new virtual methods introduced by the derived type. The CLR arranges this region of the method table such that all of the method table slots for a particular declared interface are arranged contiguously with one another. However, because different concrete types may support different interfaces, the absolute offset of this range of entries will not be the same for all types that support a given interface. To deal with this variability, the CLR adds a second level of indirection when invoking virtual methods through an interface-based object reference.

The `CORINFO_CLASS_STRUCT` contains pointers to two tables that describe the interfaces the type supports. The `isinst` and `castclass` opcodes use one of these tables to determine whether a type supports a given interface. The second of these tables is an interface offset table that the CLR uses when dispatching virtual method calls made against interface-based object references.

As shown in Figure 6.4, the **interface offset table** is an array of offsets into the type's method table. There is one entry in this table for every interface type that has been initialized by the CLR independent of whether or not the type supports the interface. As the CLR initializes interface types, it assigns them a zero-based index into this table. When the CLR initializes a concrete type, the CLR allocates a new interface offset table for the type. The interface offset table will be sparsely populated, but it must be at least as long as the index of any of its declared interfaces. When the CLR initializes a concrete type, the CLR populates its interface offset table by storing the appropriate method table offsets into the entries for supported interfaces. Because the CLR's verifier ensures that interface-based references refer only to objects that support the declared type, interface offset table entries for unsupported interfaces are never used and their contents are immaterial.

As shown in Figure 6.4, a method invocation through an interface-based reference must first locate the range of entries in the method table that corresponds to the interface. After the CLR finds this offset, the CLR adds the method-specific offset and dispatches the call. When compared with calling virtual methods through class-based references, the interface-based reference approach results in code that is slightly larger and slower because

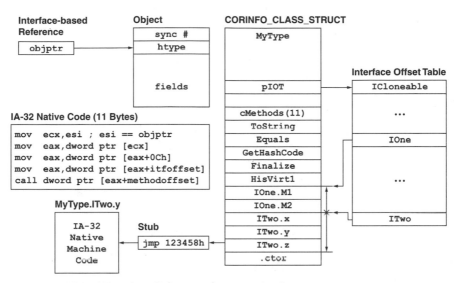

Figure 6.4: *Virtual Functions Using Interface-Based References*

an additional level of indirection is used. It is conceivable, however, for the JIT compiler to optimize away this extra indirection if the same object reference is used multiple times.

The C# language supports two techniques for implementing an interface method. Either one can implement the interface method as a public method with the same name and signature, or one can implement a private method with the same signature but with a name that follows the `InterfaceName.MethodName` convention. For example, for a method named `Display` on an interface named `IDrawable`, the implementation's method name would be `IDrawable.Display`.

The primary difference between these two techniques is that with the former, the method also becomes part of the class's public signature. With the latter approach, the method is visible only via an up-cast to the corresponding interface type. For that exact reason, the latter technique is indispensable when one must overload a given method name based on the scope of the reference used to invoke the method. One might need to do this when one desires a more type-safe version of the method for the class's contract. For example, consider the following class, which implements `System.ICloneable`:

```
using System;
public class Patient : ICloneable {

// this is part of the class's public contract
  public Patient Clone()  {
    return (Patient)this.MemberwiseClone();
  }

// this is private and accessible only via ICloneable
  Object ICloneable.Clone() {
    return this.MemberwiseClone();
  }
}
```

Note that the public contract for the Patient type contains a strongly typed Clone method that returns the precise reference type. This makes it more convenient for callers using references of type Patient to perform the clone because the second object reference is already cast to the anticipated type. In contrast, callers using ICloneable references to access the object still get correct behavior, but those clients will likely need to do a down-cast prior to using the result of the ICloneable.Clone method.

Another advantage of using scoped method names to implement the abstract members of an interface is that it lets one easily handle name collisions across interfaces. These collisions can occur when a class implements two or more interfaces with identical method declarations but differing semantics, something that is rare but in fact possible. Consider the following canonical example:

```
public interface ICowboy {
  void Draw();
}
public interface IArtist {
  void Draw();
}
public class AcePowell : ICowboy, IArtist {
  void ICowboy.Draw() { Shoot(); }
  void IArtist.Draw() { Paint(); }
  public void Draw()  { Attract(); }
}
```

Note that the `AcePowell` class has three `Draw` methods. The CLR will determine the one selected by what kind of reference is used to invoke the method.

In each of the examples shown so far, the implementation of an interface method is implicitly `final`, just as if the `sealed` and `override` modifiers were present. As illustrated in Table 6.3, when the implementation of an interface method is marked as `public`, it can also be marked as `virtual` or `abstract`, making the method nonfinal. This allows a derived type to override the method. Such an override would replace both class-based and interface-based uses of the base type's method. It is also possible for a derived type to replace any or all of the base type's interface implementation methods simply by redeclaring support for the interface. After this is done, the derived class is free to provide new implementations of any of the interface methods no matter how the base type declared them.

Listing 6.5 shows an example C# program in which the base type `Base` implements three interface methods using the techniques just described. Note that the derived type `Derived1` can replace only the base type's `Turn` method. This is because the base type did not declare any other methods as virtual. In contrast, the `Derived2` class can replace all of the interface methods. This is because `Derived2` explicitly redeclares support for the `IVehicle` interface. In this example, programs will never call the base type's implementations of `Start` on an instance of `Derived2`. This is because the only way the `Start` method can be invoked is via the `IVehicle` interface, for which the `Derived2` class has explicitly provided

TABLE 6.3 Interface Method Declaration Style

C# Declaration Style	CLR Metadata Attributes				
	virtual	abstract	newslot	final	Accessibility
void ITf.f()	1	0	1	1	private
public void f()	1	0	1	1	public
public virtual void f()	1	0	1	0	public
public abstract void f()	1	1	1	0	public

a Start method. Programs may invoke the base type's Stop and Turn methods on instances of Derived2. This can occur when a reference of type Base refers to an instance of Derived2. When such a reference is used, the Stop method in Base was nonvirtual, so no virtual method invocation (or derived-type overloading) is in effect. What is odd (but expected) is that the Turn method will still dispatch to the implementation in Base. This occurs because the developer did not use the override keyword in declaring the implementation of Turn in Derived2. The lack of an override keyword informs the C# compiler to emit the method declaration using the newslot attribute, an action that causes compilers to consider the Turn method in Derived2 unrelated to the Turn method in Base.

Listing 6.5: *Interfaces and Base Types*

```
public interface IVehicle {
  void Start(); void Stop(); void Turn();
}
public class Base : IVehicle {
  void IVehicle.Start() { a(); }
  public void Stop() { b(); }
  public virtual void Turn() { c(); }
}
public class Derived1 : Base {
// illegal - cannot override nonexistent method
  public override void Start() { d(); }
// illegal - Base.Stop not virtual
  public override void Stop() { e(); }
// legal, replaces Base.Turn + IVehicle.Turn
  public override void Turn() { f(); }
}
public class Derived2 : Base, IVehicle {
// legal - we redeclared IVehicle support
  void IVehicle.Start() { g(); }
// legal - we redeclared IVehicle support
  public void Stop() { h(); }
// legal - replaces IVehicle.Turn (but not Base.Turn)
  public void Turn() { i(); }
}
```

If the previous discussion has left you confused, consider the example shown in Listing 6.6. This example exercises most if not all combinations of overriding, overloading, and interfaces. Try to figure out what this program does. In particular, try to figure out which of the six `DoIt` method declarations the compiler and/or the CLR will choose for each of the four method invocations in `Main`.

Listing 6.6: *Inheritance Abuse*

```
public interface ICommon {
  void DoIt();
}
public class Base : ICommon {
  void ICommon.DoIt() { a(); }
  public virtual void DoIt() { b(); }
}
public class Derived : Base, ICommon {
  void ICommon.DoIt() { c(); }
  public new virtual void DoIt() { d(); }
}
public class ReallyDerived : Derived {
  public override void DoIt() { e(); }
}
public static void Main() {
  ReallyDerived r1 = new ReallyDerived();
  Derived       r2 = r1;
  Base          r3 = r1;
  ICommon       r4 = r1;

  r1.DoIt();
  r2.DoIt();
  r3.DoIt();
  r4.DoIt();
}
```

The first call would dispatch to e because the concrete type of the object has a public method named `DoIt`. The second call would dispatch to e because `Derived.DoIt` is declared as `virtual`. The third call would dispatch to b because even though `Base.DoIt` was declared as `virtual`, the subsequent derived methods overloaded its use. The fourth call would dispatch to c because `ICommon.DoIt` is implicitly `virtual`. No, you don't want to write code like this, but it may (or may not) be comforting to know that the CLR supports this without flinching.

Explicit Method Invocation

The previous discussion looked at how virtual methods introduce a level of indirection between the call site and the actual method that is executed. This level of indirection is largely transparent to the caller, with the CLR using the concrete type of the target object to automatically determine which method to use. In addition to virtual methods, the CLR provides facilities to make method invocation even more flexible, to the point where one can discover and invoke arbitrary methods without *a priori* knowledge of their signature or even their name. This facility—**explicit method invocation**—is critical for building highly dynamic systems.

Recall that one makes CLR metadata accessible through `System.Type` and friends. One of the facilities of `System.Type` is the ability to discover the methods of a given type. The `System.Reflection.MethodInfo` type exposes the metadata for a method. As described in Chapter 4, the `Method-Info` type makes the signature of the method available, including the types and names of the parameters. What was not discussed, however, is the `MethodInfo` type's capabilities for invoking the underlying method. One exposes this functionality via the `MethodInfo.Invoke` method.

`MethodInfo.Invoke` has two overloads. The more complex of the two overloads allows the caller to provide mapping code to deal with parameter type mismatches and overload resolution. This version of the `Method-Info.Invoke` method is used primarily by support plumbing in dynamically typed languages and is outside the scope of this discussion. The simpler of the two methods assumes that the caller is capable of providing the parameters exactly as the underlying method expects them to appear. Listing 6.7 shows both prototypes.

Listing 6.7: *System.Reflection.MethodInfo.Invoke*

```
using System;
using System.Globalization;
namespace System.Reflection {
  public abstract class MethodInfo : MethodBase {

    public virtual object Invoke(object target,
                                 BindingFlags invokeAttr,
                                 Binder binder,
                                 object[] args,
                                 CultureInfo culture);
```

```
public virtual object Invoke(object target,
                                object[] args);


    }
}
```

To use the simpler form of `MethodInfo.Invoke`, one needs to provide two parameters. This usage is shown in Figure 6.5. The first parameter is a reference to the target object. If the underlying method is declared `static`, then this reference is ignored. If the underlying method is not `static`, this reference must refer to an object that is type-compatible with `MethodInfo`'s reflected type. If an incompatible object is passed for this parameter, `MethodInfo.Invoke` will throw a `System.Reflection.TargetException` exception.

The second parameter to `MethodInfo.Invoke` accepts an array of object references, one array element per parameter. The length of this array must match the number of parameters expected. The type of each referenced object in the array must be type-compatible with the type of the corresponding parameter. If either of these is not the case, `MethodInfo.Invoke` will throw a `System.Reflection.TargetParameterCountException` or `System.ArgumentException` exception, respectively.

The implementation of `MethodInfo.Invoke` will call the underlying method using the parameter values and target object reference provided. To accomplish this, `MethodInfo.Invoke` will form a stack frame based on the underlying method declaration and the processor architecture under which the CLR is running. `MethodInfo.Invoke` will then copy the parameter values from the array of object references onto the stack. When the stack frame is properly formed, the `MethodInfo.Invoke` code makes a processor-specific call (e.g., `call` in IA-32) to the target method. When the method has completed execution, `MethodInfo.Invoke` will then identify any parameters that were passed by reference and copy them back to the presented array of parameter values. Finally, if the method returns a value, that value will be returned as the result of the `MethodInfo.Invoke` call.

The example in Listing 6.8 shows a C# routine that calls a method named `"Add"` on an arbitrary object. This code assumes that the object's underlying type has an `Add` method. Moreover, this example also assumes

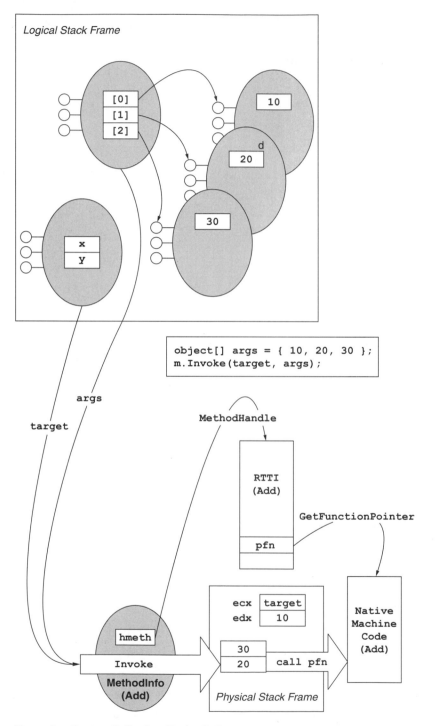

Figure 6.5: *System.Reflection.MethodInfo*

that the `Add` method takes exactly three `System.Int32`s as arguments and that the underlying method will return a `System.Int32`. As an aside, this particular example uses the `BindingFlags.NonPublic` flag to indicate that nonpublic methods are to be considered. Yes, this facility allows you to circumvent the method's access modifier (e.g., `private`); however, only trusted code can violate this encapsulation.

Listing 6.8: *Explicit Invocation via MethodInfo.Invoke*

```
public sealed class Utils
{
  static public int CallAdd(object target) {
// grab "Add" method from object's type
    Type type = target.GetType();
    MethodInfo method = type.GetMethod("Add",
                          BindingFlags.Public
                         |BindingFlags.NonPublic
                         |BindingFlags.Instance);

// check whether method exists!
    if (method == null) return 0;

// form list of argument values
    object[] args = new object[] { 10, 20, 30 };
// execute the method
    object result = method.Invoke(target, args);
// return the result
    return (int)result;

  }
}
```

Figure 6.5 shows how the `MethodInfo` object relates to the underlying method and target object. Note that there is an underlying `System.RuntimeMethodHandle` that points to CLR-managed data structures that describe the method. One can use the `System.RuntimeMethodHandle.GetFunctionPointer` method to access the address of the underlying method code. After this address is found, programmers who are comfortable with low-level programming techniques can invoke the method directly without going through the overhead of `MethodInfo.Invoke`.

The address returned by GetFunctionPointer is meant to be invoked using the CIL calli instruction. Unlike the call and callvirt instructions—which encode the metadata token of the target method directly into the instruction stream—the calli instruction expects the address of the target method to be pushed onto the stack at runtime. This level of indirection allows the CLR to support C-style function pointers. For example, suppose one has the following C# type definition:

```
public class Target {
  public static int Add(int x, int y) { return x + y; }
  public int Subtract(int x, int y) { return x - y; }
}
```

One should be able to write the following C++ code:

```
using namespace System;
using namespace System::Reflection;

typedef int (__fastcall *AddProc)(int, int);
typedef int (__fastcall *SubProc)(Target*, int, int);

void f(Target *pTarget) {
// get method pointers
  Type *ptype = pTarget->GetType();
  MethodInfo *padd = ptype->GetMethod(S"Add");
  MethodInfo *psub = ptype->GetMethod(S"Subtract");
  IntPtr pfnAdd = padd->MethodHandle.GetFunctionPointer();
  IntPtr pfnSub = psub->MethodHandle.GetFunctionPointer();

// invoke
  int r1 = ((AddProc)pfnAdd)(3, 4);
  int r2 = ((SubProc)pfnSub)(pTarget, 5, 6);
}
```

Unfortunately, under version 1.0 of the .NET framework, the C++ compiler's CLR-compliant mode (/CLR) does not support the declaration of function pointers that use the __fastcall stack discipline, which is the discipline typically used internally by the CLR. Although constructing the proper IA-32 machine code is possible, the C++ compiler also prohibits inline assembly in managed methods. This leaves the industrious developer little choice except to use **ILASM**, the CIL assembler that ships with the .NET framework SDK, to write the necessary CIL to invoke the function.

The following ILASM method definition demonstrates how to invoke the Add method shown in the previous example:

```
.method public hidebysig static int32
Call(native int pfn, int32 x, int32 y) cil managed {
  .maxstack  3
  ldarg.1                    // push x
  ldarg.2                    // push y
  ldarg.0                    // push addr. of target method
  calli int32(int32, int32)
  ret
}
```

This method would generate the same machine code that the desired C++ function pointer would generate if the C++ compiler allowed __fastcall function pointers.

To invoke the instance method Subtract, one could use this ILASM method:

```
.method public hidebysig static int32
Call(native int pfn, object pThis,
     int32 x, int32 y) cil managed {
  .maxstack  4
  ldarg.1                    // push pThis
  ldarg.2                    // push x
  ldarg.3                    // push y
  ldarg.0                    // push addr. of target method
  calli int32(object, int32, int32)
  ret
}
```

In both cases, the first parameter to Call will be a function pointer as returned by MethodBase.GetFunctionPointer. It is important to note that in both of these examples, even though it appears that every argument is passed on the stack, when the JIT compiler translates this CIL into machine code, the first two parameters will be passed in the ecx and edx registers, as per the __fastcall calling convention.

Indirect Method Invocation and Delegates

The previous discussion looked at how MethodInfo objects give developers the capability of invoking a specific method on any type-compatible object. Because a MethodInfo object is affiliated with a type but not an object, invocation using MethodInfo requires that one supply the target object reference explicitly each time one invokes a method. In many cases, this is perfectly acceptable. However, it is often desirable to bind to a particular method on a specific object, and that is the role of **delegates**.

Delegates provide a mechanism for binding to a specific method on a specific target object. Binding to a specific target object eliminates the need to explicitly supply the target object reference at invocation time, something that is required by MethodInfo.Invoke. To that end, delegates can do very little interesting work other than invoke their underlying method.

Delegates are used in CLR-based libraries to represent the capability of calling a particular method. To that end, delegates are similar to a single-method interface, the primary difference being that interfaces require the target method's type to have predeclared compatibility with the interface type. In contrast, delegates can be bound to methods on any type, provided that the method signature matches what is expected by the delegate type.

As shown in Figure 6.6, delegates are objects that maintain two fields: a method pointer and a target object reference. The method pointer is simply a C++-style function pointer such as the address returned by System.RuntimeMethodHandle.GetFunctionPointer. The target object reference is a reference of type System.Object that refers to the target object. When a delegate is bound to a static method, this reference is null.

Unlike the MethodInfo type, which is used no matter what the underlying method signature is, a delegate object must be affiliated with a delegate type that is specific to the underlying method signature. As shown in Figure 6.7, delegate types always derive directly from System.MulticastDelegate, which in turn derives from System.Delegate. These two base types provide a variety of base functions as well as signal to the CLR that the type is in fact a delegate type.

Like any other CLR type, a delegate type has a type name and can have members. However, the members of a delegate type are restricted to a finite set of methods with fixed names. The most important of these is the `Invoke` method.

The `Invoke` method must be a public instance method. Additionally, one must mark the `Invoke` method as `runtime`, which means that the CLR will synthesize its implementation rather than JIT-compile it from CIL in the type's module. Although the name and metadata attributes are hard-wired, the actual signature of the method can be any CLR-compliant signature. The signature of the `Invoke` method determines how the delegate type can be used. In particular, any method that is bound to the delegate must have a signature that is identical to that of the delegate's `Invoke` method. The CLR enforces this signature matching both at compile time and at runtime.

In addition to the `Invoke` method, delegate types must provide an instance constructor method that takes two parameters. The first parameter is of type `System.Object` and specifies the target object reference being bound. The second parameter is of type `System.IntPtr` and must point to the code for the method being bound. As with the `Invoke` method, the constructor must be marked as `runtime` because the CLR will synthesize the implementation at runtime.

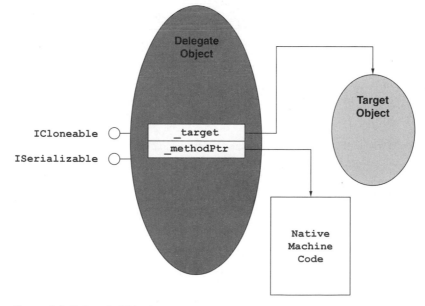

Figure 6.6: *Delegate Objects*

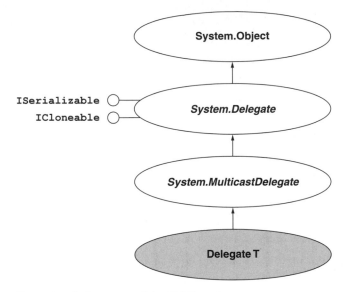

Figure 6.7: *Delegates and the CLR Type System*

Each programming language provides its own syntax for defining delegate types. C#, C++, and VB.NET all share a similar syntax, which looks like a method declaration but is in fact a type definition statement. Consider the following C# statement:

```
public delegate int AddProc(int x, int y);
```

This statement defines a new delegate type named AddProc whose Invoke method will accept two System.Int32s as parameters and will return a System.Int32 as a result. The following is the ILASM that corresponds to this C# type definition:

```
.class public auto ansi sealed AddProc
       extends [mscorlib]System.MulticastDelegate
{
  .method public hidebysig specialname rtspecialname
   instance void .ctor(object 'object',
                       native int 'method') runtime managed
   {
   }
  .method public hidebysig virtual
   instance int32 Invoke(int32 x, int32 y) runtime managed
   {
   }
}
```

As just described, the signature of the `Invoke` method corresponds to the type definition statement in C#.

To instantiate a delegate, one needs a method and optionally a target object reference. One needs the target object reference only when one is binding to an instance method; it is not used when one is binding to a static method. The `System.Delegate` type provides the `CreateDelegate` static method for creating new delegates that are bound to a particular method and object. There are four overloads of `CreateDelegate`, as shown here:

```
namespace System {
public abstract class Delegate {
// bind a delegate of type dt to method
  public static Delegate
  CreateDelegate(Type dt, MethodInfo method);

// bind a delegate of type dt to methName on target type
  public static Delegate
  CreateDelegate(Type dt, Type target, string methName);

// bind a delegate of type dt to methName on target object
  public static Delegate
  CreateDelegate(Type dt, object target, string methName);

// bind a delegate of type dt to methName on target object
  public static Delegate
  CreateDelegate(Type dt, object target, string methName,
                 bool ignoreCase);

// remaining members elided for clarity
  }
}
```

The first pair of overloads are for binding a new delegate object to a static method. The second pair are for binding to an instance method on a particular object. In all cases, the first parameter is a `System.Type` object that describes the desired delegate type. The specified target method must exactly match the signature of the delegate type's `Invoke` method.

The following C# code uses the `CreateDelegate` method to bind a delegate to a static method and an instance method:

```
using System;

public delegate int BinaryOp(int x, int y);

public class MathCode {
  internal int sum = 0;
  public int Add(int m, int n) {
    sum += m + n;
    return m + n;
  }
  public static int Subtract(int a, int b)
  { return a - b; }
}

class app {
  static void Main() {
    MathCode target = new MathCode();
    Type tt = typeof(MathCode);
    Type dt = typeof(BinaryOp);

    BinaryOp op1 = (BinaryOp)Delegate.CreateDelegate(dt,
                                         tt, "Subtract");
    BinaryOp op2 = (BinaryOp)Delegate.CreateDelegate(dt,
                                         target, "Add");

  }
}
```

Calling `CreateDelegate` is an indirect way to invoke the delegate type's constructor. Each programming language provides syntax for invoking the constructor directly. In the case of C#, one can simply specify the symbolic name of the method qualified either by the type name or by an object reference. The following `Main` method is equivalent to the previous example:

```
static void Main() {
  MathCode target = new MathCode();

  BinaryOp op1 = new BinaryOp(MathCode.Subtract);
  BinaryOp op2 = new BinaryOp(target.Add);
}
```

The C# compiler will translate these new expressions to use the underlying CIL ldftn or ldvirtftn opcode to fetch the address of the target method prior to invoking the delegate type's constructor. This technique for binding a delegate is considerably faster than calling Delegate.CreateDelegate because the method handle does not need to be looked up via metadata traversal.

After the CLR has instantiated and bound a delegate to a method and object, the delegate's primary purpose is to support invocation. One can invoke using a delegate in one of two ways. If one needs a generic mechanism (a la MethodInfo.Invoke), the System.Delegate type provides a DynamicInvoke method:

```
namespace System {
  public abstract class Delegate {
    public object DynamicInvoke(object[] args);
// remaining members elided for clarity
  }
}
```

Note that the signature for DynamicInvoke is identical to that of MethodInfo.Invoke except that the target object reference is not passed explicitly. Rather, the _target field of the delegate acts as the implicit target of the invocation. This is illustrated in Figure 6.8.

The far more common way to invoke against a delegate is to use the type-specific Invoke method. Unlike DynamicInvoke, the Invoke method is strongly typed and yields much better performance because of its lack of generality. The CLR-synthesized Invoke implementation for IA-32 is simply an eight-instruction **shim** that replaces the this pointer in ecx with that of the target object reference. The shim then jmps directly to the target method address. After the jmp occurs, the target method begins execution as if it were invoked directly by the caller. In fact, because the caller's return address is still on the stack, the target method will return directly to the caller, bypassing the delegate machinery altogether.

The shim used by the Invoke method is capable of working generically because the signature of the target method is guaranteed to match that of the Invoke method exactly. As shown in Figure 6.9, this allows one to reuse the stack frame from the call to Invoke when dispatching to the target method.

The C# programming language handles delegate invocation somewhat strangely. A C# program cannot access the Invoke method explicitly by

```
MyDelegate proc = new  MyDelegates(obj.Add);
object[] args = { 10, 20, 30 };
proc.DynamicInvoke(args);
```

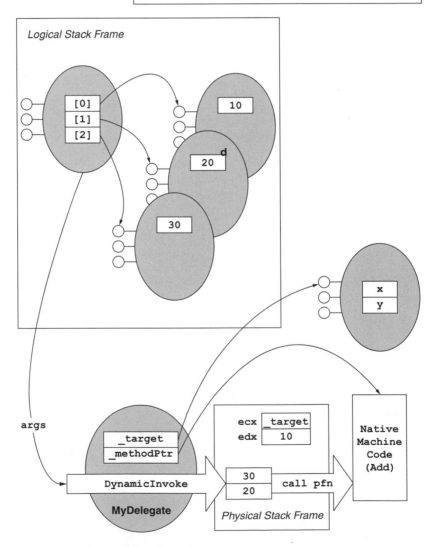

Figure 6.8: *Delegate.DynamicInvoke*

name. Rather, one omits the `Invoke` name, resulting in a usage model that resembles C-style function pointers:

```
static void Main() {
    BinaryOp op1 = new BinaryOp(MathCode.Subtract);
    int x = op1(3, 4); // this calls Invoke implicitly!
}
```

In my opinion, this slight obfuscation adds little to the usability of delegates. Fortunately, C++ and VB.NET allow developers to use the `Invoke` method explicitly.

The CLR's implementation of `Invoke` supports **chaining** together multiple delegates so that a single `Invoke` call can trigger calls to more than one method at a time. As shown in Figure 6.10, the `System.Multicast-Delegate` type adds support for chaining delegate objects into a singly linked list. When one makes a call to `Invoke` on the head of the list, the CLR-synthesized code walks the list in order, invoking the target method on each delegate in the list. Because these calls are made in sequence, any

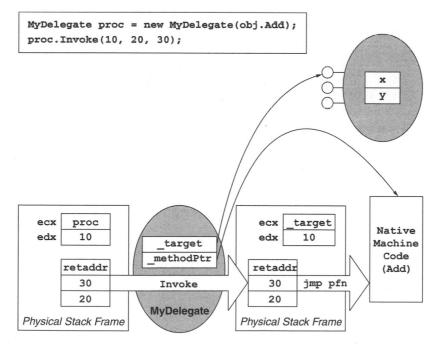

Figure 6.9: *Delegate.Invoke*

changes to pass-by-reference parameters made by one method will be visible to the next target in the chain. Additionally, if the Invoke method returns a typed value, only the last method's value will be returned to the caller. Finally, if any of the methods throws an exception, then the invocation will stop at that point and the exception will be thrown to the caller.

The System.Delegate type supports two methods for managing delegate chains: Combine and Remove.

```
namespace System {
 public abstract Delegate : ICloneable, ISerializable {
   static public Delegate Combine(Delegate a, Delegate b);
   static public Delegate Combine(Delegate[] delegates);
   static public Delegate Remove(Delegate src,Delegate node);
 }
}
```

Both of these methods return a new delegate reference that references the updated delegate chain. This reference may or may not refer to the exact delegate passed as a parameter.

Listing 6.9 shows an example that uses Delegate.Combine to conjoin two delegates into a chain. Note that the order in which the delegates are conjoined is significant because the Invoke method will walk the chain in order.

Listing 6.9: *Using Multicast Delegates*

```
public delegate void MYPROC();
public sealed class Util {
  public static void f(MYPROC first, MYPROC second) {
    Delegate pair = Delegate.Combine(first, second);
    MYPROC tpair = (MYPROC)pair;
    tpair(); // calls first() followed by second()
  }
}
```

It is possible to alter the way invocation works against a delegate chain. The System.Delegate type provides a method (GetInvocationList) that returns all of the delegates in a chain as an array. When you have access to this array, you can then decide exactly how to perform the indi-

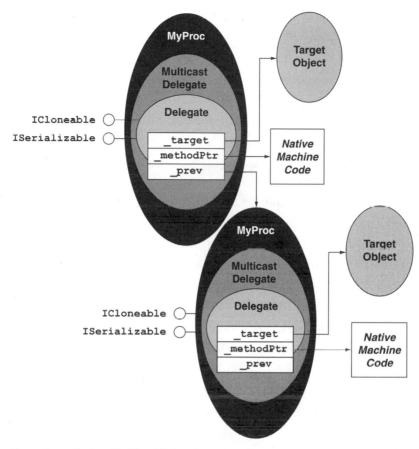

Figure 6.10: *System.MulticastDelegate*

vidual invocations. Listing 6.10 shows an example that walks the list of delegates backward. This example also looks at the intermediate results of each individual invocation. In this case, an average is taken of the results of each invocation.

Listing 6.10: *Using Multicast Delegates (Revisited)*

```
public delegate double MYPROC();
public sealed class Util {
  public static double f(MYPROC first, MYPROC second) {
// conjoin first and second
    Delegate pair = Delegate.Combine(first, second);
// get list of conjoined delegates
    Delegate[] targets = pair.GetInvocationList();
// walk through list (backward) and return average
    double total = 0;
```

```
    for (int i = targets.Length - 1; i >= 0; --i) {
      MYPROC target = (MYPROC)targets[i];
      total += target();
    }
    return total / targets.Length;
  }
}
```

Asynchronous Method Invocation

All of the invocation techniques shown so far simply route the stream of execution from one method to another. It is often desirable to fork the stream of execution into two branches, allowing one branch to execute the instructions of a given method while the remaining branch independently continues its normal processing. Figure 6.11 illustrates this concept. On a multiprocessor machine, the two branches can actually execute concurrently. On a single-processor machine, the CLR will preemptively schedule two branches of execution for execution on the shared CPU.

The primary motivation for forking execution is to allow processing to continue while part of the program is blocked, waiting for I/O to complete or for the user to enter a command. Forking execution can also increase throughput on a multi-CPU machine due to parallelism; however, this requires a very deliberate design style that avoids excessive contention for shared resources.

The primary mechanism for forking the instruction stream is to make an asynchronous method call. An asynchronous method call forks execution into two streams. The new stream executes the body of the target method. The original stream continues its normal processing.

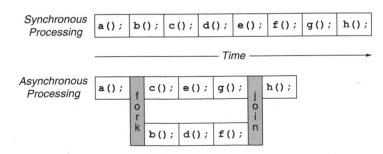

Figure 6.11: *Synchronous versus Asynchronous Processing*

The CLR implements asynchronous method invocation by using a work queue. When invoking a method asynchronously, the CLR packages the method parameters and the target method address into a request message. The CLR then queues this message onto a process-wide work queue. The CLR maintains an OS-level thread pool that is responsible for listening on the work queue. When a request arrives on the queue, the CLR dispatches a thread from its thread pool to perform the work. In the case of an asynchronous method call, the work is simply to invoke the target method.

One always performs asynchronous method invocation via a delegate object. Recall that a delegate type has two compiler-generated methods: `Invoke` and a constructor. Delegate types may also have two additional methods to enable asynchronous method invocation: `BeginInvoke` and `EndInvoke`. Like `Invoke`, these two methods must be marked as `runtime` because the CLR will provide their implementations at runtime based on their signatures.

The CLR uses the `BeginInvoke` method to issue an asynchronous method request. The CLR-synthesized implementation of `BeginInvoke` simply creates a work request containing the parameter values and queues the request onto the work queue. `BeginInvoke` typically returns before the target method begins to execute on the thread pool thread, but, because of the unpredictability of the underlying thread scheduler, it is possible (although unlikely) for the target method to actually complete before the calling thread returns from `BeginInvoke`.

The signature for `BeginInvoke` is similar to the signature for `Invoke`. Consider the following C# delegate type definition:

```
public delegate double
Add(double x, double y, out double z, ref bool overflow);
```

This delegate type would have an `Invoke` method signature that looks like this:

```
public double Invoke(double x, double y,
                 out double z, ref bool overflow);
```

The corresponding `BeginInvoke` would look like this:

```
public System.IAsyncResult
BeginInvoke(double x, double y,
            out double z, ref bool overflow,
            System.AsyncCallback complete,
            object state);
```

Note that `BeginInvoke`'s signature differs in two ways. For one thing, `BeginInvoke` accepts two additional parameters that are used to tailor how the call will be processed. These two parameters are described later in this section. The other difference between the signatures of `Invoke` and `BeginInvoke` is that `BeginInvoke` always returns a reference to a call object. The call object represents the pending execution of the method and can be used to control and interrogate the call in progress. The call object always implements the `System.IAsyncResult` interface.

As shown in Listing 6.11, `IAsyncResult` has four members. The `CompletedSynchronously` property indicates whether or not execution took place during `BeginInvoke`. Although the CLR's asynchronous invocation plumbing will never do this, objects that implement asynchronous methods explicitly may elect to process an asynchronous request synchronously.

Listing 6.11: *System.IAsyncResult and System.AsyncCallback*

```
namespace System {
  public interface IAsyncResult {
// did method execute during BeginInvoke?
    bool        CompletedSynchronously { get; }
// has method returned?
    bool        IsCompleted { get; }
// low-level thread/sync handle
    WaitHandle AsyncWaitHandle { get; }
// last argument passed to BeginInvoke
    object      AsyncState { get; }
  }
  public delegate void AsyncCallback(IAsyncResult result);
}
```

The `IAsyncResult.IsCompleted` property indicates whether or not the method has completed execution. This allows the caller to poll the call object to determine when the call has actually completed execution:

```
static void f(Add add) {
  bool overflow = true;  double z;
// issue the call
  IAsyncResult ar = add.BeginInvoke(3, 4, out z,
                                    ref overflow,
                                    null, null);
// poll until call is complete
  while (!ar.IsCompleted)
    System.Threading.Thread.Sleep(1);
}
```

As an alternative to polling, the AsyncWaitHandle property returns a System.Threading.WaitHandle object that one can use to wait via thread synchronization techniques.

```
static void f(Add add) {
  bool overflow = true;  double z;
// issue the call
  IAsyncResult ar = add.BeginInvoke(3, 4, out z,
                                    ref overflow,
                                    null, null);
// sleep until call is complete
  ar.AsyncWaitHandle.WaitOne();
}
```

This variation is considerably more efficient because the caller's underlying OS thread is put to sleep until the call is complete, giving other threads in the system more access to the CPU.

Finally, one uses the last parameter of a BeginInvoke signature to allow the caller to associate an arbitrary object with the method call. One then makes this user-provided object available via the AsyncState property of the call object. This facility is especially useful when one will use the call object outside the scope of the issuing method, because it allows the caller to provide additional information to the code that will ultimately process the completion of the call.

When an asynchronous method has completed execution, one needs some mechanism to allow the results of the call to be harvested for further processing. This mechanism is the EndInvoke method. The End-Invoke method is the fourth method of a delegate type. As with Begin-Invoke, the signature of EndInvoke is related to the signature of the delegate type's `Invoke` method. Consider the C# delegate type used throughout this discussion:

```
public double Add(double x, double y,
                    out double z, ref bool overflow);
```

The corresponding `EndInvoke` would look like this:

```
public double EndInvoke(out double z, ref bool overflow,
                        System.IAsyncResult call);
```

There are three ways in which the two method signatures relate. For one thing, `EndInvoke` returns the same typed value as `Invoke`. This is possible because `EndInvoke` will not return until the underlying method has completed execution and the return value is actually available. Second, `EndInvoke` omits any pass-by-value parameters that appear in `Invoke`. This is because the pass-by-value parameters were needed only to issue the call, and they do not represent the results of method execution. Finally, `EndInvoke` accepts an additional parameter of type `IAsyncResult`. This parameter allows the caller to indicate which call it is interested in harvesting results from. This parameter is necessary because one can issue multiple asynchronous calls against the same delegate object. The `IAsyncResult` parameter indicates which of the calls you are interested in.

Figure 6.12 shows how `BeginInvoke` and `EndInvoke` allow the caller's thread to continue processing while the target method executes. This diagram illustrates a couple of interesting points. For one thing, the CLR invokes the target method using the synchronous `Invoke` method, but one invokes it from a CLR-managed worker thread and not the caller's thread. Second, after the call has completed execution, the worker thread returns to the work queue after signaling call completion. By reusing the worker thread for additional asynchronous calls, one amortizes the thread creation costs over the lifetime of the process.

The number of threads in the thread pool will grow and shrink over time. When a work request arrives in the queue, the CLR will try to dispatch the call to an existing worker thread. If every worker thread is currently busy servicing a previous request, the CLR will start up a new thread to service the new request. To avoid saturating the system, the CLR places an upper bound on the number of worker threads it will create. The default upper bound is 25 threads per CPU, but processes that host the CLR manually can change this default using the `ICorThreadpool::CorSetMaxThreads` method. You can interrogate the upper bound from CLR-based programs by calling the `System.Threading.ThreadPool.GetMaxThreads` method.

It is possible that when a burst of work appears in the system, the number of threads can reach its upper bound. However, if that burst is a transient spike that does not represent the steady state of the application, it would be wasteful to keep every thread alive when a smaller number could accomplish the same results more efficiently. To that end, the worker threads decay after a period of time if they are not used. At the time of this writing, the decay period for a worker thread is 30 seconds.

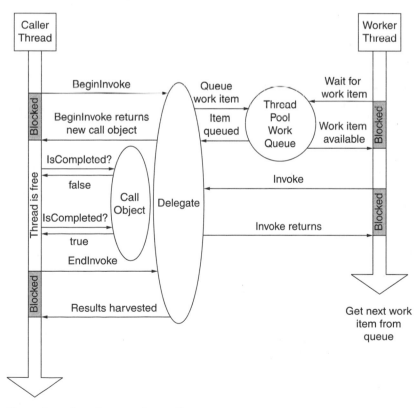

Figure 6.12: *Asynchronous Invocation*

The previous examples of asynchronous method invocation showed the caller's thread eventually making a rendezvous with the call object to process the results of the asynchronous call. Technically, it is legal to omit the call to EndInvoke if the results of the call are not important. This mode of invocation is sometimes called **fire-and-forget**, or **one-way** invocation. One typically uses this invocation style only with methods that do not have a return value and have no pass-by-reference parameters. One also uses this invocation style only when one can safely ignore method failure, because any exceptions thrown by the target method will be swallowed by the CLR in fire-and-forget scenarios.

One can process the results of an asynchronous method call without using an explicit rendezvous with the call object. One accomplishes this by passing an asynchronous **completion routine** to the BeginInvoke method when one issues the call.

Completion routines must match the prototype for the System.Async-Callback delegate, which was shown in Listing 6.11. One passes the completion routine as the second-to-last argument to BeginInvoke. When present, the completion routine will be called by the worker thread immediately following the execution of the target method. Your completion routine will be passed the call object as its lone parameter. Typically, any state that is needed to properly process the call's completion would be passed as the last parameter to BeginInvoke; the completion routine would then retrieve this state via the IAsyncResult.AsyncState property.

Listing 6.12 shows an asynchronous method call that uses a completion routine. Note that in this example, the Completed method is responsible for calling EndInvoke to harvest any results from the method call. To allow EndInvoke to be called at completion time, a reference to the delegate object was passed as the last parameter to BeginInvoke. Had more sophisticated processing been required, a more complex object could have been passed instead.

Listing 6.12: *Asynchronous Invocation with Callback*

```
public delegate double
Add(double x, double y, out double z, ref bool overflow);

public static void CallIt(Add add) {
  bool overflow = true;
```

```
//  create callback delegate
  AsyncCallback cb = new AsyncCallback(Completed);
// issue the call and return
  IAsyncResult ar = add.BeginInvoke(3, 4, out z
                                    ref overflow,
                                   cb, add);
}


// this method will be called at call completion
// by worker thread
public static void Completed(IAsyncResult call) {
  double z; bool overflow = true;
  Add add = (Add)call.AsyncState;
  double result = add.EndInvoke(out z, ref overflow, call);
  Console.Write("{0}, {1}, {2}", result, overflow, z);
}
```

As shown in Figure 6.13, the completion routine executes on the worker thread and not the caller's thread. Because the number of worker threads is limited, completion routines should avoid any long-running processing. If prolonged execution is needed, the completion routine should attempt to break the work into smaller chunks, which themselves can be executed asynchronously.

It is difficult to talk about asynchronous execution without addressing concurrency issues. Issuing an asynchronous method call inherently introduces **concurrency** into your programs. Although concurrency can allow your program to take advantage of multiple CPUs and gracefully deal with blocking system calls, concurrency can also introduce insidious problems that are extremely difficult to diagnose, debug, and repair. These problems are inevitably caused by **locking**.

It is a natural instinct to want to use locks to solve concurrency problems; most texts on multithreaded programming dedicate a great deal of space to lock primitives. However, locks introduce as many problems as they solve, and one should use them with great care and avoid them if possible. In particular, systems that use locks are often prone to **deadlock**, which can freeze the system altogether. Another common problem one encounters when using locks is poor scalability due to lock contention. This can happen when lock acquisition occurs on the critical path of an application, especially when the lock is held for a significant amount of time.

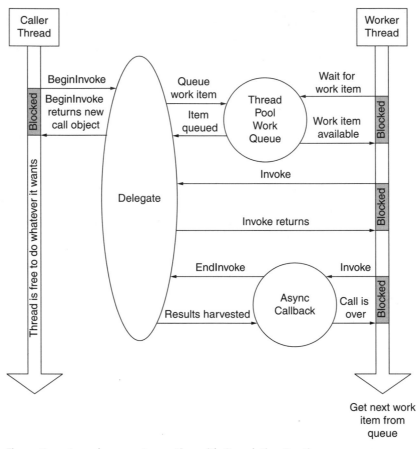

Figure 6.13: *Asynchronous Invocation with Completion Routine*

The best way to avoid using locks is to ensure that concurrent tasks do not need to share any resources. This means that asynchronous methods need to be careful not to access static fields that may also be accessed by the caller's thread. Also, if the call to `BeginInvoke` conveyed any object references, the calling thread should take care not to access the referenced object while the asynchronous method is still executing. By avoiding access to these (and other) shared resources, one can achieve lock-free concurrency.

If a resource in fact needs to be shared, one can use at least one technique short of locking. If the shared resource is simply a `System.Int32` or `System.Single`, the `System.Threading.Interlocked` type has methods that one can use to overwrite, increment, or decrement the shared value in a thread-safe fashion. These methods use processor-specific instructions to perform the operation atomically. The use of these methods is considerably faster than locking and will never result in deadlock because no locks are taken.

The CLR does support locking for cases when it is absolutely necessary. The CLR provides two basic types of locks. Locks based on `System.Threading.WaitHandle` mirror the Win32 event and mutex synchronization primitives and are suitable for cross-process synchronization. The more interesting locks are the **monitor** and `ReaderWriterLock`.

Both the monitor and `ReaderWriterLock` are limited to use within a single process (actually, within a single AppDomain). The monitor supports **exclusive locking**, which allows only one thread at a time to gain access to the lock. The `ReaderWriterLock` supports both exclusive and **shared locking**, which allows multiple threads to gain access to the lock provided that they require only read access to the resource the lock protects.

The monitor lets one associate a lock with any object in the system. However, because relatively few objects will be used with locks, objects do not have a lock when they are instantiated. Instead, the CLR lazily allocates the lock the first time a monitor tries to apply a lock to an object. To allow an object's lock to be found efficiently, the CLR stores an index into a table of **sync blocks** in the object's header. Objects that have no sync block have zero for a sync block index. The first time a monitor is used on an object, a sync block will be allocated for the object, and its index will be stored in the object's header.

One exposes monitor-based locking via the `System.Threading.Monitor` type. This type has two static methods (`Enter` and `Exit`), which acquire and release an object's lock, respectively. This lock is an exclusive lock, and only one thread at a time can acquire it. If a second thread attempts to acquire a lock on an object that is already locked, the second thread will block until the lock becomes available. C# provides an exception-safe construct for using the two monitor methods via its `lock` statement. For example, consider the following method:

```
static void UseIt(Bob bob) {
  lock (bob) {
// I have bob to myself!!!
    bob.name = "Bob Jones";
    bob.age = 32;
  }
}
```

This method is equivalent to the following:

```
static void UseIt(Bob bob) {
  try {
    System.Threading.Monitor.Enter(bob);
// I have bob to myself!!!
    bob.name = "Bob Jones";
    bob.age = 32;
  }
  finally {
    System.Threading.Monitor.Exit(bob);
  }
}
```

The CLR's monitor also offers Java-style pulse-and-wait capabilities for performing low-level thread synchronization. Readers are encouraged to look at Doug Lea's most excellent *Concurrent Programming in Java* (Addison-Wesley, 1999) for the definitive discussion of this facility.

Method Termination

The majority of this chapter has focused on how to enter a method in the CLR. Before concluding this chapter, it seems appropriate to look at how methods are left once they are invoked.

Barring termination of a process, AppDomain, or thread, there are two ways to leave a method after it has been entered: normal termination and abnormal termination. This is illustrated in Figure 6.14. The CIL `ret` instruction, which invariably terminates every method's instruction stream, triggers **normal termination**. The `ret` instruction may also appear in other locations in the instruction stream, typically due to `return` state-

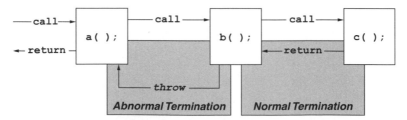

Figure 6.14: *Normal versus Abnormal Termination*

ments in C#, C++, or VB.NET. When a method terminates normally, the typed return value is available to the caller, and the CLR guarantees that any pass-by-reference parameters will reflect the changes made by the method.

Abnormal termination differs from normal termination in two ways. For one thing, the typed return value is not available to the caller when a method terminates abnormally. Second, the values of pass-by-reference parameters may or may not have been affected by the method body. Although the results of a method call are not available under abnormal termination, there is an alternative medium for conveying output to the callee. That medium is the **exception** object.

The raising of an exception triggers **abnormal termination**. The CLR itself can raise exceptions in response to any number of abnormal conditions (e.g., using a null reference, division by zero). Application code can also raise exceptions via the CIL `throw` instruction (which is triggered by the `throw` statement in C#, C++, and VB.NET). Ultimately, exception processing works the same whether the CLR or the application throws the exception, so the remainder of this discussion will focus on exceptions raised using the `throw` instruction.

The `throw` instruction requires a reference to an exception object that will convey the reason for abnormal termination. An exception object is an instance of `System.Exception` or a derived type. Rather than rely on error numbers, the CLR (like C++ and Java) uses the type of the exception to convey the reason for the error. To that end, the CLR defines two commonly used subtypes of `System.Exception`: The CLR uses `System.System-Exception` as a base type for the CLR-defined system-level exception types, and the CLR uses `System.ApplicationException` as a base type for application-specific exception types. Figure 6.15 shows many of the system-level exceptions.

Not only do exceptions carry an alternate result from a method or instruction, but also the throwing of an exception causes the CLR to change the course of normal execution. In particular, the CLR will look for an appropriate exception handler by traversing the stack of the currently executing thread. Each stack frame has an **exception table** that indicates where that method's exception handlers are located as well as which range of

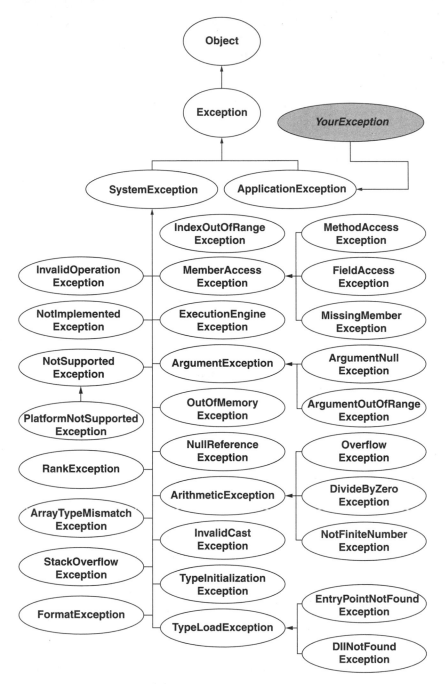

Figure 6.15: *Exceptions and the CLR Type System*

instructions they apply to. The CLR looks at the instruction counter for that stack frame to determine which handlers are applicable.

Each programming language provides its own syntax for populating the exception table of a method. Figure 6.16 shows the simplest C# exception handler. In this example, the `divide` method will have exactly one entry in its exception table. The protected body will span the assignment statement and the call to `b`. The handler will span the call to `e`. This handler is an unconditional handler, and if any exception is thrown while the method is executing in the protected body, the handler code will execute and the exception will be considered handled. After the exception is handled, execution will resume at the instructions that form the call to `g`.

The CLR will use the exception handler no matter what the type of the exception object may be. It is also possible to add a **predicate** to an exception handler that restricts the handler to exceptions that are compatible with a given type. For example, consider the C# exception handler shown in Figure 6.17. This method has an exception table with three entries. Each entry in the exception table has an identical protected range, which will correspond to the `try` block shown here. However, the first entry in the table will have a type-based predicate that causes the handler to be ignored if the current exception is not compatible with `FancyException`. The second entry in the table will have a predicate that causes the handler to be ignored if the current exception is not compatible with `NormalException`.

Finally, the third entry in the exception table has a type-based predicate that requires the exception to be compatible with `System.Object`, something that in essence makes the third entry an unconditional handler. It is important to note that the CLR will walk the exception table in order, so it is critical that handlers with more-specific types in their predicates appear before handlers that use generic types. The C# compiler will enforce this by way of compiler errors; your language's compiler may not be so watchful.

The exception table also contains entries for termination handlers. A **termination handler** fires whenever control leaves a protected range of instructions. The CLR will run termination handlers when an exception causes a protected body to be left. The CLR also runs termination handlers when a protected range of instructions completes execution normally. In C#, one creates termination handlers using the `try–finally` statement, as

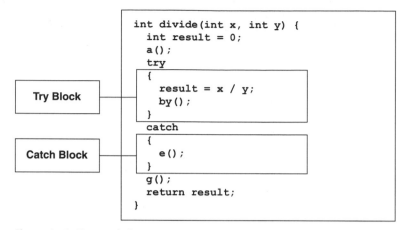

Figure 6.16: *Try–catch Statement*

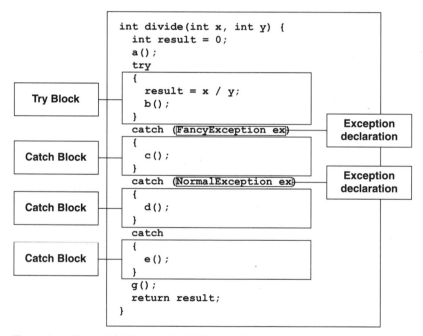

Figure 6.17: *Try–catch Statement with Declarations*

shown in Figure 6.18. In this example, the instructions in the protected range are the assignment statement and the call to b. After execution begins in this range of instructions, the CLR will guarantee that the handler clause (in this case, the call to f) will execute. If no exceptions are thrown, then the call to f will occur immediately after the call to b. If an exception is thrown

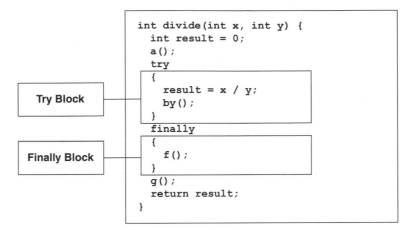

Figure 6.18: *Try–finally Statement*

while the method is executing in the protected range of instructions, the call to f will be made prior to the CLR's unwinding the method's stack frame.

Just as it was possible to specify multiple exception handlers for a given C# try block, one can also specify a termination handler after the list of exception handlers. This is shown in Figure 6.19. Again, each handler (be it a termination or an exception handler) will have its own entry in the method's exception table.

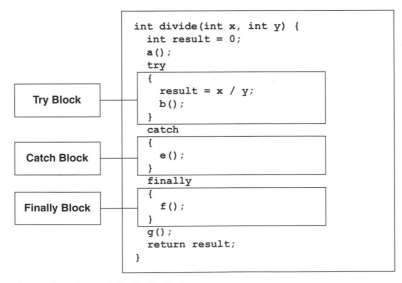

Figure 6.19: *Try–catch–finally Statement*

Where Are We?

The CLR provides a variety of mechanisms to trigger the execution of method code. Each of these mechanisms allows the developer to control the exact method that will be invoked as well as the way the parameters will be specified. Some of the mechanisms assume that method invocation will be an implicit action, whereas others make method invocation explicit. To that end, the CLR allows developers to explicitly invoke methods either synchronously or asynchronously based on the desired concurrency characteristics.

▪7▪
Advanced Methods

C HAPTER 6 LOOKED at various facilities for invoking methods. However, once the method has been invoked, control is passed to the target object's method and the fun part is over. This chapter looks at the various facilities provided by the CLR for getting between the caller and the callee and intercepting the invocation process.

It is important to note that parts of the method invocation architecture described in this chapter are likely to evolve considerably in future versions of the CLR. That stated, many of the the concepts and techniques described in this chapter will survive well into the future. The discussion of context in particular is presented here more for completeness than as a recommendation to the reader.

Motivation

Most ideas in software engineering are focused on managing complexity. Structured programming attempted to reduce complexity through coarse-grained partitioning of code and design. Object-oriented programming attempted to reduce complexity by building abstractions that marry state and behavior. Component software attempted to reduce complexity by partitioning applications based on abstract interfaces or protocols. The dream of component software was a world in which components could be assembled by less-skilled programmers using higher-level languages and tools. This, of course, assumes a world in which the problem domain can be neatly factored into discrete components that interact via simple method invocation.

The basic premise of component software ignores the fact that certain aspects of a program tend to permeate all parts of an application. Security is one such aspect. So is thread management. So is concurrency control. The list goes on.

Invariably, an application tends to become polluted with tiny snippets of code to deal with those aspects of the program that are not central to the problem domain. More often than not, such aspects tend to cross problem domains and beg for a reusable solution. Providing reuse mechanisms for these types of problems is the focus of **aspect-oriented programming** (AOP), a term coined in 1997 by Gregor Kiczales, then of Xerox PARC.

AOP focuses on providing mechanisms for factoring out pieces of the application that are not germane to the problem domain based on the principle of separation of concerns. This has two benefits. For one thing, the application code will no longer be cluttered with "plumbing" code that has no bearing on the problem at hand. The second benefit is that by factoring out aspects of the code that cross problem domains, one can conceivably reuse those solutions in other applications.

Microsoft Transaction Server (MTS) was arguably the first broadly adopted application of AOP. MTS provided an attribute mechanism that lets one express aspects of the program, such as transactioning and security, outside the normal code stream. MTS implemented these aspects through **interception**. Specifically, MTS inserted itself between the caller and the component and preprocessed or postprocessed every method call into the component. During the pre- and postprocessing, the **MTS executive** would manage transactions, handle security checks, and deal with object activation. All of this required no explicit coding on the part of the component developer. Although transactions in particular tended to impact the overall design of the component, there was no explicit code required to manage the transactions. Rather, the MTS executive would handle all of this quietly behind the scenes.

Building MTS-style interception plumbing was extremely difficult in the COM era. One reason was the lack of high-fidelity extensible metadata. That obviously is no longer a problem in the CLR-based world. The other problem, however, was dealing with the peculiarities of IA-32 call stacks in order to transparently inject one's code without stack corruption. This invariably required resorting to IA-32 assembly language in order to keep the stack from melting. One of the primary goals of the CLR architects was to provide a general-purpose interception mechanism that would allow one to inject user-defined aspects without resorting to hideous low-level coding techniques. The most fundamental concept of the CLR's interception mechanism is that calls can be viewed as message exchanges.

Messages as Method Calls

The CLR provides a rich architecture for modeling method invocation as an exchange of messages. This architecture is useful for building AOP-style interception. This architecture is useful for building RPC-style communication mechanisms. This architecture is also useful for handling asynchronous invocation and, in fact, it is used internally by the asynchronous method call facilities described in Chapter 6. The key to understanding this architecture is to reexamine what a method actually does. Ultimately, a method is simply a transformation of memory on the stack. Parenthetically, functional programming advocates would argue that this is all that a method is. The caller forms a call stack by pushing the appropriate parameters onto the stack in a format that the method has specified. After control is passed to the method, the method's primary job is to process the parameters passed on the stack and rewrite the stack to indicate the results of the processing. Figure 7.1 illustrates this process.

The CLR allows one to model this transformation of stack frames in terms of message exchanges. In this message exchange model, a method invocation has two messages: one representing the invocation request, and another representing the result of the invocation. To make this accessible programmatically, the CLR models each of these messages as an object that implements the generic `System.Runtime.Remoting.Messaging.IMessage` interface. As shown in Figure 7.2, `IMessage` acts as a base interface to several other interfaces in the suite. The most interesting of these interfaces is `IMethodMessage`:

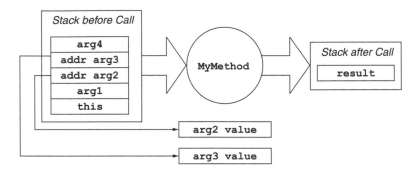

```
int MyMethod(int arg1, ref int arg2, out int arg3, int arg4);
```

Figure 7.1: *Method Invocation and Stack Frames*

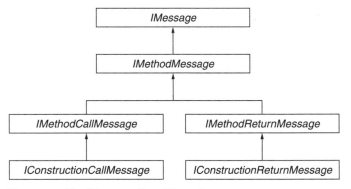

Figure 7.2: *The IMessage Type Hierarchy*

```
using System.Reflection;
using System.Collections;

namespace System.Runtime.Remoting.Messaging {
  public interface IMessage {
    IDictionary Properties { get; }
  }
  public interface IMethodMessage : IMessage {
    object              GetArg(int index);
    string              GetArgName(int index);

    int                 ArgCount { get; }
    object[]            Args { get; }
    bool                HasVarArgs { get; }
    LogicalCallContext  LogicalCallContext { get; }
    MethodBase          MethodBase { get; }
    string              MethodName { get; }
```

```
    object             MethodSignature { get; }
    string             TypeName { get; }
    string             Uri { get; }
  }
}
```

Notice that in addition to providing access to the method arguments, the `IMethodMessage` interface makes the metadata for the method available via the `MethodBase` property.

The advantage to having the stack frame exposed via this generic interface is that it allows one to access the contents of the stack without low-level knowledge of the stack frame layout. For example, consider the following code:

```
static void WireTap(IMethodMessage msg) {
  IMethodCallMessage call = (IMethodCallMessage)msg;
  Console.WriteLine("<{0}>", call.MethodName);
  for (int i = 0; i < call.ArgCount; ++i)
    Console.WriteLine("  <{0}>{1}</{0}>",
                      call.GetArgName(i),
                      call.GetArg(i), call.GetArgName(i));
  Console.WriteLine("</{0}>", call.MethodName);
}
```

Suppose that this routine were presented the message that corresponds to the following invocation:

```
int b = 2;
int c = 3;
int n = foo.MyMethod(1, ref b, out c);
```

The following would be displayed:

```
<MyMethod>
  <arg1>1</arg1>
  <arg2>2</arg2>
  <arg3>3</arg3>
</MyMethod>
```

The power of this mechanism is that the `WireTap` method did not need *a priori* knowledge of the signature of `MethodName`. This is because the `IMethodMessage` interface virtualizes the call stack into a reasonably programmable abstraction.

The parameters of a method invocation are accessible via the `IMethodMessage.GetArg` method just demonstrated. The CLR also defines two strongly typed interfaces that are specific to the request and response messages:

```
using System.Reflection;
using System.Collections;

namespace System.Runtime.Remoting.Messaging {
  public interface IMethodCallMessage : IMethodMessage {
    object          GetInArg(int index);
    string          GetInArgName(int index);

    int             InArgCount { get; }
    object[]        InArgs { get; }
  }
  public interface IMethodReturnMessage : IMethodMessage {
    object          GetOutArg(int index);
    string          GetOutArgName(int index);

    object          ReturnValue { get; }
    Exception       Exception { get; }
    int             OutArgCount { get; }
    object[]        OutArgs { get; }
  }
}
```

Note that the response message (`IMethodReturnMessage`) not only has methods that interrogate the output parameters but also provides access to the typed return value of the method via the `ReturnValue` property. Figure 7.3 shows the relationship between these two interfaces and a method invocation.

It is important to note that at the messaging level, a method invocation that results in abnormal termination simply generates a different response message. In either the normal or the abnormal termination case, there is a message that conveys the results of the invocation. However, a method

```
int Mymethod(int arg1, ref int arg2, out int arg3, int arg4);
```

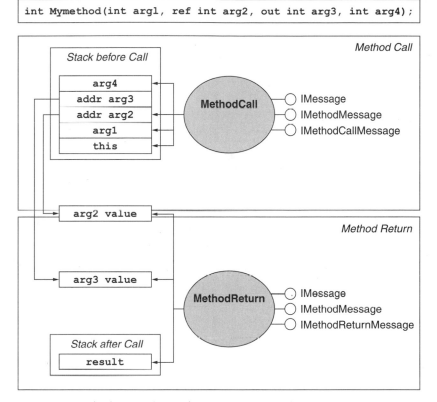

Figure 7.3: *Method Invocation and Messages*

invocation that results in abnormal termination will not have a valid
ReturnValue property. Rather, the exception object that signals the error
condition is made available via the Exception property.

At some point during message processing, someone needs to transform the request message into a response message. The CLR provides a
concrete class, System.Runtime.Remoting.Messaging.ReturnMessage,
for exactly this purpose. The ReturnMessage class implements the
IMethodReturnMessage interface and supports two constructors:
one for indicating normal termination, and one for indicating abnormal
termination.

```
namespace System.Runtime.Remoting.Messaging {
  public class ReturnMessage : IMethodReturnMessage,
                               IMethodMessage,
                               IMessage {
// normal termination constructor
```

```
      public ReturnMessage(object returnValue,
                           object[] outArgs,
                           int outArgCount,
                           LogicalCallContext callCtx,
                           IMethodCallMessage request);
// abnormal termination constructor
    public ReturnMessage(System.Exception ex,
                         IMethodCallMessage request);
// remaining members elided for clarity
  }
}
```

Note that both constructors accept a request message as the final parameter. This allows the `ReturnMessage` object to recover the metadata for the method being invoked.

At this point in the discussion, an example might be in order. First, consider the following simple interface:

```
public interface ICalculator {
  double Add(double x, double y);
  double Multiply(double x, double y);
}
```

Ultimately, each of these method definitions corresponds to a potential message exchange. For a moment, imagine that the CLR provided a way to encode a stack frame into a request message. Given this piece of CLR-based plumbing, the following code would be a reasonable implementation of this interface:

```
public static IMethodReturnMessage
ProcessMessage(IMethodCallMessage request) {
  switch (request.MethodName) {
    case "Add": {
      double x = (double)request.GetInArg(0);
      double y = (double)request.GetInArg(1);
      double result = x + y;
      return new ReturnMessage(result,null,0,null,request);
    }
    case "Multiply": {
      double x = (double)request.GetInArg(0);
      double y = (double)request.GetInArg(1);
      double result = x * y;
      return new ReturnMessage(result,null,0,null,request);
    }
```

```
    default: {
      String exm = String.Format("{0} not implemented",
                                request.MethodName);
      Exception ex = new NotImplementedException(exm);
      return new ReturnMessage(ex, request);
    }
  }
}
```

Note that the first two branches of the switch statement extract the input parameters from the request message and cache them in local variables. After the result of the method is known, the CLR constructs a new ReturnMessage object, passing the typed return value as the first constructor parameter. In the third branch of the switch statement, one indicates an abnormal termination by using the ReturnMessage constructor that accepts a System.Exception as its first parameter. By returning a valid message containing an exception, the processing code is indicating that there was no problem processing the message; rather, the processing correctly produced an exception as the result. Had there been a problem processing the message, then it would have been appropriate for the processing code to explicitly throw an exception because processing could not take place.

Although the message can be processed without a target object, the normal usage of the messaging facility is to ultimately forward the call to an actual object. This will be described in detail in the next section.

Stack and Message Transitions

The previous section ended by asking the reader to imagine a CLR-provided facility for creating request messages. Such a facility does exist, and the CLR exposes it to programmers via the transparent proxy mechanism.

A **transparent proxy (TP)** is a special kind of object that is created by the CLR and exists solely to convert method calls into message exchanges. A transparent proxy is always affiliated with a buddy object known as the **real proxy (RP)**. There is a one-to-one relationship between a transparent proxy object and a real proxy object. This relationship is shown in Figure 7.4. The real proxy is an instance of a type that derives

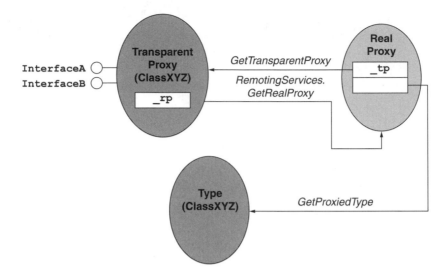

Figure 7.4: *Transparent Proxy and Real Proxy*

from the System.Runtime.Remoting.Proxies.RealProxy abstract base type. One can acquire the transparent proxy from a real proxy by calling the RealProxy.GetTransparentProxy method. One can go the other way by calling the GetRealProxy static method on the System.Runtime.Remoting.RemotingServices class. To that end, one can call the RemotingServices.IsTransparentProxy static method to test an arbitrary object reference to determine whether it points to a transparent proxy or a "real object."

The transparent proxy object ultimately must act as if it is an instance of a particular type. To that end, the constructor of the RealProxy type requires the derived type to pass a System.Type object that the CLR will use to determine the effective type of the transparent proxy object. When an isinst or a castclass CIL opcode operates on a transparent proxy, the CLR reroutes the call to simply interrogate the real proxy's System.Type object:

```
// pseudo-code for isinst, refined version
bool isinst(object obj, System.Type testType) {
// step 1 : get the type to test!
  Type targetType = null;
  if (RemotingServices.IsTransparentProxy(obj)) {
    RealProxy rp = RemotingServices.GetRealProxy(obj);
    targetType = rp.GetProxiedType();
  }
```

```
      else
        targetType = obj.GetType();
   // step 2 : perform the test!
      return testType.IsAssignableFrom(targetType);
   }
```

Given this implementation, now consider the following real proxy implementation:

```
   public class MyProxy : RealProxy {
      public MyProxy() : base(typeof(ICalculator)) {}
   // remaining members elided for clarity
   }
```

Given this proxy implementation, the following code would trigger the isinst implementation just described:

```
   MyProxy rp = new MyProxy();
   object tp = rp.GetTransparentProxy();
   ICalculator calc = tp as ICalculator; // triggers isinst
```

Because the MyProxy constructor passed the System.Type object for ICalculator to the RealProxy constructor, the GetProxiedType method will return a type object that indicates true for compatibility with ICalculator.

A real proxy implementation can override the behavior of isinst and castclass by implementing the IRemotingTypeInfo interface. This interface has two members, the main member being the CanCastTo method:

```
   namespace System.Runtime.Remoting {
     public interface IRemotingTypeInfo {
       string TypeName { get; set; }
       bool   CanCastTo(object object, System.Type testType);
     }
   }
```

Both of the CLR's implementations of isinst and castclass look for this interface when a transparent proxy is in use:

```
// pseudo-code for isinst
bool isinst(object obj, System.Type test) {
  if (RemotingServices.IsTransparentProxy(obj)) {
     RealProxy rp = RemotingServices.GetRealProxy(obj);
// special case for IRemotingTypeInfo
     IRemotingTypeInfo rti = rp as IRemotingTypeInfo;
     if (rti != null)
       return rti.CanCastTo(obj, test);
     else
       return test.IsAssignableFrom(rp.GetProxiedType());
  }
  else
     return test.IsAssignableFrom(obj.GetType());
}
```

With this refined implementation in place, now consider the following real proxy implementation:

```
public class MyProxy : RealProxy, IRemotingTypeInfo {
  public MyProxy() : base(typeof(ICalculator)) {}
  public bool CanCastTo(object obj, Type testType) {
     return true; // danger!
  }
// remaining members elided for clarity
  }
```

Assuming this implementation of IRemotingTypeInfo.CanCastTo, all casts on a MyProxy's transparent proxy will succeed no matter what the requested type is. More exotic implementations would likely look at the requested type and use some reasonable algorithm for deciding whether or not to fail the cast.

After a program acquires a reference to a transparent proxy, it is highly likely that the program will make a method call against the proxy object. When the program makes a method call against a transparent proxy object, the CLR creates a new message object that represents the invocation. The CLR then passes this message to the real proxy object for processing. One expects the real proxy object to produce a second message that represents the results of the invocation. The transparent proxy then uses this second message to transform the call stack, which transparently conveys the results to the caller. If the response message returned by the real proxy contains an exception, it is the job of the transparent proxy to rethrow this exception, again transparently conveying the results to the caller.

The message exchange between the transparent proxy and the real proxy takes place via the real proxy's `Invoke` method. The `Invoke` method accepts a request message as its sole parameter and returns a response message that conveys the results of the invocation:

```
public abstract IMessage Invoke(IMessage request);
```

Note that the `Invoke` message is marked `abstract` in the `RealProxy` type. It is the job of the derived type to implement this method and provide a meaningful implementation that produces a response message. The `ProcessMessage` routine shown in the previous section is one reasonable implementation of this processing.

Method invocations against a transparent proxy object cause a transition from the world of stack-based processing to the world of message-based processing. The real proxy's `Invoke` implementation may forward the message to any number of processing nodes prior to returning the response message. However, it is highly likely that the final processing node will ultimately need to convert the request message back into a stack frame in order to forward the call to an actual object. The CLR provides a piece of plumbing to perform this translation generically. This piece of plumbing is called the **stack builder sink** and is exposed programmatically via the `RemotingServices.ExecuteMessage` static method:

```
namespace System.Runtime.Remoting {
  public sealed class RemotingServices {
    public static IMessage
    ExecuteMessage(MarshalByRefObject target,
                   IMethodCallMessage request);
// remaining members elided for clarity
  }
}
```

The `ExecuteMessage` method accepts two parameters: a message that corresponds to a method request, and a reference to the object that will be the target of the invocation. The `ExecuteMessage` method simply creates a stack builder sink for the target object and forwards the message to the sink. The stack builder sink then does the low-level stack manipulation and invokes the actual method. When the method terminates, the stack builder sink will translate the resultant stack frame into a response message, which the CLR then returns as the result of the `ExecuteMessage` call.

Figure 7.5 shows the relationship between the transparent proxy and the stack builder sink. Note that the stack builder sink transitions from the world of message-based processing to the world of stack-based processing, effectively reversing the transition performed by the transparent proxy.

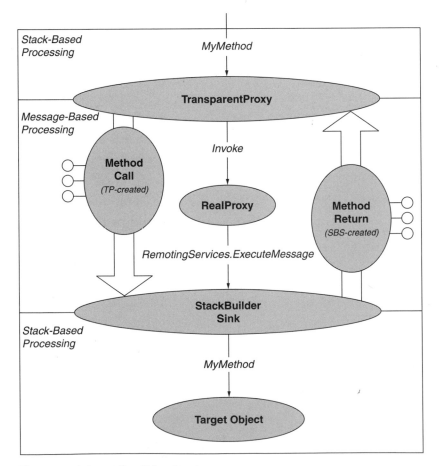

Figure 7.5: *Interception Using Proxies*

Proxiable Types

The previous section ended by looking at the `RemotingServices.ExecuteMessage` method. Careful readers may have noticed the introduction of a new type that was not explained. This type was `System.MarshalByRefObject`.

It is no coincidence that the first type used to demonstrate proxies was an interface. Interfaces have one characteristic that makes them especially proxy-friendly: Interfaces, unlike classes, always imply a virtual method dispatch. For that reason, the JIT compiler will never inline a method call through an interface-based reference. The same cannot be said for classes.

To understand the issues related to using transparent proxies with classes, consider the following class definition:

```
public sealed class Bob {
  int x;
  public void DoIt(int n) { x += n; }
}
```

In all likelihood, the JIT compiler will inline calls to `Bob.DoIt` and no method invocation will actually happen. Rather, the JIT compiler will simply insert the code for incrementing the `Bob.x` field wherever a call site to `Bob.DoIt` appears. This inline expansion bypasses the transparent proxy's attempts to intercept the call. To that end, if one were to pass `typeof(Bob)` to the `RealProxy` constructor, an exception would be thrown because the proxy infrastructure cannot guarantee that it can intercept all calls through references of type `Bob`.

This is not a problem for interfaces because the JIT compiler never inlines interface-based method calls. However, it would be useful in many circumstances to allow classes to be used for transparent proxies. Enter `System.MarshalByRefObject`.

The `System.MarshalByRefObject` type is misnamed. Its primary function is to suppress inlining by the JIT compiler, thereby allowing the transparent proxy to do its magic. When the JIT compiler tries to inline a method, it first checks to see whether the method's type derives from `System.MarshalByRefObject`. If it does, then no inlining will take place.

Moreover, any accesses to the type's instance fields will go through two little-known methods on `System.Object`: the `FieldGetter` and `FieldSetter` methods. This allows the transparent proxy to expose the public fields of a class and still be notified of their access.

Instances of classes that derive from `System.MarshalByRefObject` may or may not have a proxy associated with them. In particular, the `this` reference inside a method will never be a proxy; rather, it will always be a raw reference to the object. It is possible to indicate that a proxy is always needed to access the object. To do so, one derives from `System.ContextBoundObject`. The `System.ContextBoundObject` method derives from `System.MarshalByRefObject` and informs the runtime to always insert a transparent proxy in front of the object. For example, consider the following three types:

```
using System;
public class Bob {}
public class Steve : MarshalByRefObject {}
public class George : ContextBoundObject {}
```

Based on the descriptions of `MarshalByRefObject` and `ContextBoundObject`, one can make the following assertions:

```
using System.Runtime.Remoting;
public sealed class Utils {
  public static void Proof(Bob b, Steve s, George g) {
// g is always a TP
    Debug.Assert(RemotingServices.IsTransparentProxy(g));
// b is never a TP
    Debug.Assert(!RemotingServices.IsTransparentProxy(b));
// s may or may not be a TP
    bool whoKnows = RemotingServices.IsTransparentProxy(s);
  }
}
```

`George` derives from `ContextBoundObject` and therefore all non-null references of type `George` by definition refer to a transparent proxy (including the `this` reference!). Because `Bob` does not derive from `MarshalByRefObject`, references of type `Bob` never refer to a proxy, and, for that reason, the JIT compiler may opt to inline methods through references of type `Bob`. In contrast, `Steve` derives from `MarshalByRefObject`, and therefore references of type `Steve` may refer to a transparent proxy. This suppresses the JIT compiler from inlining method calls through references of type `Steve`.

For a class to be **proxiable**, it must derive from `MarshalByRefObject`. Armed with that knowledge, one can easily write the no-op proxy as follows:

```
public class NoOpProxy : RealProxy {
  readonly MarshalByRefObject target;
  public NoOpProxy(MarshalByRefObject target)
    : base(target.GetType())
  {
    this.target = target;
  }
  public override IMessage Invoke(IMessage request) {
    IMethodCallMessage call = (IMethodCallMessage)request;
    return RemotingServices.ExecuteMessage(target, call);
  }
}
```

This proxy does nothing other than sit between the transparent proxy and the target object and forward all method invocations through a stack builder sink.

The whole purpose of supporting interception is to enable pre- and postprocessing of method calls, typically in type-independent ways. For the remainder of this chapter, we will use the example of an interceptor that boosts thread priority prior to invoking the target method and then restores the priority prior to returning control to the caller. The following proxy implementation implements that aspect using the mechanisms described so far in this chapter:

```
public class PriorityProxy : RealProxy {
  readonly MarshalByRefObject target;
  readonly ThreadPriority level;
  public PriorityProxy(MarshalByRefObject target,
                       Type type,
                       ThreadPriority level)
    : base(type)
  { this.target = target; this.level = level; }
```

```
    public override IMessage Invoke(IMessage request) {
       IMethodCallMessage call = (IMethodCallMessage)request;
// step 1 : adjust priority
       Thread here = Thread.CurrentThread;
       ThreadPriority old = here.Priority;
       here.Priority = level;
// step 2 : forward call
       IMessage response
               = RemotingServices.ExecuteMessage(target, call);
// step 3 : restore old priority
       here.Priority = old;
// step 4 : return response message to TP
       return response;
    }
 }
```

Now one simply needs a factory method to insert the interceptor transparently:

```
public class MyCalc : MarshalByRefObject, ICalculator {

   public static MyCalc Create(ThreadPriority level) {
     MyCalc target = new MyCalc();
     PriorityProxy rp = new PriorityProxy(target,
                                 typeof(MyCalc), level);
     return (MyCalc)rp.GetTransparentProxy();
   }
   private MyCalc(){}
   public double Add(double x, double y)      {return x+y;}
   public double Multiply(double x, double y) {return x*y;}
 }
```

Note that the factory method (Create) injects the proxy between the client and the newly minted target object. The MyCalc methods do not need to deal with thread priority, and the client need only create objects using this factory method. One guarantees the use of the factory method by making the constructor private.

The previous example provided thread priority adjustment via transparent interception, which removed the priority code from the client and the target class. However, the injection of this interceptor was far from transparent. Rather, the class implementer had to write a special factory method, and the client had to use that factory method. This resulted in slightly more work for the class implementer, but, worse, it led to a somewhat unnatural usage model for the client. Of course, had the developer given the client access to the default constructor, then the new object would not have had the benefits of our interceptor.

If our target type had derived from `ContextBoundObject` rather than `MarshalByRefObject`, we could have exploited the fact that the CLR handles `newobj` requests against `ContextBoundObject`-derived types differently from the way it handles normal (non-context-bound) types. When the CLR encounters a `newobj` CIL opcode against a type that derives from `ContextBoundObject`, rather than just allocate memory, the CLR goes through a fairly sophisticated dance that allows third party extensions to become involved with the instantiation of the new object. This overall process is called **object activation**. Object activation allows us to inject our custom proxy transparently, while allowing clients to use the far more natural `new` keyword in their language of choice.

Before allocating the memory for the new context-bound object, the CLR looks at the custom attributes that have been applied to the target type being instantiated. In particular, the CLR is looking for custom attributes that implement the `System.Runtime.Remoting.Contexts.IContext-Attribute` interface. The CLR gives each of these special attributes (commonly known as **context attributes**) the opportunity to process the `newobj` request; however, because `newobj` looks only for context attributes when operating on types that derive from `ContextBoundObject`, applying a context attribute to a non-`ContextBoundObject` type has no meaningful effect. Context attributes are discussed in all their glory later in this chapter. For now, we will focus on one predefined context attribute: `System.Runtime.Remoting.Proxies.ProxyAttribute`.

The `ProxyAttribute` type hides much of the complexity of implementing a context attribute. Essentially, the `ProxyAttribute` type refactors `IContextAttribute` into two simple virtual methods, only one of which is needed to inject our custom proxy:

```
namespace System.Runtime.Remoting.Proxies {
  public class ProxyAttribute
    : Attribute,
```

```
        IContextAttribute
  {
    public virtual MarshalByRefObject CreateInstance(Type t);
  // remaining members elided for clarity
  }
}
```

When a `newobj` is executed against a type bearing a `ProxyAttribute`, the `ProxyAttribute` will call its `CreateInstance` virtual method. This method is expected to return an uninitialized instance of the presented type. Note the term *uninitialized*. Because this is happening during the activation phase, you must not call the constructor of the object you return in your overridden `CreateInstance` method. Rather, the CLR will invoke the appropriate constructor against whatever gets returned by the `CreateInstance` method.

The `ProxyAttribute.CreateInstance` method is marked as `virtual`. The default implementation simply allocates an uninitialized instance of the requested type. However, because the method is marked `virtual`, we now have an opportunity to get into the activation process without the complexity of writing our own context attribute. To inject our custom attribute, our overridden implementation of `CreateInstance` will look strikingly like the factory method implemented on the original `MyCalc`:

```
using System;
using System.Runtime.Remoting.Proxies;

[ AttributeUsage(AttributeTargets.Class) ]
public class PriorityProxyAttribute : ProxyAttribute
{
  ThreadPriority level;
  public PriorityProxyAttribute(ThreadPriority level)
  { this.level = level; }

  public override
  MarshalByRefObject CreateInstance(Type t){
  // note that we delegate to our base to get an
  // uninitialized instance!
    MarshalByRefObject target = base.CreateInstance(t);
    RealProxy pp = new PriorityProxy(target, t, level);
    return (MarshalByRefObject)pp.GetTransparentProxy();
  }
}
```

Pay close attention to the first line of the `CreateInstance` method. Because we are in the middle of a `newobj` instruction, we can't use the `new` operator or any of the other facilities for creating a new object because they would trigger yet another call to our `CreateInstance` method (which eventually would result in stack overflow). By calling `CreateInstance` on our base type, we get back an uninitialized instance of the target type, which is exactly what we need. Technically, because the target type derives from `ContextBoundObject`, we are actually holding a transparent proxy to the target object. This is illustrated in Figure 7.6.

Readers who have been around object-oriented programming for any length of time are likely concerned about the target object at this point. By calling `ProxyAttribute.CreateInstance`, we were able to acquire a reference to an object whose constructor has never executed. Your cause for concern is justified. If we were to do anything meaningful with the object, the results would be undefined. However, all we are doing is caching the reference inside our custom proxy—no more, no less. Fortunately, as soon as we return our custom proxy from our overridden `CreateInstance` method, the CLR will enter phase 2 of activation. In this phase, the constructor will be invoked; however, it will be invoked through our custom proxy, giving us the opportunity (and the responsibility) of intercepting the constructor invocation.

As with any other method call, constructor invocations against `Context-BoundObject`-derived types are represented as message exchanges. In fact messages for constructor calls implement an additional interface

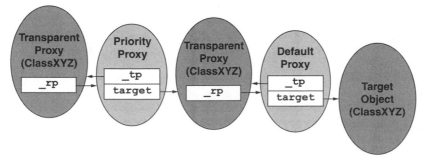

Figure 7.6: *Result of ProxyAttribute.CreateInstance*

(IConstructionCallMessage, IConstructionReturnMessage) so that one can easily detect that the call is not just another method call. Implementing custom proxies that handle constructor calls is somewhat tricky. For one thing, we cannot use RemotingServices.ExecuteMessage to forward the call. Fortunately, the RealProxy base type provides a method called InitializeServerObject that will do it for us. The Initialize-ServerObject will return a response message that our proxy's Invoke method could in fact return; however, this message contains the unwrapped object reference. To ensure that the creator gets a reference to our transparent proxy, we will need to construct a new response message that contains our custom proxy and not the "raw" object we are intercepting calls for. Ideally, we could just create a new ReturnMessage that contains our object reference. Unfortunately, we can't. Instead, we must use the EnterpriseServicesHelper.CreateConstructionReturnMessage static method.

The following code shows the modifications needed for our Invoke routine to properly handle construction calls. Note that all of the special-case handling of the construction call takes place in step 2 of the method:

```
public override IMessage Invoke(IMessage request) {
// step 1 : adjust priority
 Thread here = Thread.CurrentThread;
 ThreadPriority old = here.Priority;
 here.Priority = level;

// step 2 : forward call
 IMessage response = null;
 IMethodCallMessage call = (IMethodCallMessage)request;
 IConstructionCallMessage ctor
                    = call as IConstructionCallMessage;

 if (ctor != null)  {
// we are holding a TP, so grab its RP
  RealProxy defaultProxy
                  = RemotingServices.GetRealProxy(target);
// ask intermediate RP to invoke constructor
  defaultProxy.InitializeServerObject(ctor);
// get OUR TP
  MarshalByRefObject tp =
          (MarshalByRefObject)this.GetTransparentProxy();
```

```
   // return a message containing our TP as the result of the
   // constructor call
     response = EnterpriseServicesHelper
                   .CreateConstructionReturnMessage(ctor, tp);
    }
   else
     response = RemotingServices.ExecuteMessage(target, call);

   // step 3 : restore old priority
    here.Priority = old;
   // step 4 : return response message to TP
    return response;
   }
```

It is worth mentioning that only custom proxy implementers need to write this code. When all of this code is in place, using the code becomes as simple as applying the attribute:

```
[ PriorityProxy(ThreadPriority.Highest) ]
public class MyCalc3 : ContextBoundObject, ICalculator {
   public double Add(double x, double y)      {return x+y;}
   public double Multiply(double x, double y) {return x*y;}
}
```

Yes, the developer of the custom proxy had to go through some interesting hoops to get the proxy to work; however, users of the proxy now have an extremely simple usage model. No weird factory methods are required. Simply calling new against MyCalc3 will trigger all of the code just described.

Message Processing (Revisited)

The previous section illustrated how a custom proxy can pre- and post-process method calls simply by getting between the transparent proxy and the stack builder sink. What if one wanted to inject more than one stage of pre- and postprocessing? Yes, one could simply layer proxy upon proxy; however, redundant stack-to-message transitions would occur at each stage, resulting in undue performance costs. A far preferable approach is to chain together processing stages at the message level, thus paying the cost of stack-to-message transition only once per call and not once per stage per call. This technique is based on **message sinks**. To facilitate this in a generic manner, the CLR defines the System.Runtime.Remoting.Messaging. IMessageSink interface:

```
namespace System.Runtime.Remoting.Messaging {
  public interface IMessageSink {
    IMessageSink NextSink { get; }
    IMessage     SyncProcessMessage(IMessage request);
    IMessageCtrl AsyncProcessMessage(IMessage request,
                                     IMessageSink upcall);
  }
}
```

Note that the NextSink property models the message sink as a link in a chain. In most scenarios, the last link in the chain will be a stack builder sink, which implements IMessageSink. One expects message sinks to hold a reference to the next downstream link in the chain and return that reference in their NextSink implementation. More importantly, when an incoming method call occurs, the message sink's SyncProcessMessage method will be called. Rather than call RemotingServices.Execute-Message to forward the call, the message sink simply calls SyncPro-cessMessage on the next downstream link in the chain. Because the penultimate link in the chain typically holds a reference to the stack builder sink, the last call to SyncProcessMessage will have the same effect as a call to RemotingServices.ExecuteMessage. Figure 7.7 illustrates this process.

Message sink implementations typically provide a constructor that accepts the next downstream link in the chain. The following class shows our priority proxy functionality refactored as a message sink:

```
using System.Runtime.Remoting.Messaging;

public class PrioritySink : IMessageSink {
  readonly ThreadPriorty p;
  readonly IMessageSink next;
  public PrioritySink(ThreadPriority p,
                      IMessageSink next)
  { this.next = next; this.p = p; }
```

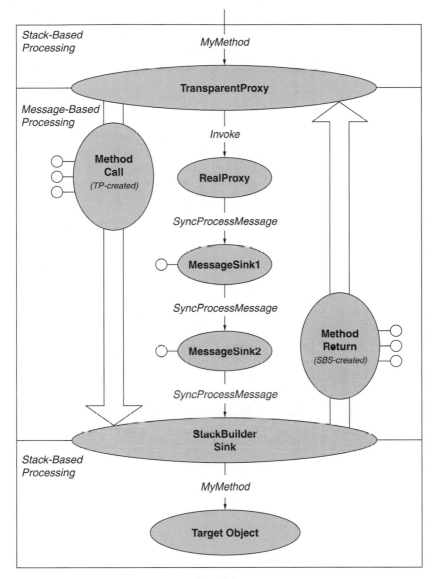

Figure 7.7: *Interception Using Message Sinks*

```
public IMessageSink NextSink { get { return next; } }

public IMessage SyncProcessMessage(IMessage request) {
// step 1 : adjust priority
   Thread here = Thread.CurrentThread;
   ThreadPriority old = here.Priority;
   here.Priority = level;
```

```
        // step 2 : forward call
           IMessage response = next.SyncProcessMessage(request);
        // step 3 : restore old priority
           here.Priority = old;
        // step 4 : return response message to TP
           return response;
        }
        // remaining methods elided for clarity
        }
```

Note that this `SyncProcessMessage` implementation looks identical to our original `PriorityProxy.Invoke` method except that in step 2, we forward the message to the next sink in the chain rather than call `RemotingServices.ExecuteMessage`.

The code fragment just shown did not illustrate the third `IMessage-Sink` method: `AsyncProcessMessage`. The CLR messaging system treats asynchronous calls differently. Specifically, the `BeginInvoke` request will trigger a call to `AsyncProcessMessage` rather than `SyncProcess-Message`. These `AsyncProcessMessage` calls will occur on a worker thread and not on the caller's thread. This means that even if your message sink took a long time to preprocess the call, the caller's thread has long since gone on to its next piece of work. That stated, the `AsyncProcess-Message` retains the asynchronous invocation style during message processing. To that end, each message sink in the chain is given the opportunity only to preprocess the call and not to postprocess it. If one needs postprocessing, one uses the second parameter to `AsyncProcess-Message` to build a reply chain to handle the results of the call. When the stack builder sink's implementation of `AsyncProcessMessage` has finished dispatching the call, it will send the response message up the reply chain. Because the reply chain was constructed in reverse order, the post-processing steps will be run in the reverse order of the preprocessing steps (which is how synchronous processing works). Figure 7.8 illustrates this overall dispatching process.

Given the mechanisms shown so far, the only way for the message sinks to communicate with one another is via messages. The type and contents of these messages are determined based on which method the caller originally invoked. It is often useful for message sinks to piggyback additional

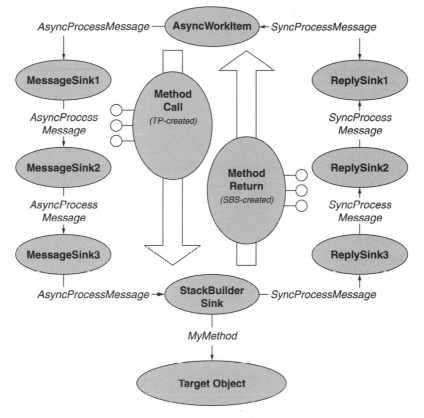

Figure 7.8: *Message Processing and Asynchronous Invocation*

data in a message, either to allow one message sink to send out-of-band information to another sink in the chain, or more interestingly, to communicate additional information to either the caller or the callee. One exposes the ability to add additional information to a message via **call context**.

Both the request and the response messages have a call context property, which is exposed via the IMethodMessage.LogicalCallContext property. Call context is a per-call property bag that allows one to associate arbitrary objects with uniquely named slots. For example, consider the following SyncProcessMessage implementation:

```
public IMessage SyncProcessMessage(IMessage request) {
  IMethodMessage method = (IMethodMessage)request;
  method.LogicalCallContext.SetData("mykey", 52);
  return next.SyncProcessMessage(request);
}
```

This message sink inserts the value 52 into the logical call context slot named mykey. Downstream message sinks can then retrieve this data as follows:

```
public IMessage SyncProcessMessage(IMessage request) {
  IMethodMessage method = (IMethodMessage)request;
// fetch data from call context
  object val = method.LogicalCallContext.GetData("mykey");
  int mykey = 0;
  if (val != null) {
    mykey = (int)val;
    method.LogicalCallContext.FreeNamedDataSlot("mykey");
  }
  return next.SyncProcessMessage(request);
}
```

This implementation simply grabs the value in slot mykey and stores it in a local variable. Notice that the implementation checks to see whether the value is actually present. Additionally, after it retrieves the value, it then releases the slot in call context, preventing downstream sinks from seeing the value. This step is optional; however, the slot will remain occupied indefinitely otherwise.

A more interesting application of call context occurs when either the caller or the callee accesses it. This capability is exposed via the System.Runtime.Remoting.Messaging.CallContext type. This type exposes three static methods (GetData, SetData, and FreeNamedDataSlot) that manipulate the implicit call context for the current thread. Both the transparent proxy and the stack builder sink use this implicit call context to keep the implicit context in sync with the explicit LogicalCallContext property used in messages.

The following client code, which manually populates the call context, is functionally identical to the SyncProcessMessage shown earlier:

```
using System.Runtime.Remoting.Messaging;
class App {
  static void Main() {
// make a new context-bound object
    ICalculator calc = new MyCalc3();
```

```
// insert 52 in implicit slot "mykey"
   CallContext.SetData("mykey", 52);
// issue the call - TP will set up
// LogicalCallContext for the call
   double val = calc.Add(3, 2);
  }
}
```

Similarly, the target method can also access the call context:

```
using System.Runtime.Remoting.Messaging;
public class MyCalc3 : ContextBoundObject, ICalculator {
  public double Add(double x, double y) {
// grab data from implicit slot "mykey"
   int n = 0;
   object val = CallContext.GetData("mykey");
   if (val != null) {
     n = (int)val;
     CallContext.FreeNamedDataSlot("mykey");
   }
// process call (using data from call context)
   return x + y + n;
  }
}
```

This target method doesn't care whether the call context was populated by the caller or by an intermediate message sink.

One can also send call context as part of the response message for a call. Had the target method called `CallContext.SetData`, the stack builder sink would have used that information to populate the response message, making any call context available to both upstream message sinks as well as the original caller.

Call context is typically bound to a particular thread. However, some message sinks may cause a thread switch or may even send a serialized version of the message over the network to a remote application. In the general case, call context will not be propagated across physical thread boundaries. However, you can change this behavior on a slot-by-slot basis. If the data stored in the slot implements the `System.Runtime.Remoting.ILogicalThreadAffinative` interface, message sinks that hop thread, application, process, or machine boundaries are required to propagate that slot to the next node in the chain. The ILogicalThreadAffinative interface has no methods; rather, it simply acts as a marker to inform the messaging plumbing which call context slots require propagation. Unfortunately, if all you want to propagate is a primitive, you will need to write a wrapper class that implements ILogicalThreadAffinative and holds the primitive as a public field.

Objects and Context

One particularly nasty problem that occurs when one is building interception plumbing is the need to prevent non-intercepted references to an object from leaking out to the outside world, thus giving callers an opportunity to bypass the services provided by the interceptors. Consider, for example, the following simple class:

```
public class Bob : MarshalByRefObject {
  public void f() {}
  public Bob GetIt() {
    return this; // danger!
  }
}
```

In this simple example, the GetIt method returns a reference to the target object. Had a transparent proxy been between the caller and the object, the client would now have two ways to reference the object: one direct and one indirect via the proxy. Now consider the following client code:

```
static void UseIt(Bob proxy) {
  Bob b = proxy.GetIt();
  proxy.f(); // goes through proxy
  b.f(); // bypasses proxy
}
```

Had the proxy performed some critical service (e.g., concurrency management or security), that service would be bypassed on the second call to Bob.f.

Some interception-based systems require programmers to explicitly protect their `this` reference using a system-provided facility. MTS provided the `SafeRef` API, and Enterprise Java Beans (EJB) provides the `EJB-Context.getEJBHome` method. In both cases, these routines force the developer to be explicit about proxy management, thereby defeating the whole idea of transparent interception.

To avoid these problems, the CLR provides an architecture by which one can simply use objects as expected, and the CLR guarantees that the appropriate interception code is run. This architecture is based on associating each object with a **context** that represents the required services that are associated with the object.

Every CLR application is divided into one or more contexts. Contexts are themselves objects that are instances of the `System.Runtime.Remoting.Contexts.Context` type. Objects that are compatible with `Context BoundObject` are bound to a particular context at creation time; these objects are referred to as **context-bound**. All other objects are considered **context-agile** and are not affiliated with any particular context (see Figure 7.9). Context-agile objects are ignorant of the context architecture and conceptually span all contexts in an application.

Threads can enter and leave contexts at will. There is a static per-thread property, `System.Threading.Thread.CurrentContext`, that returns a reference to the context the current thread is executing in. One context is allocated for each application when the application starts, and it is in this context that threads begin executing. This initial context is called the **default context**, and one can access it via the `Context.DefaultContext` static property.

To illustrate the difference between context-agile and context-bound objects, consider the following two types:

```
public class Bound : ContextBoundObject {
  Context lastContext = Thread.CurrentContext;
  public void f() {
    Context here = Thread.CurrentContext;
// this will always succeed
    Debug.Assert(here == lastContext);
    this.lastContext = here;
  }
}
```

```
public class Agile {
  Context lastContext = Thread.CurrentContext;
  public void f() {
    Context here = Thread.CurrentContext;
// this may or may not succeed!!
    Debug.Assert(here == lastContext);
    this.lastContext = here;
  }
}
```

The CLR makes no guarantees as to which context the `Agile.f` method will run because `Agile` is not a context-bound type. In contrast, the CLR ensures that the thread executing the `Bound.f` method will always run in the same context—in particular, the context the object was bound to at

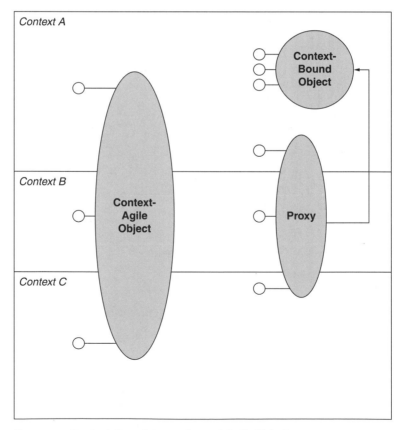

Figure 7.9: *Context-Bound versus Context-Agile Objects*

creation time. The CLR is able to make this guarantee by ensuring that all references to context-bound objects are in fact references to a proxy. It is impossible to acquire a direct reference to a context-bound object. That means that one can make the following assertion:

```
public class Bound : ContextBoundObject {
 public void f() {
  Debug.Assert(RemotingServices.IsTransparentProxy(this));
 }
}
```

As shown here, not even the this reference is a direct reference to the object. This solves our earlier problem of ensuring that no raw references escape to the client. Because not even the object can acquire a raw reference, there is no opportunity for the interception layer to be bypassed. For efficiency, the standard proxy used for context-bound objects simply forwards the call to the target object if the calling thread is already in the correct context. Otherwise, the proxy goes through the standard message processing chain described in the previous section. To ensure that the appropriate context is always used for the target object, at creation time the CLR inserts a message sink (of type CrossContextChannel) into the chain. The message sink switches the context of the calling thread to that of the target object and then switches it back to the caller's context after the call has been dispatched. The following pseudo-code illustrates how CrossContext-Channel works:

```
namespace System.Runtime.Remoting.Channels {
 public class CrossContextChannel : IMessageSink {
  IMessageSink nextSink;
  Context        targetContext;
  public IMessage SyncProcessMessage(IMessage request) {
// step 1 : preprocess call
   Context old = Thread.CurrentContext;
   Thread.CurrentContext = targetContext;
// step 2 : forward call to next sink
   IMessage resp = nextSink.SyncProcessMessage(request);
// step 3 : postprocess call
   Thread.CurrentContext = old;
```

```
  // step 4 : return message to upstream sink
    return resp;
  }
 }
}
```

This pseudo-code is a vast simplification of the actual implementation. The reader is encouraged to use ILDASM.EXE to look at the genuine code in mscorlib.dll.

Like call context, contexts are property bags that allow arbitrary data to be associated with a named slot. Unlike call context, data associated with a context will stay with the objects in that context no matter where a given method call may come from. The following code demonstrates the use of a context as a property bag:

```
public class Bound : ContextBoundObject {
  LocalDataStoreSlot slot = null;

  public void SetIt(int n) {
    if (slot == null)
      slot = Thread.CurrentContext.AllocateDataSlot();
    Thread.CurrentContext.SetData(slot, n);
  }

  public int GetIt() {
    if (slot == null)
      return 0;
    else
      return (int)Thread.CurrentContext.GetData(slot);
  }
}
```

Note that unlike call context which used simple text-based names as keys, the GetData and SetData methods use LocalDataStoreSlots.

In addition to the simple associative array just described, contexts have zero or more named **context properties**. Context properties act as logical fields of the context, and, as with fields, the set of context properties does not change for the lifetime of the context. Context properties are not arbitrary data. Rather, they are objects that implement the System.Runtime.Remoting.Contexts.IContextProperty interface. Each context property has a unique text-based name, and one can access it by calling the `Context.GetProperty` method on a particular context. Additionally, one can get references to all of a context's context properties using `Context.ContextProperties`, which returns an array of context properties.

Context properties differ from the simple `SetData` and `GetData` in that context properties are established when a context is first created. Like traditional fields, context properties are uniquely named and are bound to a context at creation time. Also like fields, context properties stay with the context throughout its lifetime. As we will see in the next section, context properties also get the opportunity to inject message sinks between the proxy and the context-bound object, a capability that arguably is their primary reason for existence.

Context attributes add context properties to a context at creation time. **Context attributes** are custom attributes that support the `IContext-Attribute` interface:

```
namespace System.Runtime.Remoting.Contexts {
  public interface IContextAttribute {
    bool IsContextOK(Context ctx,
                      IConstructionCallMessage ctor);
    void GetPropertiesForNewContext(
                      IConstructionCallMessage ctor);
  }
}
```

When a `newobj` opcode is executed against a context-bound type, the CLR enumerates all of the attributes of that type looking for context attributes. When it finds the context attributes, the CLR then presents the current context and a message representing the construction call to each context's `IsContextOK` method. The context attribute is expected to look at the current context and determine whether or not that context is appropriate. How it makes this determination is specific to each attribute; however, the attribute typically looks at the current context to see whether the appropriate context properties are present. If the current context is acceptable, the context attribute returns `true`. If the current context is not acceptable, the context attribute returns `false`, indicating that the CLR must create a new context for the new object.

If all of the context attributes return `true` from `IsContextOK`, then the CLR will bind the new object to the current context. If at least one context attribute returns `false`, then the CLR will bind the new object to a new context. To ensure that the new context is properly initialized, the CLR will make a second pass across the type's context attributes, asking each of them to contribute any context properties that it wishes to be bound to the new context. This is done via the `GetPropertiesForNewContext`.

At this point in the discussion, an example is in order. Consider our thread priority proxy from earlier in this chapter. We can refactor that proxy fairly simply to use the context infrastructure. Rather than simply force our interception code into every proxy, we would prefer to avoid doing the adjustment twice if one object calls another with the same priority setting. To accomplish this, we will add a context property that contains the priority setting to be used for all objects in that context. This will have the effect of partitioning the application into priority domains, with all objects in a particular priority domain sharing a priority level. This is illustrated in Figure 7.10.

Our context property will be fairly simple because it needs to have only one public property, that is, the thread priority:

```
using System.Runtime.Remoting.Contexts;
using System.Threading;

public class PriorityProperty : IContextProperty {

  ThreadPriority level;
  public ThreadPriority Level { get { return level; } }
  internal PriorityProperty(ThreadPriority level)
  { this.level = level;}


// IContextProperty members
  public string Name { get { return "ThreadPriority"; } }
  public bool IsNewContextOK(Context ctx) {
    return true;
  }
  public void Freeze(Context ctx) { }
}
```

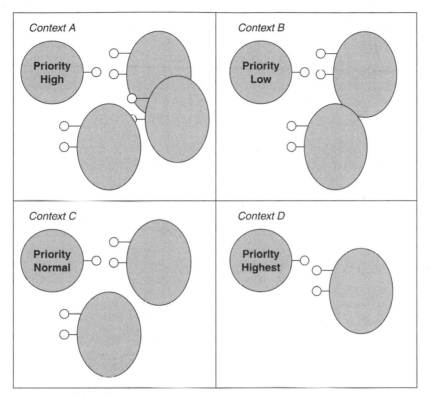

Figure 7.10: *Thread Priority as a Context Property*

To provide a way to inject our context property, we will need to define a supporting context attribute:

```
using System.Runtime.Remoting.Contexts;
using System.Threading;
using System;

[ AttributeUsage(AttributeTargets.Class) ]
public class PriorityAttribute
   : Attribute, IContextAttribute {

  ThreadPriority level;
  internal PriorityAttribute(ThreadPriority level)
  { this.level = level;}

// IContextProperty members
  public bool IsContextOK(Context current,
              IConstructionCallMessage ctor) {
```

```
// our property must be present!
   object prop = current.GetProperty("ThreadPriority");
   if (prop == null) return false;
// and its level must match the attribute's
   PriorityProperty pp = (PriorityProperty)prop;
   return pp.Level == this.Level;
 }

 public void GetPropertiesForNewContext(
                IConstructionCallMessage ctor) {
// create new property
   IContextProperty prop = new PriorityProperty(level);
// associate property with constructor call
   ctor.ContextProperties.Add(prop);
 }
}
```

The IsContextOK method checks for the presence of our property in the current context. If it is not there, we reject the current context, forcing the CLR to create a new context for the new object. Similarly, if our context property is present in the current context but has a different priority level than the one our attribute requires, then, again, we reject the current context. These two tests guarantee that all objects having a particular context will have the same thread priority level. It also allows two or more objects whose priority requirements are the same to share a context. This reduces resource consumption and speeds method invocation within a context, thereby improving the program's overall performance.

Our context attribute's GetPropertiesForNewContext simply creates a new context property and associates it with the construction call message. When the CLR allocates the object, it will also allocate a new context, initializing its context properties from the ContextProperties of the construction call message.

With our context property and attribute in place, we can now write the following code to use it:

```
[ Priority(ThreadPriority.Highest) ]
public class MyCalc5 : ContextBoundObject, ICalculator {
```

```
  public double Add(double x, double y) {
// grab the object's context
  Context here = Thread.CurrentContext;
// fetch the priority property
  IContextProperty p = here.GetProperty("ThreadPriority");
  PriorityProperty pp = (PriorityProperty)p;
// guarantee that priority level was set correctly
  Debug.Assert(pp.Level == ThreadPriority.Highest);
  }
}
```

Note that this code can rely on the context property being initialized correctly. However, based on the implementation we have seen so far, the CLR will make no actual adjustment of thread priority. Achieving that is the topic of the next and final section of this chapter.

Contexts and Interception

The CLR gives context attributes the chance to put context properties in place as a context is being created. The CLR gives context properties the chance to inject message sinks between a proxy and a context-bound object when the object's proxy is created. One could argue that the primary motivation for context properties is to act as a factory for message sinks.

The message sinks injected by a context property are responsible for implementing the aspect that their property (and its attribute) represents. For example, our thread priority property would need to inject a message sink to adjust the thread priority prior to entering the context and then reset it upon leaving the context. Message sinks typically manipulate the state of threads, contexts, and other pieces of the program's overall execution state.

Proxies to context-bound objects support the insertion of message sinks at several well-known regions. Specifically, the context architecture partitions the chain of message sinks into four distinct regions. As shown in Figure 7.11, these regions are delimited by system-provided terminator sinks that demarcate the sink chain. Recall that it is the job of the proxy to properly adjust the execution state to switch to the target object's context. Typically, the sinks injected by the context property will also adjust

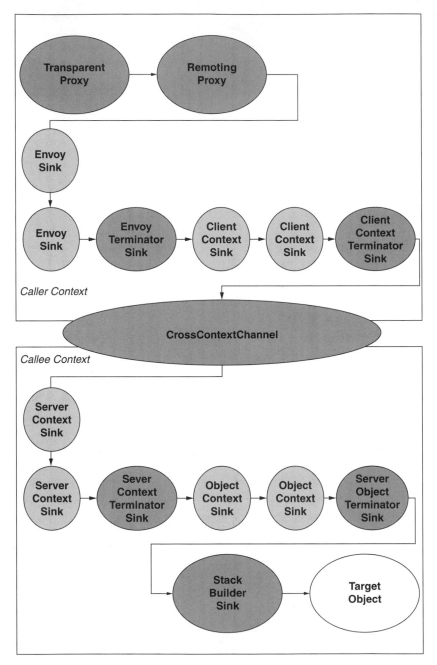

Figure 7.11: *Cross-Context Proxies and Sinks*

aspects of the execution state. Of the four distinct regions of sinks, the CLR runs envoy sinks and client context sinks prior to switching the context. That means that if an envoy sink were to call `Thread.CurrentContext`, it would get back the context of the caller and not that of the target object. In contrast, object and server context sinks run after switching the context, and this means that if either of these sinks were to call `Thread.Current-Context`, it would receive the context of the target object and not that of the caller.

To understand exactly why four regions of sinks are needed, it is useful to examine who needs to inject these sinks. For the remainder of this discussion, we will consider only the case in which a proxy is called from a context different from that of the target object. In this case, there are two contexts to consider: the caller's context and the target object's context.

It should be obvious that the properties of the target context will likely want to adjust the execution state prior to entering the context. This adjustment is the role of server context sinks. The CLR gives each context property in the target context that implements the `IContributeServer-ContextSink` the opportunity to inject a message sink in this region. **Object sinks** are similar to server context sinks. Like server context sinks, object sinks execute after the context has been switched to the target context. Unlike server context sinks, which execute no matter which object the call is destined for, object sinks are specific to one particular object in the target context. Object sinks are useful for implementing features that are specific to one object, such as MTS-style just-in-time activation. Object sinks are contributed by context properties that implement the `ICon-tributeObjectSink` interface.

Server context sinks intercept calls coming into the target context. However, if a context property wishes to adjust the execution state as calls are made from the current context, that context property must contribute a **client context sink**. Client context sinks are contributed by context properties that implement the `IContributeClientContextSink` interface. Client context sinks typically undo or suspend the work done by the server context sink. The canonical example of using client and server context sinks together is to implement call timing. If a server context sink were used by itself, one could imagine easily recording the time that elapsed between entering the context and leaving the context:

```
public class ServerTimingSink : IMessageSink {
  [ ContextStatic ]
  static internal long totalTicks = 0;

  public IMessage SinkProcessMessage(IMessage r) {
    long start = DateTime.Now.Ticks;
    IMessage p = next.SyncProcessMessage(r);
    long end = DateTime.Now.Ticks;
    totalTicks += end - start;
    return p;
  }
// remaining members elided for clarity
}
```

However, this sink will consider the time spent in this context as well as in any child contexts that the target object may call into. To eliminate from consideration the time spent calling outside the target context, one could also inject a client context sink that would note that we are leaving the current context and adjust the accumulated time accordingly:

```
public class ClientTimingSink : IMessageSink {
  public IMessage SinkProcessMessage(IMessage r) {
    long start = DateTime.Now.Ticks;
    IMessage p = next.SyncProcessMessage(r);
    long end = DateTime.Now.Ticks;
    ServerTimingSink.totalTicks -= end - start;
    return p;
  }
// remaining members elided for clarity
}
```

To inject both sinks in the appropriate places, the following context property would suffice:

```
using System.Runtime.Remoting.Contexts;
using System.Threading;

public class TimingProperty
    : IContextProperty,
      IContributeServerContextSink,
      IContributeClientContextSink
  {
   IMessageSink GetServerContextSink(IMessageSink next) {
```

```
      return new ServerTimingSink(next);
    }

    IMessageSink GetClientContextSink(IMessageSink next) {
      return new ClientTimingSink(next);
    }

  // IContextProperty members
    public string Name { get { return "TimingProperty"; } }
    public bool IsNewContextOK(Context ctx) {
      return true;
    }
    public void Freeze(Context ctx) { }
  }
```

The `GetServerContextSink` method will be called for all proxies com-ing into the current context. The CLR will call the `GetClientContextSink` method for all proxies that call out of the current context.

The last region of message sinks to be discussed is envoy sinks. Like client context sinks, **envoy sinks** execute prior to the switching of context. However, client context sinks are contributed by the caller's context. In contrast, envoy sinks are contributed by the target context. Envoy sinks act as ambassadors for the server context sinks in the caller's context. Envoy sinks typically exist to inspect pieces of the caller's context (e.g., security information, locale, transaction identifiers) and send them to the server context sink via call context properties. That communication can work both ways; a server context sink can ship information upstream to its envoy sink as part of a response message, and the envoy sink can then adjust the exe-cution state of the caller prior to finally returning control from the proxy. Envoy sinks are contributed by context properties in the target context; these properties must implement the `IContributeEnvoySink` interface.

To understand the role of envoy sinks, we need to look at our thread pri-ority aspect one last time. Our previous implementations always set the thread priority to an absolute level without regard to the existing priority. What if we wanted to implement an interceptor that boosted the thread pri-ority by one level? One approach would be to do the following in a server context sink:

```
IMessage SyncProcessMessage(IMessage m) {
// cache
  Thread here = Thread.CurrentThread;
  ThreadPriority oldp = here.Priority;
  ThreadPriority newp = old;
// boost
  if (newp != ThreadPriority.Highest)
    here.Priority = newp + 1;
// dispatch call
  IMessage r = next.SyncProcessMessage(m);
// restore
  if (newp != ThreadPriority.Highest)
    here.Priority = old;
  return r;
}
```

Unfortunately, this works only if we are still running on the original thread of the caller. We cannot make this guarantee in the face of arbitrary message sinks. Rather, we need to build an envoy sink that propagates the original priority to our server context sink as an additional piece of call context. Moreover, to ensure that this call context is always propagated, we will need our extra data to support the ILogicalThreadAffinative interface. Here is all we need:

```
internal class EnvoyData : ILogicalThreadAffinative {
  internal ThreadPriority clientPriority;
  internal EnvoyData(ThreadPriority p)
  { clientPriority = p; }
}
```

Our envoy sink will simply add the priority to the message prior to forwarding it down the chain:

```
public class PriorityEnvoySink : IMessageSink {
  public IMessage SyncProcessMessage(IMessage m)    {
    IMethodCallMessage call = (IMethodCallMessage)m;
    ThreadPriority p = Thread.CurrentThread.Priority;
    EnvoyData ed = new EnvoyData(p);
    call.LogicalCallContext.SetData("clientpriority", ed);
    return next.SyncProcessMessage(call);
  }
// remaining methods elided for clarity
}
```

This allows our downstream server context sink to scrape the caller's priority out of call context as follows:

```
public class PriorityServerSink : IMessageSink {
  public IMessage SyncProcessMessage(IMessage m)    {

// grab caller's priority from call context
    IMethodCallMessage call = (IMethodCallMessage)m;
    LogicalCallContext cc = call.LogicalCallContext;
    EnvoyData ed = (EnvoyData)cc.GetData("clientpriority");
    cc.FreeNamedDataSlot("clientpriority");

// proceed to boost-dispatch-unboost!
    Thread here = Thread.CurrentThread;
    ThreadPriority old = here.Priority;
    if (ed.clientPriority != ThreadPriority.Highest)
      here.Priority = ed.clientPriority + 1;
    IMessage resp = next.SyncProcessMessage(call);
    if (ed.clientPriority != ThreadPriority.Highest)
      here.Priority = old;
    return resp;
  }
// remaining methods elided for clarity
}
```

Now all that we need is a simple context property to inject both message sinks:

```
public class BoostProperty
    : IContextProperty,
      IContributeEnvoySink,
      IContributeServerContextSink
{
  public IMessageSink GetEnvoySink(MarshalByRefObject obj,
                                   IMessageSink n)
  {
    return new PriorityEnvoySink(n);
  }
  public IMessageSink GetServerContextSink(IMessageSink n)
  {
    return new PriorityServerSink(n);
  }
  public string Name { get { return "Boost"; } }
```

```
public bool IsNewContextOK(Context ctx) { return true; }
public void Freeze(Context ctx) {}

}
```

The context attribute that inserts this property is extremely boilerplate, with one exception. Because the `newobj` opcode executes prior to our envoy sink's being in place, the first call to our server context sink's `SyncProcessMessage` will not have the benefit of our `EnvoyData`. To address this, our context attribute will need to insert our call context property into the construction call message in its `GetPropertiesForNewContext` method:

```
public void
GetPropertiesForNewContext(IConstructionCallMessage ctor) {
// add our property to the new context
  ctor.ContextProperties.Add(new BoostProperty());
// store the current thread priority in call context
  ctor.LogicalCallContext.SetData("clientpriority",
          new EnvoyData(Thread.CurrentThread.Priority));
}
```

In essence, the context attribute is playing the role of the envoy sink for the constructor call.

Where Are We?

The CLR provides a rich architecture for viewing method invocation as an exchange of messages. The key to this architecture is the transparent proxy facility provided by the CLR's remoting library. Transparent proxies live at the boundary of the world of call stacks and allow developers to view the world as a pipeline of message filters. The CLR also provides a strong notion of context, which allows one to transparently integrate interception into a type-centric programming model.

▓ 8 ▪
Domains

MANY PROGRAMMING TECHNOLOGIES and environments define their own unique models for scoping the execution of code and the ownership of resources. For an operating system, the model is based on processes. For the Java VM, it is based on class loaders. For Internet Information Services (IIS) and Active Server Pages (ASP), the scoping model is based on a virtual directory. For the CLR, the fundamental scope is an AppDomain, which is the focus of this chapter.

Execution Scope and the CLR

AppDomains fill many of the same roles filled by an operating system process. AppDomains, like processes, scope the execution of code. AppDomains, like processes, provide a degree of fault isolation. AppDomains, like processes, provide a degree of security isolation. AppDomains, like processes, own resources on behalf of the programs they execute. In general, most of what you may know about an operating system process probably applies to AppDomains.

AppDomains are strikingly similar to processes, but they are ultimately two different things. A process is an abstraction created by your operating system. An AppDomain is an abstraction created by the CLR. Whereas a given AppDomain resides in exactly one OS process, a given OS process can host multiple AppDomains. Figure 8.1 shows this relationship.

It is less costly to create an AppDomain than it is to create an OS process. Similarly, it is cheaper to cross AppDomain boundaries than it is to cross OS process boundaries. However, as is the case with OS processes, it is difficult (but not impossible) to share data between AppDomains. One reason that sharing is difficult is due to the way that objects and AppDomains relate.

An object resides in exactly one AppDomain, as do values. Moreover, object references must refer to objects in the same AppDomain. In this respect, AppDomains behave as if each one has its own private address space. However, this behavior is only an illusion because all it takes is an unverifiable method to start walking over memory to shatter this illusion. If only verifiable code is executed, then this illusion is in fact the rule of the land. The ability of nonverifiable code to shatter the illusion of the CLR

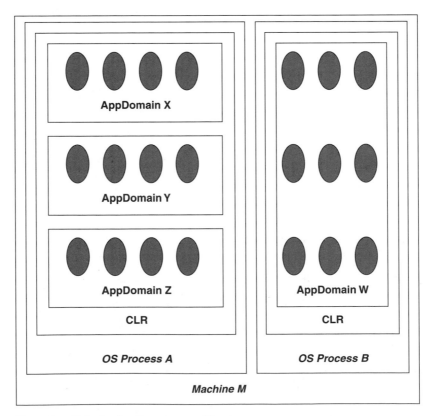

Figure 8.1: *Objects, AppDomains, and Processes*

AppDomain is analogous to kernel-mode code's ability to shatter the illusion of an OS process.

Like objects, types reside in exactly one AppDomain. If two App-Domains need to use a type, one must initialize and allocate the type once per AppDomain. Additionally, one must load and initialize the type's module and assembly once for each AppDomain the type is used in. Because each AppDomain in a process maintains a separate copy of the type, each AppDomain has its own private copy of the type's static fields. Figure 8.2 shows the relationship among AppDomains, objects, and types.

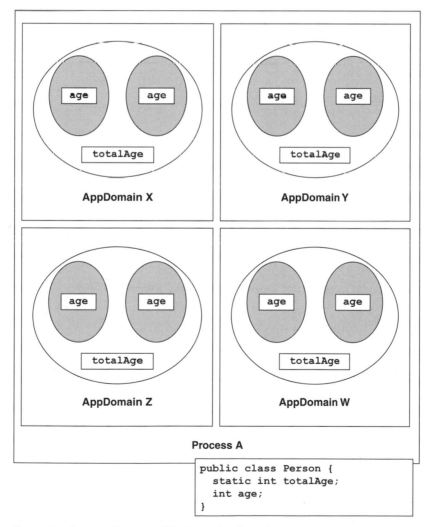

```
public class Person {
    static int totalAge;
    int age;
}
```

Figure 8.2: *Scoping Types and Statics to AppDomains*

Like processes, AppDomains are a unit of ownership. The resources that are owned by an AppDomain include loaded modules, assemblies, and types. These resources are held in memory as long as the owning AppDomain is loaded. Unloading an AppDomain is the only way to unload a module or assembly. Unloading an AppDomain is also the only way to reclaim the memory consumed by a type's static fields.

It is difficult to talk about processes without quickly steering the conversation to the topic of threads. The CLR has its own abstraction for modeling the execution of code that is conceptually similar to an OS thread. The CLR defines a type, `System.Threading.Thread`, that represents a schedulable entity in an AppDomain. A `System.Threading.Thread` thread object is sometimes referred to as a **soft thread** because it is a construct that is not recognized by the underlying operating system. In contrast, OS threads are referred to as **hard threads** because they are what the OS deals with.

There is no one-to-one relationship between hard threads and CLR soft thread objects. However, certain realities are known to be true based both on the programming model and empirical analysis of the current CLR implementation. For one thing, a CLR soft thread object resides in exactly one AppDomain. This is a byproduct of how AppDomains work and what they mean and must be true no matter how the CLR's implementation changes over time. Second, a given AppDomain may have multiple soft thread objects. In the current implementation, this happens when two or more hard threads execute code in a single AppDomain. All other assumptions about the relationship between hard and soft threads are implementation-specific. With that disclaimer in place, there are a few other observations worth noting.

In the current implementation of the CLR, a given hard thread will have at most one soft thread object affiliated with it for a given AppDomain. Also, if a hard thread winds up executing code in multiple AppDomains, each AppDomain will have a distinct soft thread object affiliated with that thread. However, if a hard thread never enters a given AppDomain, then that AppDomain will not have a soft thread object that represents the hard thread. Figure 8.3 illustrates these observations.

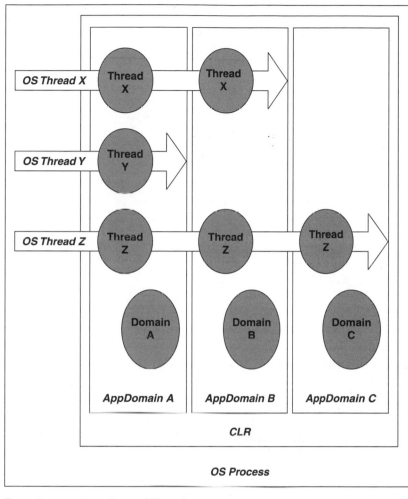

Figure 8.3: *AppDomains and Threads*

Finally, each time a given hard thread enters an AppDomain, it gets the same soft thread object. Again, please note that these observations are based on the behavior of the current CLR implementation. In particular, when the CLR is hosted in a fiber-based environment (such as SQL Server), it is likely that one or more of these assumptions may break, most likely the assumption that a hard thread has at most one soft thread object per App-Domain.

The CLR maintains a fair amount of information in the hard thread's **thread local storage (TLS)**. In particular, one can find hard TLS references to the current AppDomain and soft thread object. When a hard thread crosses over from one AppDomain to another, the CLR automatically adjusts these references to point to the new "current" AppDomain and soft thread. The current implementation of the CLR maintains a per-App-Domain thread table to ensure that a given hard thread is affiliated with only one soft thread object per AppDomain.

It is worth noting that a soft thread object has its own private thread local storage that is accessible via the `Thread.GetData` and `Thread.SetData` methods. Because this TLS is bound to the soft thread object, when a hard thread crosses AppDomain boundaries, it cannot see the soft TLS that was stored while the hard thread was executing in the previous AppDomain.

Programming with AppDomains

One exposes AppDomains to programmers via the `System.AppDomain` type. Listing 8.1 shows a subset of the public signature of `System.AppDomain`. The most important member of this type is the `CurrentDomain` static property. This property simply fetches the AppDomain reference that is stored in the hard thread's TLS. As a point of interest, one can extract the current soft thread object from the hard thread's TLS via the `Thread.CurrentThread` property.

Listing 8.1: *System.AppDomain (Excerpt)*

```
using System.Security.Policy;
namespace System {
  public sealed class AppDomain : MarshalByRefObject,
                _AppDomain, // for COM-based hosting
                System.Security.IEvidenceFactory
  {
// get "current" domain
    public static AppDomain CurrentDomain { get; };

// get/set domain-specific environment variables
    public object GetData(string name);
    public void SetData(string name, object value);

// get all assemblies loaded in domain
    public Assembly[] GetAssemblies();

// spawn new AppDomain
    public static AppDomain
```

```
    CreateDomain(
            string friendlyName,      // name for debugger
            Evidence secinfo,         // top-of-stack sec
            AppDomainSetup ldrinfo); // fusion env vars

// unload existing AppDomain
    public static void Unload(AppDomain target);

// load EXE-based assembly and run Main (synchronously)
    public int ExecuteAssembly(string assemblyFile,
                                Evidence assemblySecurity,
                                string[] argv);

// execute method in target AppDomain
    public void DoCallBack(CrossAppDomainDelegate cb);

// other members elided for clarity
    }
}
```

After you have a reference to an AppDomain, there are a variety of things you can do with it. For one thing, each AppDomain has its own set of environmental properties that is accessible via the SetData and Get-Data methods. These properties act like the environment variables of an OS process, but, unlike process environment variables, these properties are scoped to a particular AppDomain. These properties are functionally equivalent to static fields; however, unlike static fields, they are not duplicated per assembly or assembly version, and that makes them a handy replacement for static fields in side-by-side versioning scenarios.

One can create and destroy AppDomains programmatically. Although this is normally done by hosting environments such as ASP.NET, your application can access these same facilities to spawn new AppDomains. The AppDomain.CreateDomain method creates a new AppDomain in the current process and returns a reference to the new domain. The domain will remain in memory until a call to AppDomain.Unload causes it to be removed from memory. After you have created an AppDomain, you can force it to load and execute code using a variety of techniques. The most direct way to do this is to use the AppDomain.ExecuteAssembly method.

`AppDomain.ExecuteAssembly` causes the target AppDomain to load an assembly and execute its main entry point. `ExecuteAssembly` will not load or initialize the specified assembly in the parent AppDomain; rather, `ExecuteAssembly` will first switch AppDomains to the child domain and will load and execute the code while running in the child domain. If the specified assembly calls `AppDomain.CurrentDomain`, it will get the child AppDomain object. If the specified assembly uses any of the same assemblies as the parent program, the child AppDomain will load its own independent copies of the types and modules, including its own set of static fields.

Listing 8.2 shows an example of the `ExecuteAssembly` method in action. `ExecuteAssembly` is a synchronous routine. That means that the caller is blocked until the child program's `Main` method returns control to the runtime. One can use the asynchronous method invocation mechanism discussed in Chapter 6 if nonblocking execution is desired.

Listing 8.2: *Spawning New Applications*

```
using System;

public class MyApp {

  public static int Main(string[] argv) {
// create domain
    AppDomain child = AppDomain.CreateDomain("childapp");
// execute yourapp.exe
    int r = child.ExecuteAssembly("yourapp.exe",null,argv);
// unload domain
    AppDomain.Unload(child);
// return result
    return r;
  }
}
```

It is also possible to inject arbitrary code into an AppDomain. The `AppDomain.DoCallBack` method allows you to specify a method on a type that will be executed in the foreign domain. The specified method should be static and should have a signature that matches the `CrossAppDomainDelegate`'s signature. Additionally, one will have to load the specified method's type, module, and assembly in the foreign AppDomain in order to execute the code. If the specified method needs to share information between the AppDomains, it can use the SetData and GetData methods on the foreign AppDomain. Listing 8.3 shows an example of this technique.

Listing 8.3: *Calling into Foreign AppDomains*

```
using System;
using System.Reflection;

public class MyApp {

// simple routine that stores the number of
// loaded assemblies in an AppDomain property
  public static void CallbackProc()
  {
    AppDomain current = AppDomain.CurrentDomain;
    current.SetData("XX_assmcount",
                    current.GetAssemblies().Length);
  }

// This routine does the work!
  static int GetAssemblyCount(AppDomain target) {
// create the delegate
    CrossAppDomainDelegate cb =
        new CrossAppDomainDelegate(CallbackProc);
// inject and execute the code
    target.DoCallBack(cb);
// extract the property
    return (int)target.GetData("XX_assmcount");
  }

// spawn a domain and inject the code
  static void Main() {
    AppDomain child = AppDomain.CreateDomain("childapp",
                                             null, null);
    Console.WriteLine(GetAssemblyCount(child));
    AppDomain.Unload(child);

  }
}
```

AppDomain Events

The `AppDomain` type supports a handful of events that allow interested parties to be notified of significant conditions in a running program. Table 8.1 lists these events. Four of these events are related to the assembly resolver and loader. Three of these events are related to terminal conditions in the process. `DomainUnload` is called just prior to the unloading of an AppDomain. `ProcessExit` is called just prior to the termination of the CLR in a process. `UnhandledException` acts as the last-chance exception handler to deal with threads that do not handle their own exceptions.

The runtime eventually handles unhandled exceptions. If the thread that caused the exception to be raised does not have a corresponding exception handler on the stack, then the CLR invokes its own global exception handler. This global exception handler is a last chance for the application to recover from the error. It is not good design to rely on the global exception handler, if for no other reason than the offending thread is long gone and very little execution scope may be left to recover.

TABLE 8.1 AppDomain Events

Event Name	EventArg Properties	Description
AssemblyLoad	Assembly LoadedAssembly	Assembly has just been successfully loaded
AssemblyResolve	string Name	Assembly reference cannot be resolved
TypeResolve	string Name	Type reference cannot be resolved
ResourceResolve	string Name	Resource reference cannot be resolved
DomainUnload	None	Domain is about to be unloaded
ProcessExit	None	Process is about to shut down
UnhandledException	bool is Terminating, object ExceptionObject	Exception escaped thread-specific handlers

The CLR's global exception handler first checks a configuration setting to see whether a debugger needs to be attached. One can make this setting on a per-process, per-user, and per-machine basis. Under Windows NT, the CLR picks up the per-process setting from a process-wide environment variable (COMPLUS_DbgJITDebugLaunchSetting). For per-user and per-machine settings, the CLR reads the value from a registry key. As shown in Figure 8.4, the value of DbgJITDebugLaunchSetting is either 0, 1, or 2. If the DbgJITDebugLaunchSetting is 1, then the CLR will not attach a debugger. If the DbgJITDebugLaunchSetting is 2, then the CLR attaches the JIT debugger. The CLR reads the exact debugger that will be used from the registry. By default, the DbgManagedDebugger registry value points to VS7JIT.EXE, which starts by giving the user the choice of debuggers to use. Figure 8.5 shows the initial prompt of VS7JIT.EXE. If the DbgJITDebugLaunchSetting is 0, then the CLR will prompt the user to find out whether a debugger should be attached. Figure 8.6 shows this dialog box. If the user selects Cancel, then processing continues as if DbgJIT-DebugLaunchSetting were 2. If the user selects OK, then processing continues as if DbgJITDebugLaunchSetting were 1.

After the user has indicated the decision about attaching a debugger, the CLR then checks to see whether the application has registered an UnhandledException event handler. The exception handler must be registered from the default domain, which is the initial domain created by the CLR. Registering the event handler from child domains will have no effect.

Listing 8.4 shows the use of an UnhandledException event handler. The CLR will run our handler prior to terminating the process. Had no UnhandledException event handler been registered, then the stack dump from the exception would be printed to the console. Figure 8.7 shows the overall process of unhandled exception processing.

Value	Meaning
0	Prompt user to attach debugger.
1	Don't attach debugger.
2	Always attach debugger.

Figure 8.4: *Configuring JIT Debugging for Unhandled Exceptions*

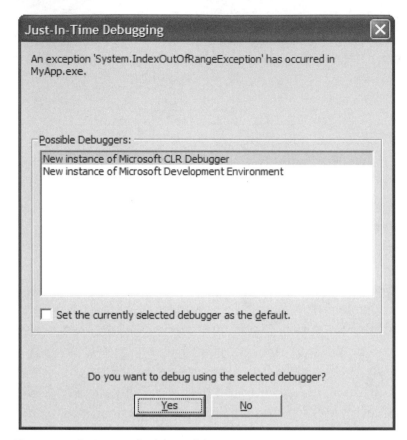

Figure 8.5: *DbgManagedDebugger/VS7JIT.EXE*

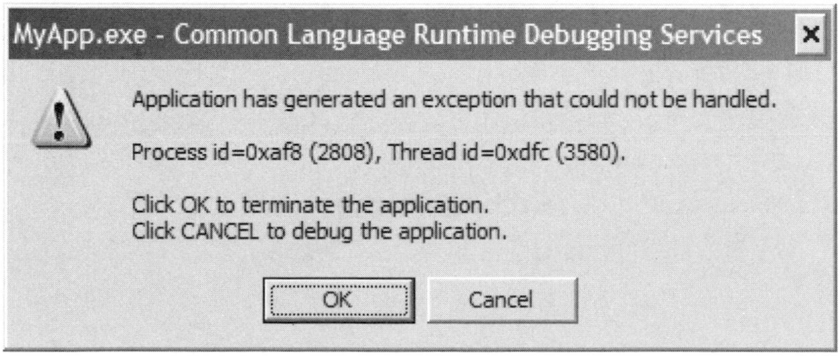

Figure 8.6: *Dialog Box Presented If DbgJitDebugLaunchSetting = 0*

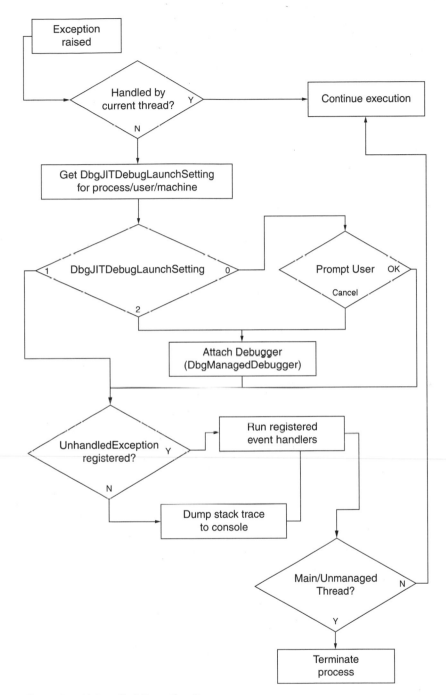

Figure 8.7: *Unhandled Exception Sequence*

Listing 8.4: *Registering an Unhandled Exception Event Handler*

```csharp
using System;

class BadApp {
// this method is our handler
  static void AppHurts(Object sender,
                          UnhandledExceptionEventArgs args) {
    Exception offender = args.ExceptionObject;
    if (args.IsTerminating)
      CleanUpBeforeDying();
  }
  static void Main() {
// this registers the handler for the entire process
    AppDomain.CurrentDomain.UnhandledException +=
            new UnhandledExceptionEventHandler(AppHurts);

    int x = 3 / 0; // causes exception
  }
}
```

There are four AppDomain events related to assembly resolution and loading. One uses one of the events (`AssemblyLoad`) to notify interested parties when a new assembly has successfully been loaded. The assembly resolver uses the other three of these events when it cannot resolve a type (`TypeResolve`), assembly (`AssemblyResolve`), or manifest resource (`ResourceResolve`). For these three events, the CLR gives the event handler the opportunity to produce a `System.Reflection.Assembly` object that can be used to satisfy the request. It is important to note that the resolver calls these three methods only after it has gone through its standard techniques for finding the desired assembly. These events are useful primarily for implementing an application-specific "last-chance" assembly resolver that uses some app-specific policy for converting the requested `AssemblyName` into a codebase that can be passed to `Assembly.LoadFrom`.

Listing 8.5 shows an example that uses the `AssemblyResolve` event to supply a backup policy for finding assemblies. In this example, the CLR munges the simple name of the requested assembly into an absolute pathname into the `windows\system32` directory. After the new pathname is constructed, the event handler uses the `Assembly.LoadFrom` method to pass control to the low-level loader.

Listing 8.5: *Retro-Programming in C#*

```csharp
using System;
using System.Reflection;

class oldhack {
  static oldhack() {
// register the event handler at type-init time
    AppDomain.CurrentDomain.AssemblyResolve +=
                        new ResolveEventHandler(Backstop);
  }
// here is the event handler
  static Assembly Backstop(object sender,
                  ResolveEventArgs args) {
// extract the simple name from the display name
    string displayName = args.Name;
    string simpleName = displayName.Split(',')[0];

// build the retro-file name
    string fullPath = String.Format(
            "C:\\windows\\system32\\{0}.dll", simpleName);

// delegate to LoadFrom
    return Assembly.LoadFrom(fullPath);
  }

  static void Main()  {
    Console.WriteLine(MyCode.GetIt());
  }
}
```

AppDomains and the Assembly Resolver

AppDomains play a critical role in controlling the behavior of the assembly resolver. The AppDomain's properties control most of the assembly resolver's behavior. In fact, one stores the properties used by the assembly resolver in a single data structure of type AppDomainSetup, which is maintained on a per-AppDomain basis. The CLR exposes this data structure via the AppDomain.SetupInformation property.

Each AppDomain can have its own APPBASE and configuration file. By virtue of this fact, each AppDomain can have its own probe path and version policy. One can set the properties used by the assembly resolver either by using the AppDomain's `AppDomainSetup` property or by calling `Set-Data` and `GetData` with the right well-known property name. Listing 8.6 shows an example of three ways to access the same property.

Listing 8.6: *Accessing AppDomain Properties*

```
using System;

static void Main() {
// fetch current domain
  AppDomain here = AppDomain.CurrentDomain;

// fetch the base directory path 3 different ways
  string dir1 = here.BaseDirectory;
  string dir2 = here.SetupInformation.ApplicationBase;
  string dir3 = (string)here.GetData("APPBASE");
}
```

Table 8.2 shows the properties of an AppDomain that are used by the assembly resolver. This table shows both the `AppDomainSetup` member name and the well-known name to use with `AppDomain.SetData` and `GetData`. Chapter 2 has already discussed several of the properties shown in this table. However, there are two sets of properties that have not yet been discussed. One set alters the probe path; the other set controls how code is actually loaded.

Recall that when an assembly is not found in the GAC or via a codebase hint, the assembly resolver looks in the **probe path** of the application. One sets this path using the `probing` element in the configuration file, and it is visible programmatically via the `AppDomain.RelativeSearchPath`. Also recall that this relative search path is in fact relative; it cannot refer to directories that are not children of the APPBASE directory.

Now consider the case in which an application needs to generate code dynamically. If that code is to be stored on disk, then it is an open question as to where it should be stored. If the generated assembly is to be loaded via probing (something that is likely if the code is specific to the generating application), then the application must have write access to a directory underneath APPBASE. However, there are many scenarios in which it is desirable to execute an application from a read-only part of a file system

TABLE 8.2 AppDomain Environment Properties

AppDomainSetup Property	Get/SetData Name	Description
ApplicationBase	APPBASE	Base directory for probing
ApplicationName	APP_NAME	Symbolic name of application
ConfigurationFile	APP_CONFIG_FILE	Name of .config file
DynamicBase	DYNAMIC_BASE	Root of codegen directory
PrivateBinPath	PRIVATE_BINPATH	Semicolon-delimited list of subdirs
PrivateBinPathProbe	BINPATH_PROBE_ONLY	Suppress probing at APPBASE ("*" or null)
ShadowCopyFiles	FORCE_CACHE_INSTALL	Enable/disable shadow copy (Boolean)
ShadowCopyDirectories	SHADOW_COPY_DIRS	Directories to shadow-copy from
CachePath	CACHE_BASE	Directory th shadow-copy to
LoaderOptimization	LOADER_OPTIMIZATION	JIT-compile per-process or per-domain
DiablePublisherPolicy	DISALLOW_APP	Suppress component-supplied version policy

AppDomain Property	Description
BaseDirectory	Alias to AppDomainSetup.ApplicationBase
RelativeSearchPath	Alias to AppDomainSetup.PrivateBinPath
DynamicDirectory	Directory for dynamic assemblies (<DynamicBase>/<ApplicationName>)
FriendlyName	Name of AppDomain used in debugger

(e.g., a secured server or CD-ROM), and this means that one must use some alternative location for dynamically generated code. This is the role of the `AppDomain.DynamicDirectory` property.

Each AppDomain can have at most one **dynamic directory**. The CLR searches the dynamic directory during probing prior to looking in the probe path specified by the `probing` element in the configuration file. One derives the name of the dynamic directory is derived by catenating two other properties of the AppDomain: `APP_NAME` (a.k.a. `AppDomainSetup.ApplicationName`) and `DYNAMIC_BASE` (a.k.a. `AppDomainSetup.DynamicBase`). ASP.NET, which is one of the more notorious generators of code, uses this feature extensively. On the author's machine, the `DYNAMIC_BASE` property for the default virtual directory is currently

```
C:\WINDOWS\Microsoft.NET\Framework\v1.0.3705\
   Temporary ASP.NET Files\root\2135a508
```

The `APP_NAME` for the Web application running in the default virtual directory is currently

```
8d69a834
```

This means that the resultant `DynamicDirectory` for that Web application is

```
C:\WINDOWS\Microsoft.NET\Framework\v1.0.3705\
   Temporary ASP.NET Files\root\2135a508\8d69a834
```

The CLR stores in this directory every DLL that the ASP.NET engine generates for that Web application. Because the CLR searches this directory as part of the probing process, DLLs found in that directory can be successfully loaded, despite the fact that they are not under the `APPBASE` for the AppDomain (which in this case is `C:\inetpub\wwwroot`). As a point of interest, ASP.NET sets the `BINPATH_PROBE_ONLY` property to suppress probing in the `APPBASE` directory itself. This is why you cannot simply put a DLL into your virtual directory and get ASP.NET to find it. Rather, ASP.NET sets the probe path to `bin`, which is where you must store any prebuilt DLLs used by an ASP.NET application.

The second set of AppDomain properties that warrant discussion relates to a feature known as shadow copying. **Shadow copying** addresses a common (and annoying) problem related to server-side development and deployment. Prior to .NET, developing and deploying DLLs that load into server-side container environments (e.g., IIS, COM+) was somewhat problematic because of the way the classic Win32 loader works. When the Win32 loader loads a DLL, it takes a read lock on the file to ensure that no changes are made to the underlying executable image. Unfortunately, this means that after a DLL is loaded into a server-side container, there is often no way to overwrite the DLL with a new version without first shutting down the container to release the file lock. Shadow copying solves this problem. When the CLR loads an assembly using shadow copying, a temporary copy of the underlying files is made in a scratch directory and the temporary copies are loaded in lieu of the "real" assembly files. When shadow copying is enabled for an AppDomain, you must specify two directory paths: `SHADOW_COPY_DIRS` and `CACHE_BASE`. The `SHADOW_COPY_DIRS` path (a.k.a. `AppDomainSetup.ShadowCopyDirectories`) indicates the parent directories of the assemblies that you want to be shadow-copied. `CACHE_BASE` (a.k.a. `AppDomainSetup.CachePath`) indicates the root of the scratch directory where you want the assemblies to be copied to. As shown in Figure 8.8, the actual directory used is a mangled pathname beneath `CACHE_BASE`. To avoid collisions between applications, the pathname takes into account the `APP_NAME`.

Again, ASP.NET is a heavy user of this feature, and that is appropriate given its status as the de facto server-side container for the CLR. On the author's machine, the `SHADOW_COPY_DIRS` property simply points to the Web application's `bin` directory (`C:\inetpub\wwwroot\bin`, to be exact). The `CACHE_BASE` points to the same directory as the `DYNAMIC_BASE` property.

When one uses shadow copying, the assembly's `CodeBase` property will still match the original location of the assembly manifest. This is important for code-access security, which will be discussed in Chapter 9. To discover the actual path used to load the assembly, one can use the `Assembly.Location` property, as is shown in Figure 8.8.

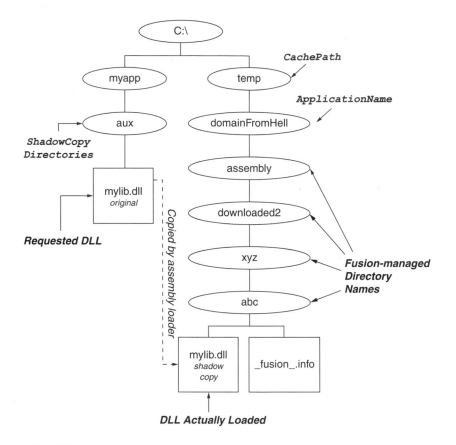

Figure 8.8: *Loading Using Shadow Copy*

AppDomains and Code Management

Each AppDomain has its own private copy of a type's static data. An App-Domain may or may not need a private copy of the type's executable code, depending on any number of factors. To understand why this is the case, we first must look at how the CLR manages code.

AppDomains influence the way the JIT compiler works. In particular, the JIT compiler can generate code on either a per-process or a per-AppDomain basis. When all AppDomains in a process share machine code, the impact on the working set is reduced; however, raw invocation speed suffers slightly whenever a program accesses static fields of a type. In contrast, when the CLR generates machine code for each AppDomain, static field access is faster, but the working set impact is much greater. For that reason, the CLR allows the developer to control how JIT-compiled code is managed.

When the CLR first initializes an AppDomain, the CLR accepts a loader optimization flag (`System.LoaderOptimization`) that controls how code is JIT-compiled for modules loaded by that AppDomain. As shown in Table 8.3, this flag has three possible values.

The `SingleDomain` flag (the default) assumes that the process will contain only one AppDomain and therefore that the machine code should be JIT-compiled separately for each domain. This makes static field access faster, and, because only one AppDomain is expected, there is no impact on the working set because only one copy of the machine code will be required. Of course, if multiple AppDomains are created, each will get its own copy of the machine code, and that is why the `MultiDomain` flag exists.

The `MultiDomain` flag assumes that the process will contain several AppDomains running the same application and therefore that only one copy of the machine code should be generated for the entire process. This makes static field access slightly slower but significantly reduces the memory impact of having multiple AppDomains.

Figure 8.9 shows the effects of the loader optimization setting. This figure shows a simple C# type definition and the JIT-compiled IA-32 machine code that would be generated for each setting. Note that when one uses

TABLE 8.3 LoaderOptimization Enumeration/Attribute

Value	Expected Domains in Process	Each Domain Expected to Run ...	Code for MSCORLIB	Code for Assemblies in GAC	Code for Assemblies not in GAC
SingleDomain	One	N/A	Per-process	Per-domain	Per-domain
MultiDomain	Many	Same Program	Per-process	Per-process	Per-process
MultiDomainHost	Many	Different Programs	Per-process	Per-process	Per-domain

C# Source Code

```
class Bob {
  static int x = 0;
  static int y = 0;
  static void Method() {
    x += 10;
    y -= 10;
  }
}
```

LoaderOptimization.SingleDomain

```
push ebp
move ebp, esp
  add dword ptr ds:[3e5110h],
  0Ah
  add dword ptr ds:[3e5114h],
  0FFFFFFF6h
movc ebp, esp
pop ebp
ret
```

LoaderOptimization.MultiDomain

```
push ebp
move ebp, esp
  move ecx,588h
  call GetCurrentDomainData; load ptr to domain-block from TLS
                          ; into eax
  move edx,eax
  add dword ptr [edx], 0Ah
  add dword ptr [edx+4], 0FFFFFFF6h
move esp, ebp
pop ebp
ret
```

Figure 8.9: *The Effects of Loader Optimization*

SingleDomain, the JIT compiler literally injects the addresses of the static fields (e.g., ds:[3E5110h]) into the native code stream. This is reasonable because each AppDomain will have its own copy of the method code, each with a different field address. When one uses the MultiDomain loader optimization, methods that access static fields have an additional prolog that calls the internal GetCurrentDomainData routine inside the CLR. This routine loads the base address of the AppDomain's static data from hard TLS. This extra step adds roughly 15 IA-32 instructions to every method that uses static fields. However, the code is generic, and only one copy needs to be in memory no matter how many AppDomains are in use.

Clearly, there are costs and benefits to both loader optimization policies. For many applications, there is a compromise that yields the best of both worlds. That compromise is the MultiDomainHost flag.

The MultiDomainHost flag assumes that the process will contain several AppDomains, each of which will run different application code. In this hybrid mode, only assemblies loaded from the global assembly cache share machine code (a la MultiDomain). Assemblies not loaded from the GAC are assumed to be used only by the loading AppDomain and use private machine code for each AppDomain that loads them (a la `SingleDomain`).

It is important to note that no matter which loader optimization one uses, all AppDomains in a process always share the machine code for `mscorlib`. The `LoaderOptimization` has no impact on the way `mscorlib` is treated.

When `mscoree` first initializes the runtime in an OS process, the host application can specify which of the three loader optimization policies to use for the default domain. For managed executables that the OS process loader loads directly (e.g., `CreateProcess` under Windows NT), the main entry point method (`Main` in a C# program) can use the `System.LoaderOptimizationAttribute` attribute to indicate which policy to use. Listing 8.7 shows an example of a managed executable program that sets the policy to `MultiDomain`.

Listing 8.7: *Setting LoaderOptimization for a Managed Executable*

```
using System;

public class MyApp {

// override default of SingleDomain
  [ LoaderOptimization(LoaderOptimization.MultiDomain) ]
  public static void Main() {
// spawn domains and do work here
  }
}
```

As a point of interest, worker processes in ASP.NET use the `MultiDomainHost` option. In an ASP.NET worker process, the code from each (private) Web application directory uses the faster per-AppDomain code; but common code that all Web applications use (e.g., the data access and XML stacks) is JIT-compiled only once per process, reducing the size of the overall working set.

AppDomains and Objects (Revisited)

This chapter began by framing AppDomains as scopes of execution. A large part of that discussion was dedicated to portraying an AppDomain as a "home" for objects and types. In particular, an object is scoped to a particular AppDomain, and object references can refer only to objects in the same AppDomain. However, there is a slight inconsistency in the AppDomain interface that has yet to be discussed. That slight inconsistency is the SetData and GetData mechanism.

Listing 8.3 showed an example of injecting code into a foreign AppDomain. In that example, the code used the SetData and GetData mechanism to pass the number of loaded assemblies from one AppDomain to another. When one reviews the signatures of the following two methods, however, it appears that one can store an object reference into a common property from one AppDomain and fetch (and use!) it from another.

```
static public void   SetData(string name, object value);
static public object GetData(string name);
```

In fact, that is exactly what the code in Listing 8.3 did. One might ask how an object reference from one AppDomain can be smuggled into another domain given that object references are AppDomain-specific. The answer is **marshaling**.

The CLR scopes all objects, values, and object references to a particular AppDomain. When one needs to pass a reference or value to another AppDomain, one must first marshal it. Much of the CLR's marshaling infrastructure is in the System.Runtime.Remoting namespace. In particular, the type System.Runtime.Remoting.RemotingServices has two static methods that are fundamental to marshaling: Marshal and Unmarshal.

RemotingServices.Marshal takes an object reference of type System.Object and returns a serializable System.Runtime.RemotingServices.ObjRef object that can be passed in serialized form to other AppDomains. Upon receiving a serialized ObjRef, one can obtain a valid object reference using the RemotingServices.Unmarshal method. When calling AppDomain.SetData on a foreign AppDomain, the CLR calls RemotingServices.Marshal. Similarly, calling AppDomain.GetData on a foreign AppDomain returns a marshaled reference, which is converted via `RemotingServices.Unmarshal` just prior to the method's completion.

When one marshals an object reference, the concrete type of the object determines how marshaling will actually work. As shown in Table 8.4, there are three possible scenarios.

By default, types are **remote-unaware** and do not support cross-AppDomain marshaling. Attempts to marshal instances of a remote-unaware type will fail.

If a type derives from `System.MarshalByRefObject` either directly or indirectly, then it is **AppDomain-bound**. Instances of AppDomain-bound types will marshal by reference. This means that the CLR will give the receiver of the marshaled object (reference) a proxy that **remotes** (forwards) all member access back to the object's home AppDomain. Technically, the proxy remotes only access to instance members back to the object's home AppDomain. Proxies never remote static methods.

Types that do not derive from `MarshalByRefObject` but do support object serialization (indicated via the `[System.Serializable]` pseudo-custom attribute) are considered **unbound** to any AppDomain. Instances of unbound types will marshal by value. This means the CLR will give the

TABLE 8.4 Agility and Objects

Category	AppDomain-Bound	Unbound	Remote-Unaware
Applicable types	Types derived from MarshalbyRefObject	Types marked [Serializable]	All other types
Cross-domain marshaling behavior	Marshal-by-reference across AppDomain	Marshal-by-value across AppDomain	Cannot leave AppDomain
Inlining behavior	Inlining disabled to support proxy access	Inlining enabled	Inlining enabled
Proxy behavior	Cross-domain proxy Same-domain direct	Never has a proxy	Never has a proxy
Cross-domain identity	Has distributed identity	No distributed identity	No distributed identity

receiver of the marshaled object (reference) a disconnected clone of the original object. Figure 8.10 shows all three behaviors.

Marshaling typically happens implicitly when a call is made to a cross-AppDomain proxy. The CLR marshals the input parameters to the method call into a serialized request message that the CLR sends to the target App-Domain. When the target AppDomain receives the serialized request, it first

```
public class A { }
[ Serializable ]
public class B { }

public class C
  : MarshalByRefObject
{
}
```

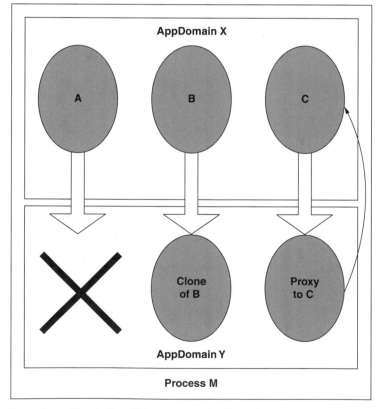

Figure 8.10: *Marshaling Objects across AppDomains*

deserializes the message and pushes the parameters onto a new stack frame. After the CLR dispatches the method to the target object, the CLR then marshals the output parameters and return value into a serialized response message that the CLR sends back to the caller's AppDomain where the CLR unmarshals them and places them back on the caller's stack.

Figure 8.11 shows the cross-AppDomain remoting architecture. It is the job of the `CrossAppDomainChannel` to take the BLT-ed stack frame and serialize it into a buffer that is sent to the **channel** plumbing in the target AppDomain. The channel infrastructure in the target AppDomain deserializes the message and passes it onto the appropriate message sink, which will ultimately form the stack frame and invoke the method on the target object. Each AppDomain maintains an identity table that maps a unique identifier (called a URI) onto the appropriate message sink for the

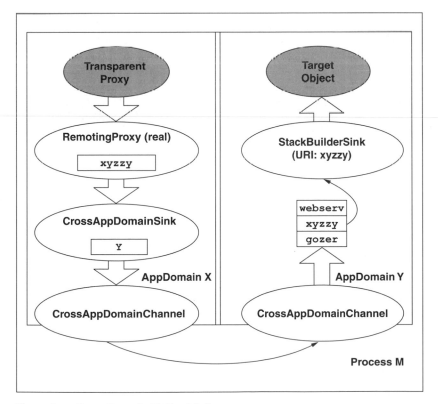

Figure 8.11: *Cross-Domain Method Calls*

marshaled object. This URI appears in the marshaled object reference, and the proxy sets it in every outbound request message.

When one use cross-AppDomain proxies, it is important to note that the CLR must load in both AppDomains the metadata for all types used by the proxy. This means that both AppDomains must have access to the same assemblies. Moreover, when the two AppDomains reside on different machines, both machines must have access to the shared types' metadata.

For example, consider the following program, which creates an object in a child AppDomain:

```
using System;

class App {
  static void Main() {
// create domain
    AppDomain child = AppDomain.CreateDomain("c", null);
// create object in new domain
    Object proxy = child.CreateInstance("someassm",
                                       "Bob").Unwrap();
// downcast and invoke
    Bob b = (Bob)proxy;
    b.f();
  }
}
```

Because the proxy needs the metadata for Bob, both the child domain and the parent domain need access to the someassm assembly that contains Bob's metadata.

Observant readers may have noted the call to Unwrap in the previous example. The AppDomain.CreateInstance method does not return a normal object reference. Rather, it returns an **object handle**. Object handles are similar to marshaled object references. AppDomain.CreateInstance returns an object handle rather than a real object reference to avoid requiring metadata in the caller's AppDomain. For example, consider the following variation on the previous program:

```
using System;

class App {
  static void Main() {
```

```
// create 2 domains
   AppDomain c1 = AppDomain.CreateDomain("c1", null);
   AppDomain c2 = AppDomain.CreateDomain("c2", null);
// create object in first domain
   Object handle = c1.CreateInstance("someassm", "Bob");
// store handle to object in c2's property
   c2.SetData("HeresYourHandle", handle);
// run some program
   c2.ExecuteAssembly("foo.exe", null, null);
  }
}
```

In this program, because the result of AppDomain.CreateInstance is never unwrapped in the parent domain, the CLR never needs to load the "someassm" assembly in the parent. That is because the metadata is not needed until the call to Unwrap, which the CLR will perform only in the second child domain.

Where Are We?

AppDomains scope types and objects at runtime. One uses AppDomains to model independent applications that may or may not share an OS process. AppDomains interact extensively with the assembly resolver and loader and support a fairly rich marshaling layer to support controlled interapplication communication.

9

Security

O NE OF THE ADVANTAGES of virtualized execution environments such as the CLR is that one can develop new security models that transcend the underlying operating system's security model. To that end, the CLR implements its own secure execution model that is independent of the host platform. Beyond the benefits of bringing security to platforms that have never had it (e.g., Windows 98), this also is an opportunity to impose a more component-centric security model that takes into account the nature of dynamically composed systems. This component-centric model is known as **code-access security (CAS)**, which is the focus of this chapter.

Components and Security

Systems that are dynamically composed from components have unique security requirements. Because the individual components of an application often come from disparate organizations, it is likely that different aspects of the application may warrant different degrees of trust. For example, components from trusted organizations may need access to private information or critical resources that one normally would need to protect from malicious code. Unfortunately, the classic principal-based security model of Windows NT and UNIX ignores where the code came from and focuses only on who is running the code. For classic 1980s-era programs built before the widespread advent of components, this model made sense. However, for a component-centric world in which an application's code may come from all corners of the globe, this model is far too coarse-grained to be useful by itself. Hence code-access security.

The CLR implements a code-access security model in which privileges are granted to code, not users. Upon loading a new assembly, the CLR gathers **evidence** about the code's origins. The CLR associates this evidence with the in-memory representation of the assembly, and the security system uses it to determine what privileges to grant to the newly loaded code. The CLR makes this determination by running the evidence through a **security policy**. The security policy accepts evidence as input and produces a **permission set** as output. To avoid undue performance costs, the system typically does not run security policy until an explicit security demand is made.

Permission sets, such as those returned by policy, are simply a collection of permissions. A **permission** is a right to perform some trusted operation. The CLR ships with a set of built-in permission types to protect the integrity of the system and the privacy of the user; however, this system is extensible, and one can transparently integrate user-defined permission types into the model.

The determination of which code is assigned which permissions is called **policy**. The CLR uses a distinct set of mechanisms to enforce security policy. Prior to executing a privileged operation, trusted code is expected to enforce the security policy by explicitly demanding that the callers have sufficient privileges to perform the operation. Note the use of the plural *callers*. By default, enforcement will demand that all callers, direct and indirect, have sufficient permissions to perform the privileged operation. This prevents untrusted components from luring a gullible (yet trusted) piece of code into performing an operation on their behalf, thus assuming the privileges of the gullible piece of code.

Like garbage collection, code-access security requires an omniscient and omnipotent runtime. In particular, that means that calling code that is not written to a strict format can thwart the security system. To that end, the CLI categorizes code into two broad families: verifiable code and non-verifiable code. **Verifiable code** can be mathematically proven to adhere to the type-safe execution model that the CLI encourages. VB.NET and C#

produce verifiable code by default. However, certain language features are not verifiably type-safe, C++'s `reinterpret_cast` being the canonical example. For that reason, code emitted by the C++ compiler is explicitly **nonverifiable**, and the use of this code can compromise the security of the system. To protect the integrity of the system, the ability to load nonverifiable code is itself a permission that one must explicitly grant to code through policy. The default policy that is installed with the CLR grants this permission only to code that is installed on a local file system. Similarly, the ability to call out to classic C-based or COM DLLs (which by definition are nonverifiable) is also a trusted operation that, by default, is granted only to code installed on the local file system.

In general, the performance impact of code-access security is slight. The assembly loader has additional work to do to gather evidence; however, this occurs only at load time and the cost is amortized over the lifetime of the assembly in memory. The key performance concern is policy enforcement, which can cause a potentially expensive traversal of the entire call stack. Fortunately, you can minimize the cost of enforcement by factoring security into your design, typically by avoiding excessive enforcement through explicit programming techniques. These techniques will be discussed later in this chapter.

Evidence

The code-access security story begins with evidence. Evidence acts as testimony as to the origins of a given piece of code. The assembly loader is responsible for gathering evidence at load time based on where the code is loaded from as well as the metadata for the assembly itself.

The CLR ships with seven types of evidence. Four of these evidence types (`Site`, `Url`, `Zone`, and `ApplicationDirectory`) relate to where the code was loaded from. Two of these evidence types (`StrongName` and `Publisher`) relate to who wrote the code. Finally, the seventh evidence type, `Hash`, is based on the overall contents of the assembly and allows the detection of a particular compilation of a piece of code, independent of version number.

Collectively, these seven types of evidence are called **host evidence** because they are implemented by the host environment. It is possible to define your own evidence types, which collectively are called **assembly evidence** because they are explicitly provided by the assembly itself. Defining new assembly evidence types also involves extending the policy mechanism to recognize them, something that is beyond the scope of this book. For the remainder of this chapter, the focus will be on the built-in host evidence types.

Recall that the assembly loader ultimately works in terms of codebase URLs, some of which may be file-based. The CLR uses the codebase URL to determine three of the four location-based evidence types: Url, Zone, and Site. The Url evidence is the easiest to understand because it is simply the codebase URL in its "raw" form. The Site and Zone types are derived from the codebase URL based on its contents.

The Site evidence type is simply the host name portion of an HTTP-based or FTP-based URL. For example, if an assembly's codebase is http://www.acme.com/foo.dll, its Site would be www.acme.com. However, had the codebase been a file-based URL (e.g., file:///C:/usr/bin/foo.dll), then there would be no Site in the evidence for the assembly. One typically uses the Site evidence type to grant blanket trust to code downloaded from a trusted repository.

The Zone evidence type is also derived from the codebase URL. The CLR splits the world into five possible security zones, which are represented by the System.Security.SecurityZone enumeration:

```
namespace System.Security {
  public enum SecurityZone {
    MyComputer,
    Intranet,
    Trusted,
    Internet,
    Untrusted,
    NoZone = 0xFFFFFFFF
  }
}
```

The MyComputer zone applies to all code loaded from a local file system. The CLR categorizes code that originates from remote file systems based on settings made in the Internet Options dialog box of Internet Explorer.

Internet Explorer defines three special-case categories of URLs. The Local Intranet category (represented by `SecurityZone.Intranet`) applies to all code loaded off of a remote file system using UNC-style paths (e.g., `\\server\share\code.dll`). This zone also applies to HTTP-based URLs that use WINS-style names rather than DNS or IP-based host names (e.g., `http://server/vroot/code.dll`). Internet Explorer allows you to further refine what constitutes qualification in this zone, but these are the default tests used.

Internet Explorer also defines two categories for recognized trustworthy and malicious sites. By default, these categories are empty; however, users or system administrators may add any number of pattern-based URLs to these categories. These categories are represented by `SecurityZone.Trusted` and `SecurityZone.Untrusted`, respectively. Codebase URLs that do not fall into any of the three special-case categories just described are placed in the generic `SecurityZone.Internet` zone.

The final location-based evidence type is `ApplicationDirectory`. The host application must explicitly provide this evidence type, which specifies the base directory for the running application. This evidence type is similar to the `Zone` type in that it partitions codebase URLs into categories. One typically uses the `ApplicationDirectory` evidence type in concert with the `Url` evidence type to grant special permissions to DLLs loaded from the `APPBASE` directory of an application.

The CLR provides a programmatic type for each type of evidence. These types all reside in the `System.Security.Policy` namespace and are in the `mscorlib` assembly. For example, the following code creates the `Url`, `Site`, and `Zone` objects for a given codebase URL:

```
using System;
using System.Security;
using System.Security.Policy;

class App {
  static void Main(string[] argv) {
// accept codebase URL as command-line argument
    string codebase = argv[0];
```

```
// create the three evidence objects
   Url url = new Url(codebase);
   Zone zone = Zone.CreateFromUrl(codebase);
   Site site = null;
   try { site = Site.CreateFromUrl(codebase); }
   catch (ArgumentException) { /* ignore */ }

// display the interesting bits
   Console.WriteLine("url: {0}", url.Value);
   Console.WriteLine("zone: {0}", zone.SecurityZone);
   if (site != null)
     Console.WriteLine("site: {0}", site.Name);
  }
}
```

Note that the `Site` type is special-cased. This is because file-based URLs do not have an associated `Site`, and the `Site.CreateFromUrl` method will throw a `System.ArgumentException` if passed a file-based URL.

The discussion so far has looked at the location-based forms of evidence. The CLR also supports two evidence types that pertain to who developed the code independent of where it was loaded from. Of the two, the `StrongName` type is the easier to understand.

Assemblies that have public keys as part of their name will be assigned a `StrongName` evidence type at load time. The three properties of the `StrongName` correspond to three of the four properties of an assembly name. The loader will initialize the `Name`, `Version`, and `PublicKey` properties based on the metadata of the assembly being loaded. As was the case with `Site`, `Url`, and `Zone`, you can construct a `StrongName` evidence object programmatically, as shown here:

```
using System;
using System.Reflection;
using System.Security;
using System.Security.Permissions;
using System.Security.Policy;

class App {
  static StrongName CreateFromAssembly(Assembly assm) {
// get the name and public key
    AssemblyName name = assm.GetName();
    byte[] pk = name.GetPublicKey();
```

```
// construct a new StrongName evidence object
  StrongNamePublicKeyBlob blob =
    new StrongNamePublicKeyBlob(pk);
  return new StrongName(blob, name.Name, name.Version);
}
static void Main(string[] argv) {
// accept assembly name as command-line argument
  string name = argv[0];

// load the assembly and grab the strong-name evidence
  Assembly assm = Assembly.Load(name);
  StrongName sn = CreateFromAssembly(assm);

// display the interesting bits
  Console.WriteLine(sn.Name);
  Console.WriteLine(sn.Version);
  Console.WriteLine(sn.PublicKey);
}
}
```

Be aware that one can create `StrongName` evidence only for assemblies with public keys. Also note that, in this example, one needs a wrapper object of type `System.Security.Permissions.StrongNamePublic-KeyBlob` to wrap the byte array containing the public key. This wrapper object accepts either public keys or public key tokens.

Evidence based on `StrongName` assumes that all parties recognize the public key as identifying a particular development organization. Unrecognized public keys are useless because there is no way to algorithmically discern the identity of the public key's owner. This capability is provided by **X.509 certificates**, which are used by the sixth evidence type, `Publisher`.

The assembly loader adds the `Publisher` evidence type to code that is signed with an X.509 certificate. Unlike public/private key pairs, which can be reliably generated autonomously on the developer's machine, certificates assume the presence of a trusted **certificate authority (CA)**, such as VeriSign, Entrust, or Thawte. These authorities issue certificates only to known entities who can prove their identity via out-of-band techniques. To allow developers to get started with certificates, Microsoft ships two tools that emit untrustworthy certificates for testing purposes: `make-cert.exe` and `cert2spc.exe`. These two tools produce X.509 certificates and **Software Publisher Certificates (SPCs)**, respectively; however, the certificates they produce have no meaningful CA, so they are useful only for kicking the tires, not for shipping code. For more details on acquiring legitimate certificates, visit your favorite CA's Web site.

One can apply certificates to an assembly using the `signcode.exe` tool. The `signcode.exe` tool places the certificate in a well-known location in the DLL and calculates a digital signature to prevent tampering. The assembly loader notices this certificate at load time and attaches a `Publisher` evidence object to the loaded assembly. The following code demonstrates how to construct a `Publisher` evidence object based on a raw X.509 certificate loaded from disk:

```
using System;
using System.Reflection;
using System.Security;
using System.Security.Permissions;
using System.Security.Policy;
using System.Security.Cryptography.X509Certificates;


class App {
  static void Main(string[] argv) {
// accept cert file name as command-line argument
    string name = argv[0];

// load the certificate and grab the Publisher evidence
    X509Certificate cert =
      X509Certificate.CreateFromCertFile(name);
    Publisher pub = new Publisher(cert);

// display the interesting bits
    X509Certificate value = pub.Certificate;
    Console.WriteLine(value.GetName());
    Console.WriteLine(value.GetIssuerName());
    Console.WriteLine(value.GetExpirationDateString());
    Console.WriteLine(value.GetEffectiveDateString());

    Console.WriteLine(value.GetCertHashString());
    Console.WriteLine(value.GetSerialNumberString());
    Console.WriteLine(value.GetPublicKeyString());
    Console.WriteLine(value.GetKeyAlgorithm());
  }
}
```

The first three properties of the certificate (Name, IssuerName, and ExpirationDate) convey most of what developers and system administrators care about. The remaining properties keep crypto-wonks from losing sleep and are beyond the scope of this book.

The final evidence type to be discussed is the Hash evidence type. The Hash evidence is simply a compact identifier that uniquely identifies a particular compilation of a component. The assembly loader adds the Hash evidence to all assemblies to allow security policy to recognize particular builds of an assembly even when the assembly version numbers have not changed.

The CLR defines a built-in type (System.Security.Policy.Evidence) for holding the pieces of evidence that are used by the security policy. The Evidence type is itself a simple collection and implements the System.Collections.ICollection interface. The Evidence type differs from a generic collection in that it keeps two internal collections: one for built-in host evidence objects and one for user-defined assembly evidence objects.

The following code demonstrates how to construct a new Evidence object that contains Url, Zone, and Site evidence:

```
using System;
using System.Security.Policy;

class App {
  static void Main(string[] argv) {
// accept codebase URL as command-line argument
    string codebase = argv[0];

// create and populate an Evidence object
    Evidence evidence = new Evidence();
    evidence.AddHost(new Url(codebase));
    evidence.AddHost(Zone.CreateFromUrl(codebase));
    try { evidence.AddHost(Site.CreateFromUrl(codebase)); }
    catch (ArgumentException) { /* ignore */ }

// display the interesting bits
    foreach (object part in evidence) {
      Console.WriteLine(part);
    }
  }
}
```

When run against the codebase URL `http://www.microsoft.com/foo.dll`, this program emits the following:

```
<System.Security.Policy.Url version="1">
   <Url>http://www.microsoft.com/foo.dll</Url>
</System.Security.Policy.Url>

<System.Security.Policy.Zone version="1">
   <Zone>Internet</Zone>
</System.Security.Policy.Zone>

<System.Security.Policy.Site version="1">
   <Name>www.microsoft.com</Name>
</System.Security.Policy.Site>
```

Note that each evidence object emits an XML-based representation of itself. The use of this syntax will be explained later in this chapter.

Constructing `Evidence` objects programmatically is occasionally useful; however, the assembly loader is the primary user of this facility. The assembly loader makes an assembly's evidence available to security policy and to programmers via the `System.Reflection.Assembly.Evidence` property. The following code fragment illustrates how to access the evidence for an arbitrary object's assembly:

```
using System.Reflection;
using System.Security.Policy;
public sealed class Util {
  public static Zone WhichZone(object obj) {
    Evidence ev = obj.GetType().Module.Assembly.Evidence;
    IEnumerator i = ev.GetHostEnumerator();
    while (i.MoveNext()) {
      Zone zone = i.Current as Zone;
      if (zone != null) return zone;
    }
    return null; // no zone
  }
}
```

As we will see throughout this chapter, evidence is used primarily by security policy and is rarely accessed explicitly by programmers.

Policy

Evidence by itself is relatively useless. Rather, the *raison d'être* for evidence is to act as input to a security policy. The CLR uses security policy to determine what permissions to assign to a given assembly based on the assembly's evidence. System administrators and users can configure CLR security policy. The CLR security policy is also extensible, allowing one to plug in custom policy algorithms to the existing infrastructure.

One can specify security policy at up to four levels, which are represented by the `System.Security.PolicyLevelType` enumeration:

```
namespace System.Security {
  public enum PolicyLevelType {
    User,
    Machine,
    Enterprise,
    AppDomain
  }
}
```

The `User` policy level is specific to an individual user, whereas the `Machine` policy level applies to all users on a specific host machine. The `Enterprise` policy level applies to a family of machines that are part of an Active Directory installation. Finally, the `AppDomain` policy level is specific to a particular application running inside an operating system process.

Of the four policy levels, all but the `AppDomain` level are loaded automatically from XML-based configuration files that one can edit as raw XML or by using the `caspol.exe` tool or `mscorcfg.msc` MMC snap-in. The `Machine` and `Enterprise` levels are read from the files `security.config` and `enterprisesec.config`, respectively. These files reside in the `CONFIG` subdirectory of the version-specific installation directory for the CLR. The `User` policy level is read from the `Application Data\Microsoft\CLR Security Config\v1.0.nnnn\security.config` file found under the user-specific profile directory. One must specify the `AppDomain` policy programmatically by calling the `System.AppDomain.SetAppDomainPolicy` method.

The combination of the four policy levels is called the **policy hierarchy** of the system. Each level in the hierarchy grants a set of permissions based on the presented evidence. One derives the resultant set of permissions that will be granted by taking the intersection (not the union) of the permissions granted by each of the four policy levels, as shown in Figure 9.1.

The policy hierarchy uses the intersection rather than the union because the security model of the CLR is based on granting, not denying, privilege. For readers familiar with Windows NT security, this model is similar to the notion of Win32 privileges or COM+ roles—that is, the only way to deny access is to neglect to grant the appropriate permissions. Unlike Win32 DACLs, this model gives one no way to explicitly deny access to a protected operation or resource. To that end, the default Enterprise, User, and AppDomain policy levels all grant full-trust permission regardless of the presented evidence. However, the default Machine policy level grants full-trust permissions only to code loaded from the MyComputer security zone or code that carries the Microsoft or ECMA public keys. The Machine policy grants considerably fewer permissions to non-Microsoft or non-ECMA code loaded from other security zones.

Like evidence, the policy hierarchy is used implicitly by the security infrastructure but is also available for programmatic access. The CLR

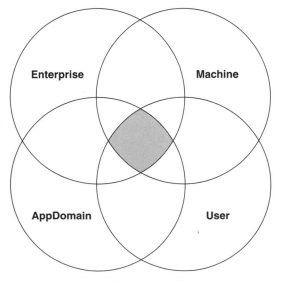

Figure 9.1: *Security Hierarchy and Levels*

exposes each level in the hierarchy via the `System.Security.Policy.PolicyLevel` type, and one exposes the collection of policy levels via the `System.Security.SecurityManager.PolicyHierarchy` method. The following code uses this method to enumerate the policy levels used by the current program and to display the file names used to load the policies:

```
using System;
using System.Collections;
using System.Security;
using System.Security.Policy;

class App {
  static void Main() {
    IEnumerator i = SecurityManager.PolicyHierarchy();
    while (i.MoveNext()) {
      PolicyLevel level = (PolicyLevel)i.Current;
      Console.WriteLine("{0,10}: {1}",
              level.Label,
              level.StoreLocation);
    }
  }
}
```

On the author's machine, this program displays the following:

```
Enterprise:
C:\WINNT\Microsoft.NET\Framework\v1.0.3705\config\
enterprisesec.config
Machine:
C:\WINNT\Microsoft.NET\Framework\v1.0.3705\config\
security.config
User: C:\Documents and Settings\dbox\Application Data\
                Microsoft\CLR Security Config\
                v1.0.3705\security.config
```

Note that, by default, there is no `AppDomain`-specific policy.

Each policy level consists of three components. A policy level contains a list of named **permission sets** (visible via the `PolicyLevel.NamedPermissionSets` property), each of which grants zero or more privileges. A policy level also contains a **code group** hierarchy (visible via the `PolicyLevel.RootCodeGroup` property) that one uses to determine which permission sets to apply given a particular body of evidence. Finally, a policy level contains a list of **full-trust assemblies** (visible via the `Policy-Level.FullTrustAssemblies` property) that explicitly lists the assemblies that contain types needed to enforce policy. For example, if a custom permission type is defined, its assembly must appear in this list in order for the security policy to recognize it. Because extending security policy is outside the scope of this book, we will focus on the code groups and named permission sets.

Code groups are used to grant permissions based on evidence. To that end, a code group has two primary properties: a membership condition and the name of a permission set. This is illustrated in Figure 9.2. The **membership condition** uses the presented evidence to determine whether or not the assembly in question is a member of this code group. If the membership condition acknowledges that the evidence satisfies the condition, then the policy will grant the rights contained in the named permission set.

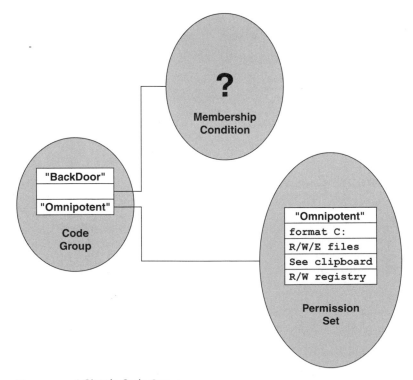

Figure 9.2: *A Simple Code Group*

Membership conditions are strongly typed and are represented by CLR types that implement the System.Security.Policy.IMembership-Condition interface. This interface has one interesting method, Check:

```
namespace System.Security.Policy {
  public interface IMembershipCondition {
    bool Check(Evidence evidence);
// remaining methods elided for clarity
  }
}
```

Given an arbitrary policy level, the following method determines whether or not a given assembly is a member of the root code group:

```
static bool IsInRootGroup(Assembly assm,
                          PolicyLevel level) {
// grab evidence for assembly
  Evidence evidence = assm.Evidence;
// grab condition for root code group
  CodeGroup group = level.RootCodeGroup;
  IMembershipCondition cond = group.MembershipCondition;
// check for membership
  return cond.Check(evidence);
}
```

Because the root code group for all built-in policies matches all assemblies, this method would always return true.

The system ships with eight built-in membership condition types. The Check method for the AllMembershipCondition always returns true independent of the evidence (and is used on the root code group in each policy level). The Check method for the ApplicationDirectoryMembershipCondition checks to see whether the assembly in question is loaded from the application directory. This condition uses the Url evidence to determine the assembly's code base. This condition also relies on an ApplicationDirectory evidence object being present in the host-provided evidence. The host application, such as ASP.NET, must establish this evidence. The remaining six membership condition types (UrlMembershipCondition, ZoneMembershipCondition, etc.) correspond directly to the six host evidence types (e.g., Url, Zone, etc.) and allow membership to be determined directly by a particular piece of evidence.

To allow more than one permission set to be applied to a particular assembly, code groups are hierarchical and may contain child code groups. These child groups are visible via the `CodeGroup.Children` property. Most code groups that appear in a security policy are instances of type `System.Security.Policy.UnionCodeGroup`. If its membership condition is satisfied, the `UnionCodeGroup` enumerates all child code groups and takes the union of the permission sets of each child whose membership condition is also satisfied. Because a child code group may itself have children, this process may result in the evaluation of a large number of permission sets. However, if the membership condition for a given code group is not satisfied, none of its children will be considered. For example, consider the code group hierarchy shown in Figure 9.3. If the membership

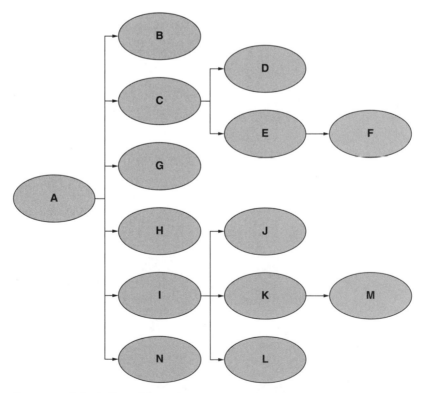

Figure 9.3: *A Code Group Hierarchy*

condition for group A is not satisfied, then no other code groups will be considered (and the resultant permission set would be empty). If the membership condition for group A is satisfied, the groups B, C, G, H, I, and N will be considered. If group C's membership condition is satisfied, then groups D and E will be considered.

One can set two properties on a code group that alter its interpretation. The `PolicyStatementAttribute.Exclusive` property indicates that no other sibling code groups may be combined with this code group. Had this attribute been set on group B in the previous example, then if B's membership condition were satisfied, groups C, G, H, I, and N could not be considered. It is considered a policy error if the presented evidence matches more than one exclusive group in a given level of the hierarchy. The second property that can alter the interpretation of a code group is the `Policy-StatementAttribute.LevelFinal`. This property informs the security manager to disregard any lower policy levels. For example, had this attribute been set on a matching code group in the `SecurityLevel.Machine` policy level, the `SecurityLevel.User` and `Security-Level.AppDomain` policy levels would have been ignored. This prevents less-privileged users and administrators from disabling critical components by neglecting to grant them the needed permissions.

One uses the `CodeGroup.ResolveMatchingCodeGroups` method to expose the ability to resolve a body of evidence into a collection of matching code groups. This method simply runs the membership condition on the current code group and all children to determine which code groups match. As a convenience, the `PolicyLevel` type has a `ResolveMatching-CodeGroups` method that simply forwards the call to the root code group of the policy level after ensuring that the policy level has in fact been loaded:

```
namespace System.Security.Policy {
 public class Policylevel {
  CodeGroup ResolveMatchingCodeGroups(Evidence ev) {
   this.CheckLoaded(true); //
   if (ev == null)
    throw new ArgumentException("evidence");
   return this.RootCodeGroup.ResolveMatchingCodeGroups(ev);
  }
```

```
// remaining members elided for clarity
  }
}
```

To find the matching code groups across all applicable policy levels, one can instead call the `SecurityManager.ResolvePolicyGroups` static method. This method simply calls `PolicyLevel.ResolveMatching-CodeGroups` on each policy level in the policy hierarchy (e.g., machine, enterprise, etc). The following C# program uses `SecurityManager.ResolvePolicyGroups` to enumerate all groups that a given assembly is a member of:

```csharp
using System;
using System.Collections;
using System.Reflection;
using System.Security;
using System.Security.Policy;

class App {
  static void DumpGroup(CodeGroup group, string prefix) {
    Console.WriteLine("{0}{1}['{2}']:{3}",
                      prefix, group.GetType().Name,
              group.Name, group.PermissionSetName);
    foreach (CodeGroup child in group.Children)
      DumpGroup(child, prefix + "  ");
  }

  static void Main(string[] argv) {
    string assmname = argv[0];
    Evidence ev = Assembly.Load(assmname).Evidence;
    IEnumerator i = SecurityManager.ResolvePolicyGroups(ev);
    while (i.MoveNext())
      DumpGroup((CodeGroup)i.Current, "  ");
  }
}
```

The `SecurityManager.ResolvePolicyGroups` method is somewhat limited because the permission set names in the resultant code groups make sense only when one knows which policy level the code group came from. Fortunately, there are also several higher-layer methods that will resolve the permission sets. These methods will be described later in this section.

The default policy files that ship with the CLR include a built-in set of code groups.[1] Figure 9.4 shows these groups. Note that there is a distinct code group for each of the five SecurityZone values, as well as a distinguished group for assemblies with the Microsoft and ECMA public keys. One typically adds new user-defined code groups as children to the All_Code group, unless one will be using the security zone as part of the membership condition.

For example, running the example program just described on the mscorlib assembly would produce the following:

```
UnionCodeGroup['All_Code']:FullTrust
UnionCodeGroup['All_Code']:Nothing
   UnionCodeGroup['ECMA_Strong_Name']:FullTrust
   UnionCodeGroup['My_Computer_Zone']:FullTrust
UnionCodeGroup['All_Code']:FullTrust
```

Note that in the first and third policy levels (shown on lines 1 and 5), the only matching code group is All_Code and that it grants the FullTrust permission set to the code. That is because the first and third policy levels are the enterprise and user levels, both of which default to simply granting FullTrust to every assembly no matter what the evidence. The second policy level (shown on lines 2–4) corresponds to the machine policy level. In that policy level, the All_Code group grants no permissions; however, the mscorlib also matched the membership conditions for the My_Computer_Zone and ECMA_Strong_Name code groups, both of which grant FullTrust permissions to the code.

The previous discussion mentioned several built-in named permission sets. The default policy files that ship with the CLR each contain seven predefined named permission sets. Table 9.1 shows these sets. The Nothing set grants no permissions, and the root code group uses it in the Machine

---

1 Microsoft periodically updates the default security policy to address security issues discovered after the initial release of the CLR. The exact policy shown here corresponds to the RTM version of the CLR. Subsequent updates and service packs are likely to alter these defaults.

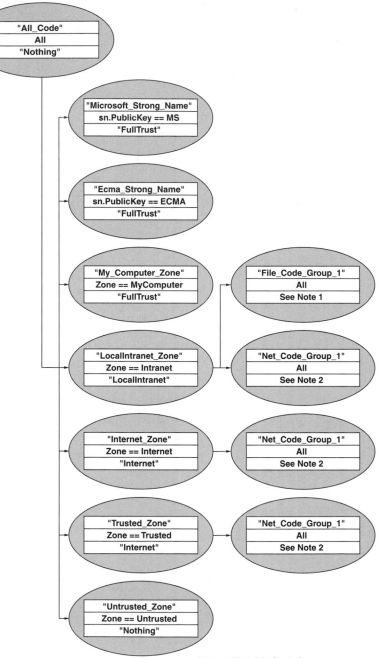

Note1: The FileCodeGroup grants read-only FileIOPermission to the directory containing the assembly.

Note2: The NetCodeGroup grants WebPermission to the assembly's site of origin.

Figure 9.4: *Built-in Code Groups*

TABLE 9.1 Built-in Permission Sets

Nothing	The empty permission set (grants nothing)
FullTrust	Implicitly grants unrestricted permissions for all permission types
Everything	Explicitly grants unrestricted permissions for all built-in permission types
SkipVerification	SecurityPermission: SkipVerification
Execution	SecurityPermission: Execution
Internet	SecurityPermission: Execution FileDialogPermission: Open Isolated Storage Permission: DomainIsolationByUser (quota=10240) UIPermission: OwnClipboard | SafeTopLevelWindows PrintingPermission: SafePrinting
LocalIntranet	SecurityPermission: Execution | Assert | RemotingConfiguration FileDialogPermission: Unrestricted Isolated Storage Permission: AssemblyIsolationByUser (no quota) UIPermission: Unrestricted PrintingPermission: DefaultPrinting EnvironmentPermission: Read-only (USERNAME/TMP/TEMP) ReflectionPermission: ReflectionEmit DNSPermission: Yes EventLog: Instrument

policy level. This allows the root code group to safely match any assembly without granting any permissions. The `FullTrust` and `Everything` permission sets are both used only for highly trusted components. The `Everything` group explicitly specifies all known permissions, whereas the `FullTrust` permission set simply acts as a signal to implicitly grant all possible permissions, including those that cannot be known *a priori*. As shown earlier in Figure 9.4, the `FullTrust` permission set is granted to all code loaded from a local file system.

The `Internet` and `LocalIntranet` provide only a limited subset of permissions and are used for code loaded from remote file systems or the Internet. In both cases, only verifiable code may be run, and no access to unmanaged code is allowed. Moreover, access to the local file system is restricted based on file dialog boxes that require the end user to explicitly select the file name. The Internet code group is more restrictive because it does not allow code to be generated, nor does it allow the clipboard to be read or DNS names to be resolved.

In addition to the predefined permission sets, the CLR provides two special types of code groups that dynamically produce a permission set based on the presented evidence. These two code group types are NetCodeGroup and FileCodeGroup. The NetCodeGroup produces a permission set that contains a dynamically calculated WebPermission that grants connect access to the site from which the code was downloaded. The FileCode-Group produces a permission set that contains a dynamically calculated FileIOPermission that grants read-only file access to the directory from which the code was loaded. As shown in Figure 9.4, the default machine policy uses the NetCodeGroup to grant Web access to code from the Internet, Intranet, and Trusted security zones, and one uses the FileCode-Group to grant file access to code from the Intranet security zone.

It is important to remember that the result of running a body of evidence through a security policy is a permission set. The CLR exposes this functionality via the Resolve method on the CodeGroup and Policy-Level types. This method accepts a body of evidence and returns the corresponding permission set based on which code groups are matched. The Resolve methods return not only a System.Security.Policy.Policy-Statement object, which indicates the resultant permission set, but also the PolicyStatementAttribute, which indicates whether the policy statement is exclusive and/or level final. This is illustrated in the following C# program:

```
using System;
using System.Collections;
using System.Security;
using System.Security.Policy;

class App {
  static void Main(string[] argv) {
    string codebase = argv[0];
// construct evidence
    Evidence evidence = new Evidence();
```

```
      evidence.AddHost(new Url(codebase));
      evidence.AddHost(Zone.CreateFromUrl(codebase));
      try { evidence.AddHost(Site.CreateFromUrl(codebase)); }
      catch (ArgumentException) { /* ignore */ }

// walk each policy level resolving evidence along the way
      IEnumerator i = SecurityManager.PolicyHierarchy();
      while (i.MoveNext()) {
        PolicyLevel level = (PolicyLevel)i.Current;
        PolicyStatement statement = level.Resolve(evidence);
        Console.WriteLine("Level: {0} (attributes = {1})",
                level.Label, statement.Attributes);
        Console.WriteLine(statement.PermissionSet);
      }
    }
  }
```

The `Resolve` method first finds the matching code groups and then takes the union of the permissions granted by each code group's permission set. To find the permissions used in the aggregate, one would need to take the intersection of each permission set, taking the `PermissionStatementAttribute.LevelFinal` into account. Fortunately, the CLR provides this functionality via the higher-level `SecurityManager.ResolvePolicy` static method. The example just shown could be rewritten to use `ResolvePolicy` as follows:

```
using System;
using System.Security;
using System.Security.Policy;

class App {
  static void Main(string[] argv) {
    string codebase = argv[0];
// construct evidence
    Evidence ev = new Evidence();
    evidence.AddHost(new Url(codebase));
    evidence.AddHost(Zone.CreateFromUrl(codebase));
    try { evidence.AddHost(Site.CreateFromUrl(codebase)); }
    catch (ArgumentException) { /* ignore */ }

// get the aggregate permissions from all levels
    PermissionSet ps = SecurityManager.ResolvePolicy(ev);
    Console.WriteLine(ps);
  }
}
```

Note how the `ResolvePolicy` method returns only a permission set, not a policy statement as did `PolicyLevel.Resolve`. This is because one needs the additional `Attribute` property on the policy statement only when combining permissions from multiple policy levels. Because `SecurityManager.ResolvePolicy` has already taken into account every applicable policy level, there is no need to return anything beyond the resultant permission set.

In addition to properly intersecting each level's permission set, the `SecurityManager.ResolvePolicy` method adds identity permissions based on the presented evidence. Each type of host evidence (e.g., `Url`, `Zone`, `StrongName`) has a corresponding permission type. `SecurityManager.ResolvePolicy` walks the list of host evidence and gathers an extra permission from each piece of evidence that supports the `IIdentityPermissionFactory` interface. All of the built-in evidence types support this interface. Identity permission is always added by policy and can be used to demand that a caller or callers belong to a particular security zone or originate from a particular site.

Permissions

Permission sets are ultimately just a collection of zero or more individual permissions. The CLR exposes permission sets programmatically via `System.Security.PermissionSet`. Because `PermissionSet` implements the `System.Collections.ICollection` interface, one can treat the permission set as a standard collection. The elements of that collection are guaranteed to implement at least the `System.Security.IPermission` interface.

The `IPermission` interface is the primary interface for dealing with permissions. The `IPermission` interface models the permission settings for one category of operations. The CLR ships with a dozen or so built-in categories, each of which supports the `IPermission` interface. For a particular category of permission, there may be multiple protected operations in that category. The `IPermission` interface provides the following methods to support set operations on permission objects:

```
namespace System.Security {
  public interface IPermission {
    IPermission Union(IPermission rhs);
    IPermission Intersect(IPermission rhs);
    bool        IsSubsetOf(IPermission rhs);
    IPermission Copy();
    void        Demand();
  }
}
```

The first three methods allow one to treat permission objects of the same type as sets. This is illustrated in Figure 9.5.

Programming against IPermission is fairly intuitive. For example, consider the following C# method:

```
static void DoIt() {
  SecurityPermissionFlag f1
        = SecurityPermissionFlag.Execution;
  SecurityPermissionFlag f2
        = SecurityPermissionFlag.SkipVerification;
  IPermission p1 = new SecurityPermission(f1);
  IPermission p2 = new SecurityPermission(f2);
```

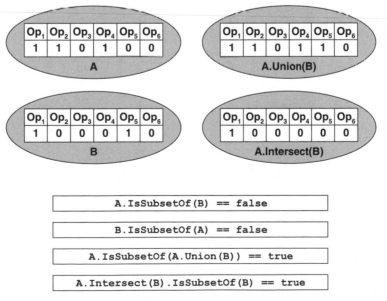

Figure 9.5: *Combining Permissions*

```
    // add p1's and p2's permissions together
      IPermission p3 = p1.Union(p2);

    // take permissions that are in  p1 and p3
      IPermission p4 = p3.Intersect(p1);

      Debug.Assert(p4.IsSubsetOf(p3));
      Debug.Assert(p1.IsSubsetOf(p3));
    }
```

In this example, the `SecurityPermission` type supports a bitmask that indicates which operations are allowed. The call to the `Union` method returns a new `SecurityPermission` object that has both the `Execution` and the `SkipVerification` bits set (as if a bitwise OR had been performed). When the `Intersect` method is called in this example, the result is a new `SecurityPermission` object that has only the `Execution` bit set (as if a bitwise AND had been performed). The `IsSubsetOf` method simply tests whether every operation supported by p1 is also supported by p3, an answer that one can calculate by comparing p1's bitmask to the result of intersecting p1 and p3.

The `IPermission` methods assume that the provided permission is of the same type. For example, it would be an error to pass a `FileIOPermission` object to the `Intersect` method of a `WebPermission` object. Also, whereas most permission types support a bitmask to indicate which operations are enabled, many permission types also carry additional information, such as a file path or host name. The CLR factors this type-specific information into the `IPermission` method implementations. For example, consider the following example, which uses the `FileIOPermission` type:

```
    static void DoIt() {
    FileIOPermissionAccess all
              = FileIOPermissionAccess.AllAccess;
    IPermission p1 = new FileIOPermission(all,@"C:\etc");
    IPermission p2 = new FileIOPermission(all,@"C:\etc\bin");

    IPermission p3 = p1.Union(p2);       // C:\etc allowed
    IPermission p4 = p1.Intersect(p2); // C:\etc\bin allowed

    Debug.Assert(p2.IsSubsetOf(p1));
    Debug.Assert(p1.IsSubsetOf(p2) == false);
    }
```

The exact semantics of Union, Intersect, and IsSubsetOf are type-specific. Consult the documentation for details for a particular permission type.

Permission types typically support a constructor that accepts a System. Security.Permissions.PermissionState enumeration to allow one to set the new permission object to a well-known state. The Permission-State enumeration is simple:

```
namespace System.Security.Permissions {
  public enum PermissionState {
    None,
    Unrestricted
  }
}
```

Permission objects that are initialized with PermissionState.None represent the most restrictive set of permissions for that type. Permission objects that are initialized with PermissionState.Unrestricted represent the least restrictive set of permissions for that type. Moreover, to allow permission objects to be checked for this least-restrictive state generically, permission types that support unrestricted access must also support the System.Security.Permissions.IUnrestrictedPermission interface:

```
namespace System.Security.Permissions {
  public interface IUnrestrictedPermission {
    bool IsUnrestricted();
  }
}
```

Permission types that support this interface indicate that they support the notion of unrestricted permissions, which are an implicit granting of all possible permissions for that permission type. When a permission object grants unrestricted permissions, all possible operations in that permission object's type are implicitly allowed.

PermissionState and IUnrestrictedPermission allow one to treat permission objects uniformly despite the details of how unrestricted access may be specified, allowing the following generic code to always hold true for all permission types T:

```
IUnrestrictedPermission perm
        = new T(PermissionState.Unrestricted);
Debug.Assert(perm.IsUnrestricted());
```

Be aware, however, that a permission object may be unrestricted even if it is not explicitly initialized that way. For example, passing the `SecurityPermissionFlag.AllAccess` parameter to the constructor for `SecurityPermission` is equivalent to passing `PermissionState.Unrestricted`. Additionally, performing union operations on permission objects may produce an unrestricted permission object as the result.

Although it is possible to define your own permission types by implementing the `IPermission` interface (and a few of its close cousins that are used to encode a permission object into XML), the CLR provides a family of built-in permission types that are used to protect various system-level resources. Table 9.2 lists the most commonly used permission types. Note that all but the identity permissions support `IUnrestrictedPermission`. Also, many of the permission types allow one to set permissions based on pattern matching. This is true for permissions that protect location-based resources such as the file system and network resources.

It is often useful to combine permissions of different types together. To that end, the CLR provides the `PermissionSet` type, which is used to aggregate permission objects of arbitrary type together. A `PermissionSet` object holds at most one permission object per permission type. Adding a permission object that is an instance of a type already held by the permission set results in the presented permission object being unioned with the permission object already held. For example, consider the following C# method:

```
static void DoIt() {
  FileIOPermissionAccess all
          = FileIOPermissionAccess.AllAccess;
  SecurityPermissionFlag f1
          = SecurityPermissionFlag.Execution;
  SecurityPermissionFlag f2
           = SecurityPermissionFlag.SkipVerification;

  PermissionSet ps
      = new PermissionSet(PermissionState.None);
```

TABLE 9.2 Built-in Permission Types

Namespace	Name	Description	Unrestricted	Pattern-based
System. Security. Permissions	Security	Basic execution environment capabilities	Yes	No
	Reflection	Read and write CLR metadata	Yes	No
	Environment	Access to OS environmental variables	Yes	Yes
	UrlIdentity	Asserts codebase URL in assembly evidence	No	Yes
	SiteIdentity	Asserts Site in assembly evidence	No	Yes
	ZoneIdentity	Asserts SecurityZone in assembly evidence	No	No
	StrongNameIdentity	Asserts public key in assembly evidence	No	No
	PublisherIdentity	Asserts certificate in assembly evidence	No	No
	Registry	Access to Windows registry	Yes	Yes
	FileIO	Access to directories and files	Yes	Yes
	IsolatedStorage	Access to per-user storage system	Yes	No
	FileDialog	Display file dialogs to user	Yes	No
	UI	Access to window hierarchy and clipboard	Yes	No

(Continued)

TABLE 9.2 (Continued)

Namespace	Name	Description	Unrestricted	Pattern-based
System. Drawing	Printing	Access to attached and default printer	Yes	No
System.NET	Dns	DNS address translation	Yes	No
	Socket	Low-level socket usage (accept/connect)	Yes	Yes
	Web	High-level Web access (accept/connect)	Yes	Yes
System. Messaging	MessageQueue	Access to MSMQ features	Yes	Yes
System.Data. Common	DBData	Access to database provider features	Yes	No

```
    ps.AddPermission(new SecurityPermission(f1));
    ps.AddPermission(new SecurityPermission(f2));
    ps.AddPermission(new FileIOPermission(all, @"C:\etc"));
}
```

At the end of this method, the newly created permission set will contain two permission objects: one of type `FileIOPermission` and one of type `SecurityPermission` that allows both `Execution` and `SkipVerification`.

The `PermissionSet` type supports the three set-oriented operations of `IPermission` (i.e., `Union`, `Intersect`, and `IsSubsetOf`). The `PermissionSet` implementations of these methods simply traverse the individual permission objects and perform the set operations on the matching permission object in the second permission set. This is illustrated in Figure 9.6.

Performing set operations on `PermissionSet` objects is trivial. For example, consider the following C# code:

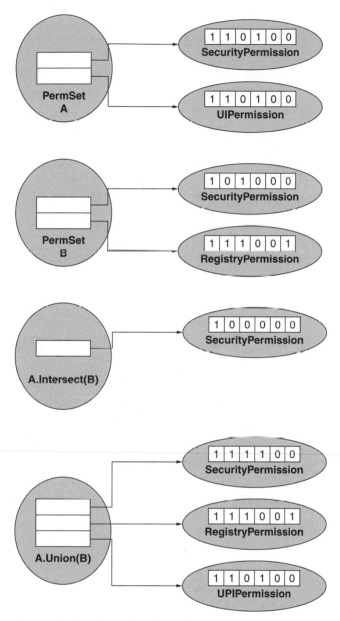

Figure 9.6: *Combining Permission Sets*

```
static void DoIt() {
  FileIOPermissionAccess all
              = FileIOPermissionAccess.AllAccess;
  SecurityPermissionFlag f1
              = SecurityPermissionFlag.Execution;
  SecurityPermissionFlag f2
              = SecurityPermissionFlag.SkipVerification;

  PermissionSet ps1 = new PermissionSet(null);
  PermissionSet ps2 = new PermissionSet(null);
  PermissionSet ps3 = new PermissionSet(null);
  ps1.AddPermission(new SecurityPermission(f1));
  ps2.AddPermission(new SecurityPermission(f2));
  ps2.AddPermission(new FileIOPermission(all, @"C:\etc"));
  ps3 = ps1.Union(ps2);
}
```

This code produces the same permission set that the previous example did, albeit in a somewhat less direct manner.

Permission sets may also grant unrestricted permissions. One accomplishes this by passing `PermissionState.Unrestricted` to the permission set's constructor. When a permission set grants unrestricted permissions, all possible operations in all possible permission types are implicitly supported, provided that the permission type supports `IUnrestrictedPermission`. A permission set that grants unrestricted permissions does not implicitly grant any rights for permission types that do not support `IUnrestrictedPermission` (e.g., the identity permissions). However, it is legal to call `AddPermission` on an unrestricted permission set to explicitly grant those specific permissions.

Enforcement

As important as security policy is, it spends most of its life lying dormant until it is time for enforcement. The CLR itself sometimes implicitly enforces security policy; however, security policy is most often enforced explicitly by trusted libraries that wish to protect a secure resource. One enforces security policy by demanding that all callers have been granted a particular permission or set of permissions. To that end, both the

IPermission interface and the PermissionSet class support a Demand method to allow explicit policy enforcement.

The Demand method triggers a stack walk in which the permissions of every method are inspected. The CLR calculates the permissions of each method by running the evidence from the method's assembly through the security policy. If at least one method on the stack does not have the permission being demanded, then the Demand method will throw a System.Security.SecurityException. If, however, all methods on the stack do have the permission being demanded, then the Demand method will indicate this by not throwing the exception.

To call the Demand method, one first needs either a permission or a permission set object that specifies which permissions are being demanded. Consider the following C# method:

```
using System.Net;

public sealed class Utils {
  public static IPAddress LookupHost(string host) {
    return Dns.GetHostByName(host).AddressList[0];
  }
}
```

The Dns.GetHostByName method calls Demand internally to require that all callers have the System.Net.DnsPermission:

```
using System.Security.Permissions;
namespace System.Net {
  public sealed class Dns {
    public static IPHostEntry GetHostByName(string host) {
// enforce security policy
      DnsPermission perm
         = new DnsPermission(PermissionState.Unrestricted);
      perm.Demand();
// if we get here, DNS lookups are allowed by policy so
// do the actual work (elided here for clarity)
  }
}
```

Note that the GetHostByName method worries about security only at the beginning of the method. If policy prohibits DNS lookups, then the

`Demand` method will prevent the remainder of the method from executing. Of course, if our `Utils.LookupHost` method wants to deal with this, the exception would need to be handled explicitly:

```
using System.Net;
using System.Security;

public sealed class Utils {
  public static IPAddress LookupHost(string host) {
    try {
      return Dns.GetHostByName(host).AddressList[0];
    } catch (SecurityException) {
      return IPAddress.Loopback;
    }
  }
}
```

For applications that care, the type of permission that was not satisfied is available as a property of the security exception object via the `SecurityException.PermissionType` property.

As shown in Figure 9.7, the `Demand` method requires that each method on the stack have at least the permissions being demanded, where "at least" is defined by the implementation of the `IsSubsetOf` method for the permission type. This figure also illustrates the **top-of-stack permission set**. The top of stack permission set is established when a thread begins using the CLR. For threads that are explicitly created by CLR-based programs, this permission set is simply the intersection of permissions for each method in the spawning thread's call stack. Similarly, when a thread pool thread begins to service a work request, the CLR uses a similar snapshot from the spawning thread to set the top-of-stack permissions. In both cases, this prevents the secondary thread from performing operations that the spawning thread could not legally perform itself. For all other threads (including the "main" thread of a CLR-based application), the CLR calculates the top-of-stack permissions based on the evidence provided when the AppDomain was created. The `AppDomain.CreateDomain` method accepts a parameter of type `System.Security.Policy.Evidence` for this very purpose.

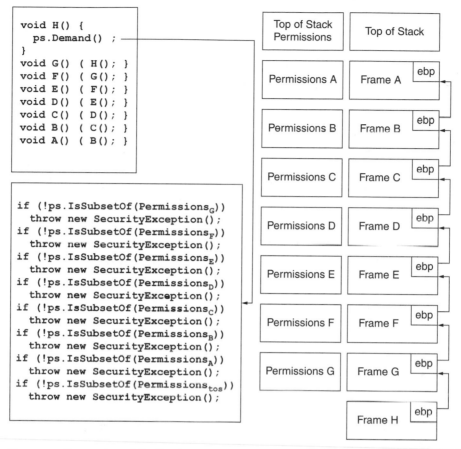

Figure 9.7: *Demands and the Stack*

The example from the `System.Net.Dns` class just shown was an example of an **imperative** security demand. It is called "imperative" because an explicit programmatic statement was executed. The CLR also supports **declarative** security demands based on attributes. For each permission type, the CLR defines a permission-specific custom attribute that derives from `System.Security.Permissions.CodeAccessSecurityAttribute`. These permission-specific attributes all accept a mandatory constructor parameter of type `System.Security.Permissions.SecurityAction`:

```
namespace System.Security.Permissions {
  public enum SecurityAction {
    Demand = 1,
    Assert,
```

```
        Deny,
        PermitOnly,
        LinkDemand,
        InheritanceDemand,
        RequestMinimum,
        RequestOptional,
        RequestRefuse,
    }
}
```

For this part of the discussion, the only `SecurityAction` to consider is `Demand`. Consider the following imperative demand:

```
using System.Security.Permissions;
namespace System.Net {
  public sealed class Dns {
    public static IPHostEntry GetHostByName(string host) {
      DnsPermission perm
          = new DnsPermission(PermissionState.Unrestricted);
      perm.Demand();
// if we get here, then the demand succeeded!
    }
  }
}
```

This security action allows one to rewrite the preceding imperative demand as follows:

```
using System.Security.Permissions;
namespace System.Net {
 public sealed class Dns {

   [DnsPermission(SecurityAction.Demand, Unrestricted=true)]
   public static IPHostEntry GetHostByName(string host) {
// if we get here, then the demand succeeded!
   }
 }
```

The advantage of the latter example is that one can determine the security requirements of the code strictly by looking at the metadata for the type. The disadvantage to declarative security demands is that they cannot support permissions requiring dynamic information (for example, file paths) that cannot be known at compile time. One can apply security attributes such as `DnsPermission` to either individual methods or to a type. The latter in effect applies the attribute to all methods of the type.

It is often desirable to tune the permissions that are granted to a given method. One typically does this to restrict the permissions that a given piece of code will run with. The CLR provides two ways to do this. One way is to restrict the effective permissions to a subset of those granted by policy. The other way is to explicitly deny one or more permissions. One can take both of these actions either declaratively or imperatively. One can use the `SecurityAction.PermitOnly` and `SecurityAction.Deny` with a `SecurityAttribute` to accomplish this declaratively. For example, consider the following code:

```
using System.Net;
using System.Security.Permissions;

public sealed class Utils {
  [
    DnsPermission(SecurityAction.PermitOnly,
                Unrestricted=true)
  ]
  public static IPAddress LookupHost(string host) {
    return Dns.GetHostByName(host).AddressList[0];
  }
}
```

This example using declarative security is equivalent to the following imperative security-based example:

```
using System.Net;
using System.Security.Permissions;

public sealed class Utils {
  public static IPAddress LookupHost(string host) {
    DnsPermission perm
        = new DnsPermission(PermissionState.Unrestricted);
    perm.PermitOnly();
    return Dns.GetHostByName(host).AddressList[0];
  }
}
```

In either example, if the DnsGetHostByName method were to demand any permission beyond DnsPermission, the demand would be denied even if the LookupHost method (and all of its callers) were in fact granted the requested permission by policy. Had the LookupHost simply wanted to deny the use of one particular permission, the following code would have sufficed:

```
using System.Net;
using System.Security.Permissions;

public sealed class Utils {
  [
    FileIOPermission(SecurityAction.Deny,
                     Unrestricted=true)
  ]
  public static IPAddress LookupHost(string host) {
    return Dns.GetHostByName(host).AddressList[0];
  }
}
```

This is the imperative equivalent:

```
using System.Net;
using System.Security.Permissions;

public sealed class Utils {
  public static IPAddress LookupHost(string host) {
    FileIOPermission perm
      = new FileIOPermission(PermissionState.Unrestricted);
    perm.Deny();
    return Dns.GetHostByName(host).AddressList[0];
  }
}
```

In this case, any demands for FileIOPermission in Dns.GetHostByName would be denied; however, any other permission types would be subject to policy.

It is important to note that for a given stack frame, one can have only one permission set in place using Deny or PermitOnly. For example, consider the following method:

```
using System.Net;
using System.Security.Permissions;

public sealed class Utils {
 public static IPAddress LookupHost(string host) {
   FileIOPermission p1
       = new FileIOPermission(PermissionState.Unrestricted);
   RegistryPermission p2
    = new RegistryPermission(PermissionState.Unrestricted);
   p1.Deny();
   p2.Deny();
   return Dns.GetHostByName(host).AddressList[0];
 }
}
```

In this example, the second call to Deny would cause an exception to be raised because there is already a Deny in place. To prohibit both permissions, one would need to use a permission set as follows:

```
using System.Net;
using System.Security.Permissions;

public sealed class Utils {
 public static IPAddress LookupHost(string host) {
   FileIOPermission p1
       = new FileIOPermission(PermissionState.Unrestricted);
   RegistryPermission p2
    = new RegistryPermission(PermissionState.Unrestricted);
   PermissionSet ps = new PermissionSet(null);
   ps.AddPermission(p1);
   ps.AddPermission(p2);
   ps.Deny();
   return Dns.GetHostByName(host).AddressList[0];
 }
}
```

In this case, both permissions would be denied to Dns.GetHostByName.

Trusted components often need permissions that their callers may not necessarily have been granted. For example, the System.Net.Dns type needs to call the underlying gethostbyname API function, which, like all API calls, causes the CLR to demand the SecurityPermissionFlags. UnmanagedCode permission. However, requiring all callers to have this permission would make the Dns type useless to all but the most trusted components. To address this situation, the CLR supports the Assert security action.

When a method asserts a given security permission, any demands for that permission will stop walking the stack at that method frame. As shown in Figure 9.8, by asserting a permission, one is indicating that the caller's permissions are not to be considered. Ironically, the act of asserting a permission is itself a protected operation that requires the asserting method to have the SecurityPermissionFlag.Assertion permission. Methods that assert a permission typically do so in concert with a demand for a lesser permission that callers are likely to have. For example, the Dns.GetHostByName method might carry the following security attributes:

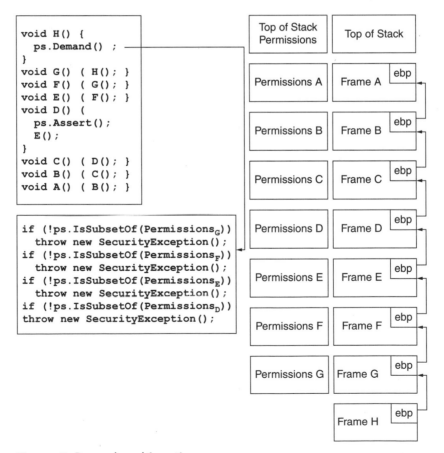

Figure 9.8: *Demands and Assertions*

```
using System.Security.Permissions;
namespace System.Net {
 public sealed class Dns {

   [
     DnsPermission(SecurityAction.Demand,
             Unrestricted=true),
     SecurityPermission(SecurityAction.Assert,
             Flags=SecurityPermissionFlag.UnmanagedCode)
   ]
   public static IPHostEntry GetHostByName(string host) {
// if we get here, then the demand and assertion succeeded!
   }
  }
 }
```

It is important to note that an assertion will succeed only if the requesting method was granted the permission being asserted. One cannot use assertion to gain permissions not already granted to the requesting method.

It is also possible to annotate an entire assembly to influence which permissions are actually granted. The `SecurityAction.RequestMinimum` action indicates that the specified permission must be granted to the assembly in order to successfully load. If the specified permissions cannot be granted by policy, then the assembly loader will fail the load. Moreover, the actual permissions that will be granted to the assembly's methods will be a subset of those granted by policy. Specifically, the effective permissions of the method will simply be all of the permissions marked `SecurityAction.RequestMinimum` unioned with any permissions marked with a `SecurityAction.RequestOptional` attribute (policy allowing) less those permissions marked with a `SecurityAction.RequestRefuse` attribute. For example, consider the following C# code:

```
using System.Net;
using System.Security.Permissions;

[assembly:
   DnsPermission(SecurityAccess.RequestMinimum,
             Unrestricted=true),
   EnvironmentPermission(SecurityAction.RequestMinimum,
             Unrestricted=true),
```

```
        FileIOPermission(SecurityAccess.RequestOptional,
                  Unrestricted=true)
        FileIOPermission(SecurityAccess.RequestRefuse,
                  Write=@"C:\autoexec.bat")
]

public sealed class Utils {
  public static IPAddress LookupHost(string name) {
    return Dns.GetHostByName(name).AddressList[0];
  }
}
```

In this example, all methods in the assembly will have at least the `DnsPermission` and `EnvironmentPermission`. If policy neglects to grant either of these permissions, then the loading of the assembly will fail. Additionally, the CLR will grant the assembly any `FileIOPermissions` allowed by policy. However, the CLR will explicitly deny the ability to write to the file `C:\autoexec.bat`. Figure 9.9 shows how the effective permissions for a given stack frame are calculated.

There are two other security actions that have not been discussed: `SecurityAction.InheritanceDemand` and `SecurityAction.LinkDemand`. A `SecurityAction.InheritanceDemand` attribute allows a base type to demand that a derived type has been granted a given permission. For example, consider the following C# abstract base class:

```
using System.Security.Permissions;

[ UIPermission(SecurityAction.InheritanceDemand,
               Unrestricted=true) ]
public abstract class MyWindow {
  public abstract void ShowMe();
}
```

Any types that derive from `MyWindow` must have the `UIPermission`. The CLR will perform this security demand implicitly as part of the loading of the derived type.

The `SecurityAction.LinkDemand` attribute is similar to the `SecurityAction.Demand` attribute; however, `SecurityAction.LinkDemand` is used to place demands on the direct caller and not the entire stack. When

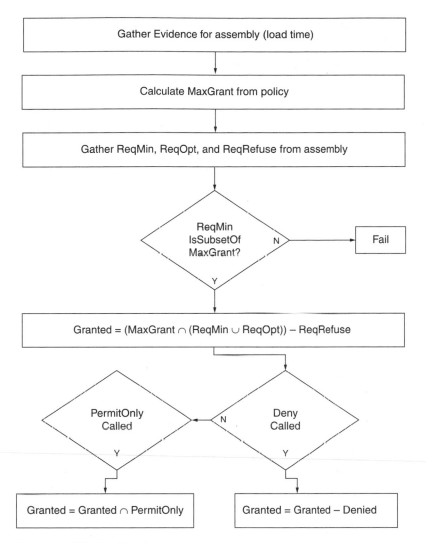

Figure 9.9: *Effective Permissions*

the JIT compiler attempts to JIT-compile a particular method, any calls within that method to methods marked with the LinkDemand attribute will force a security check. Unlike a normal Demand call, this check will look only at the direct caller (in this case, the method being JIT-compiled). Also, unlike a normal SecurityAction.Demand attribute, which is evaluated each time the method is called, a SecurityAction.LinkDemand is evaluated only at JIT-compile time, and that makes it considerably cheaper to enforce.

Both LinkDemand and InheritanceDemand provide an ideal venue for using identity permissions. For example, consider the case in which a collection of assemblies from the same vendor need to work closely together. Unfortunately, the normal access modifiers (e.g., public, internal) are extremely coarse-grained and don't allow you to grant access to a method to particular assemblies. However, by applying a LinkDemand attribute to the method that demands that the caller have a particular identity permission (e.g., StrongNameIdentityPermission), one could demand that all callers have a particular public key in their assembly name. For example, consider the following simple C# class:

```
using System;
using System.Security.Permissions;
using System.Reflection;

[assembly: AssemblyKeyFile("pubpriv.snk") ]

public sealed class Utils {
  [ StrongNameIdentityPermission(SecurityAction.LinkDemand,
                   PublicKey=
       "002400000480000094000000060200000024000" +
       "0525341310004000001000100cb3cec5f0ac3e5" +
       "30b73fe823ce6084be139df6119fdc0d4ff3a65" +
       "680da90f2819a10ef6a1db0eb5c5e6ea3822456" +
       "92a1505f88ad8f6716d366fb2d9d553e0f680b3" +
       "09f7e78dca447a23ec892d13f150e7c7b7997e8" +
       "50dc64273860e752c1ffb75ed244522d293b46f" +
       "74d511e17f76b2874ee80cb82babea3b624b745" +
       "baca48b7") ]
  public static void DoIt() {
    Console.WriteLine("Hello, world");
  }
}
```

Despite the fact that the DoIt method is marked as public, it can be called only by methods bearing the public key that is specified in the LinkDemand attribute. Attempts to call this method from assemblies not bearing the designated public key will fail at JIT-compile time. In the same vein, one could mark an abstract base class with an InheritanceDemand attribute:

```
[
    StrongNameIdentityPermission(
        SecurityAction.InheritanceDemand, PublicKey=
            "0024000004800000940000000602000000024000" +
            "0525341310004000001000100cb3cec5f0ac3e5" +
            "30b73fe823ce6084be139df6119fdc0d4ff3a65" +
            "680da90f2819a10ef6a1db0eb5c5e6ea3822456" +
            "92a1505f88ad8f6716d366fb2d9d553e0f680b3" +
            "09f7e78dca447a23ec892d13f150e7c7b7997e8" +
            "50dc64273860e752c1ffb75ed244522d293b46f" +
            "74d511e17f76b2874ee80cb82babea3b624b745" +
            "baca48b7")
]
public abstract class PersonImpl {
  // members elided for clarity
}
```

Given this type definition, any types that derive from `PersonImpl` must belong to assemblies bearing the specified public key. Attempts to load and initialize a type that derives from `PersonImpl` from assemblies not bearing this public key will fail at type initialization time.

Where Are We?

The CLR supports a component-centric security model known as code-access security. Code-access security assumes that each assembly can provide evidence as to its origins, both in terms of who wrote the code and where it was downloaded from. Code-access security uses a configurable security policy to grant permissions to code based on evidence. Although the CLR implicitly enforces some aspects of security policy, it is the job of trusted libraries to enforce security explicitly, using either imperative programmatic interfaces or declarative attributes.

◼ 10 ◼
CLR Externals

T HIS ENTIRE BOOK has been focused on the core programming model that applies to programs written for the CLR. At every step, I have tried to keep the discussion focused on the virtualized world of the CLR, avoiding discussion of OS-isms or memory management whenever possible. It is appropriate that, in this last chapter, we will do a reality check and see how CLR-based programs relate to the world around them.

Memory

One of the key characteristics of modern runtime environments such as the CLR is that they raise the level of abstraction from manual memory management to a type-centric model based on types, objects, and values. In such a model, the use of memory is implicit, not explicit. For the lion's share of programs, the resultant increase in productivity far outweighs any inconvenience that the lack of low-level control may impose. However, there is a class of problem for which explicit memory manipulation is vital, the most common of which is the direct access of memory buffers. This sort of direct access is critical in high-performance I/O processing, dealing with memory-mapped devices, and interfacing with existing C-based libraries or system calls.

Most runtimes (including the CLR) provide a way to integrate with C-based libraries through a thunking layer (e.g., J/Direct, P/Invoke, Java Native Interface [JNI]). However, these thunking layers do not come without a cost. In all cases, the transition from "runtime mode" to "C mode" incurs a nontrivial performance cost. This leads to unnatural designs that minimize transitions between the two worlds in order to maintain respectable performance. Additionally, in at least one of these thunking layers, JNI, one must write an adapter library in C or C++ to map between the Java VM and the target library.

What makes the CLR unique is that the CLR type system and instruction set allow the use of classic C-style memory manipulation for programs that absolutely require it. The explicit use of memory is fully supported in CIL and does not require machine-dependent native code. The explicit use of memory is completely consistent with the runtime semantics of the CLR and does not require a "mode switch" to disable the services provided by the CLR. The explicit use of memory does require an understanding of how the CLR distinguishes between object references and pointers.

The CLR treats object references as distinct from pointers, despite the fact that both are ultimately addresses of memory locations. Object references support a set of operations distinct from those of pointers. In particular, object references support assignment, identity comparison, and member access. Period. There is no notion of "dereferencing" an object reference, nor any notion of "object reference arithmetic." Finally, object references are assumed to refer to distinct objects on the garbage-collected heap, and this means that the address contained in an object reference is subject to change when the garbage collector compacts the heap.

The CLR supports pointers as a construct distinct from object references. Unlike object references, pointers are meant to be dereferenced. Unlike object references, pointers are ordered and can be compared using the < and > operators. Also, unlike object references, pointers support arithmetic operations, allowing random access to memory. This last difference imposes problems that bear closer scrutiny.

Because C-style pointers allow programs to access arbitrary memory, the use of C-style pointers makes program verification intractable. Program verification is a key feature of the CLR that is used to ensure that components do not compromise the security of the CLR or the host environment. Programs that do not use C-style pointers can be verified because all accesses to objects and values can be verifiably type-safe. However, in the presence of random memory access, it is possible to spoof the system into believing that arbitrary memory is in fact an instance of a highly trusted component. For this reason, the CLR supports two types of pointer: one that does not compromise verifiability, and one that does.

CLR-based programs routinely use pointers that are verifiable. These kinds of pointers are referred to as **managed** pointers. The C# and VB.NET compilers use managed pointers whenever a method parameter is declared as pass-by-reference. Unlike C-style pointers, managed pointers do not support arithmetic operations. Additionally, the initialization and assignment of a managed pointer are constrained to ensure that there is no compromise of the CLR type system. To that end, managed pointers are strongly typed and are themselves instances of a type. For example, a managed pointer to `System.Int32` is an instance of type `System.Int32&`. The ultimate reason that managed pointers are called "managed" is that the garbage collector is capable of adjusting the pointer value when the referent is moved during heap compaction.

Managed pointers exist largely to implement pass-by-reference for method parameters. The CLR also supports a second style of pointer that behaves exactly like a C-style pointer. This style of pointer is called an **unmanaged** pointer. The adjective *unmanaged* is used because the garbage collector ignores unmanaged pointers during heap compaction. Like managed pointers, unmanaged pointers are instances of a type. For example, an unmanaged pointer to `System.Int32` is an instance of type `System.Int32*`.

Unlike managed pointers, unmanaged pointers support pointer arithmetic and unchecked type casts. With unmanaged pointers, it is completely legal to write code that looks like this:

```
int x = 0x12345678;
void *pv = &x;
double *pd = (double*)(pv);
*(pd + 5) = 2.0;
```

The C# compiler is perfectly happy to turn this very dangerous code into CIL. Moreover, the CLR is happy to turn the CIL into native code and then execute it. However, neither of these things will happen without an explicit action on the part of the developer and the system administrator or user.

The use of unmanaged pointers results in code that is not verifiably type-safe. The ability to execute code that is not verifiably type-safe is a highly trusted security permission that, by default, the CLR denies to all code not originating from the local file system. In particular, the assembly containing the nonverifiable code must request (and be granted) the `Secu-rityPermissionFlag.SkipVerification` permission in its assembly manifest. On a default installation of the CLR, this permission is not granted to code loaded from remote file systems, so the only way to get nonverifiable code to execute is to dupe a user into copying it to an executable area of the local file system. Of course, the administrator or end user may explicitly grant permission to run code that is known to be trusted, but this as well requires that someone with trusted access to the deployment machine take a deliberate action.

Because of the role of C-style pointers in C++ programs, the C++ compiler emits only nonverifiable code. In contrast, VB.NET emits only verifiable code. C# supports both verifiable and nonverifiable code. By default, the C# compiler emits verifiable code. This allows one to deploy C# code easily from remote file systems or Web servers. To keep programmers from randomly generating nonverifiable code, the C# compiler forces them to explicitly state that they intend to use unmanaged pointers in their programs. This statement takes the form of a compiler switch and of a language keyword.

To compile C# programs that use unmanaged pointers, one must use the `/unsafe` or `/unsafe+` command-line switch. This switch causes the compiler to emit the permission set requesting the `SkipVerification` permission. This switch also allows the use of unmanaged pointers in the source code of the program.

To discourage the use of unmanaged pointers, C# requires that any use of an unmanaged pointer appear inside a surrounding scope (e.g., method, type) that is declared as `unsafe`. For example, the following code will not compile because of the absence of the `unsafe` keyword:

```
public class Bob {
  public void Hello() {
```

```
        int x = 3;
        int *px = &x; // use of unmanaged pointer
    }
}
```

The following code would compile:

```
public class Bob {
  public unsafe void Hello() {
    int x = 3;
    int *px = &x; // use of unmanaged pointer
  }
}
```

This code would also compile:

```
public unsafe class Bob {
  public void Hello() {
    int x = 3;
    int *px = &x; // use of unmanaged pointer
  }
}
```

Of course, these latter two programs will compile only if the /unsafe or /unsafe+ command-line switch is used.

The use of unmanaged pointers requires even more attention to detail than the use of pointers in classic C. This is because unmanaged pointers need to be respectful of the memory that is "owned" by the CLR. This issue is especially contentious when one is dealing with memory on the garbage-collected heap.

The CLR can (and will) relocate objects on the garbage-collected heap. This means that taking the address of a field in an object requires great care because the garbage collector does not adjust unmanaged pointers when compacting the heap. To allow unmanaged pointers to refer to fields in objects, the CLR allows unmanaged pointers to be declared as pinned. A **pinned** pointer prevents the surrounding object from being relocated for as long as the pinned pointer is in scope. Each programming language exposes pinned pointers differently. In C++, one uses the __pin pointer modifier. In C#, one uses the fixed statement as shown here:

```
public unsafe class Bob {
  double y; // instance field in object
  static public void Hello(Bob b) {
    fixed (double *py = &b.y) {
      System.Console.WriteLine((int)py);
      *py = 300.00;
    }
    Debug.Assert(b.y == 300.00);
  }
}
```

For the duration of the `fixed` statement, the object referred to by b is guaranteed not to move, even if `Console.WriteLine` blocks for a significant duration of time. However, the object may move prior to the execution of the last statement of the `Hello` method. If this happens, the garbage collector will adjust the b reference accordingly. Note, however, that if a garbage collection occurs while a pinned pointer is in scope, the CLR cannot relocate the underlying object. For this reason, programmers are encouraged to hold pinned pointers for as short a time as possible to avoid heap fragmentation.

It is important that programmers not cache unmanaged pointers to memory on the garbage-collected heap. For example, the following program is a crash waiting to happen:

```
unsafe class Bob {
  static int *pi;
  int x;
  static void Main() {
    Bob o = new Bob();
    fixed(int *p = &o.x) {
      pi = p;                // watch out!!
    }
    System.GC.Collect(2); // force memory movement
    *pi = 100;               // use stale ptr
    System.Console.WriteLine(o.x);
  }
}
```

This program will compile without warning or error. However, the assignment of a pinned pointer (p) to a nonpinned pointer (pi) should give experienced C# programmers concern. In this example, the use of pi after the fixed statement will result in random behavior. This is exacerbated by the explicit call to System.GC.Collect, but by no means would the program be valid in the absence of such a call because garbage collection can happen at any time because of library calls, work done by secondary threads, or the use of the concurrent garbage collector.

It is important to note that you do not need to use pinned pointers when accessing memory on the stack. This means that taking the address of a local variable (or the field of a local variable of value type) does not require any special treatment. In fact, the following code will result in a compiler error because the CLR never relocates values declared as local variables:

```
public class Target {
  public static void f() {
    int x = 0; // x is on the stack and won't move
    fixed (int *px = &x) { // error: x is already fixed!
    }
  }
}
```

C++ and C# support scaled addition and subtraction only on unmanaged pointers. To perform arbitrary numeric operations, one must first cast to a numeric type. The CLR supports two generic numeric types for this purpose that are guaranteed to be large enough to hold a pointer. One usually exposes these types (native int and native uint) to programmers via the System.IntPtr and System.UIntPtr type, respectively. Because different architectures use different pointer sizes, the size of these two types is indeterminate and not known until runtime. The following code demonstrates the use of native int to round a pointer up to an 8-byte boundary.

```
static IntPtr RoundPtr(IntPtr ptr) {
  if (IntPtr.Size == 4) {  // specialize for 32-bit
    int n = ptr.ToInt32();
    n = (n + 7) & ~7;
    return (IntPtr)n;
  }
  else if (IntPtr.Size == 8) {  // specialize for 64-bit
    long n = ptr.ToInt64();
```

```
      n = (n + 7) & ~7;
      return (IntPtr)n;
    }
    else
      throw new Exception("Unknown pointer size");
  }
```

Note that this code uses the `System.IntPtr.Size` property to select the appropriate numeric type. Also note that this code takes advantage of the fact that one can freely cast `System.IntPtr` to and from `System.Int32`, `System.Int64`, or `void*`. This also makes `System.IntPtr` the most appropriate type to use when one is representing Win32 handle types such as HANDLE or HWND.

It is difficult to look at pointer use without dealing with the layout of types. Consider the following C# program:

```
using System;

unsafe class Bob {
  short a;
  double b;
  short c;
  static void Main() {
    Bob bob = new Bob();
    fixed (void *pa = &bob.a) {
      fixed (void *pb = &bob.b) {
        fixed (void *pc = &bob.c) {
// watch out - will these assertions succeed?
          Debug.Assert(pa < pb);
          Debug.Assert(pb < pc);
          Debug.Assert(pa < pc);
        }
      }
    }
  }
}
```

Had the equivalent program been written in classic C or C++, the three assertions would succeed because C and C++ guarantee that the in-memory layout of a type is based on order of declaration. As discussed in Chapter 3, the CLR uses a virtualized layout system and will lay out types based on performance characteristics. For most programs, this is ideal. However, for programs that explicitly manipulate memory based on the in-memory format of a type, one needs some mechanism to override the automatic layout rules and explicitly control the layout of a type.

There are three metadata attributes that control the layout of a type: `auto`, `sequential`, or `explicit`. Each type has exactly one of these attributes set. The CLR calculates the layout of types marked `auto` at runtime, and these types are said to have "no layout." The CLR guarantees that types marked as `sequential` will be laid out in order of declaration using the default packing rules for the host platform (on Win32, this is the equivalent to Microsoft C++'s `#pragma pack 8` option). One specifies the precise format of types marked as `explicit` via additional metadata entries that indicate the offset of each individual field of the type. Types marked as `sequential` or `explicit` are sometimes called **formatted types** because their format is under the control of the programmer.

When emitting the metadata for a type, compilers are free to use whichever attribute the language designer prefers. In C# and VB.NET, classes are marked `auto` and structs are marked `sequential` by default. To allow programmers to express the layout attributes in a consistent manner, the CLR defines two pseudo-custom attributes: `System.Runtime.InteropServices.StructLayout` and `System.Runtime.InteropServices.FieldOffset`. These attributes simply inform the compiler how to emit the metadata and do not appear as custom attributes in the target executable.

To understand the impact of these attributes, consider the following three C# type definitions:

```
using System.Runtime.InteropServices;

[ StructLayout(LayoutKind.Auto) ]
public struct Jane {
  public short  a;
  public double b;
  public short  c;
}
[ StructLayout(LayoutKind.Sequential) ]
public struct Helen {
  public short  a;
  public double b;
```

```
      public short   c;
   }
   [ StructLayout(LayoutKind.Explicit) ]
   public struct Betty {
      [ FieldOffset(0) ] public short   a;
      [ FieldOffset(8) ] public double b;
      [ FieldOffset(2) ] public short   c;
   }
```

The three types are logically equivalent, but each has a different in-memory representation. On the author's machine, Jane's fields will be ordered { b, a, c }, Helen's fields will be ordered { a, b, c}, and Betty's fields will be ordered { a, c, b }. Because C# assumes sequential for structs by default, the StructLayout attribute on Helen is superfluous.

It is important to note that when using the explicit layout option, one must take care to maintain the platform-agnostic nature of the CLR. Specifically, the sizes of object references, managed pointers, and unmanaged pointers are all indeterminate and cannot be known until the code is loaded on the deployment machine. For that reason, one should use explicit layout with care on types that contain object references or pointers to ensure that ample space is available for each field. Failure to do so will result in a type initialization error at runtime (specifically, a System.TypeLoadException). As an aside, it is legal to have overlapping fields that are not object references. This is one way to implement C-style unions in CLR-based programs. The following C# type illustrates this technique:

```
   using System.Runtime.InteropServices;

   [ StructLayout(LayoutKind.Explicit) ]
   public struct Number {
    private enum NumType { Double, Int64 }

    [ FieldOffset(0) ] double  dblVal;
    [ FieldOffset(0) ] long    longVal;// same loc. as dblVal
    [ FieldOffset(8) ] NumType type;

    public void Set(double val) {
       type = NumType.Double;
       dblVal = val;
```

```
    }
    public void Set(long val) {
      type = NumType.Int64;
      longVal = val;
    }
    public double GetDouble() {
      if (type == NumType.Double) return dblVal;
      else return (double)longVal;
    }
    public long GetInt64() {
      if (type == NumType.Int64) return longVal;
      else return (long)dblVal;
    }
  }
```

Note that instances of Number have enough storage for either a System.Double or a System.Int64 but not both.

There is one final topic related to types and layout that needs to be addressed. As just discussed, the explicit metadata attribute completely sacrifices the virtualized layout provided by the CLR. However, even types that are marked explicit have rich metadata, and the CLR is aware of the fields, methods, and other members of the type. This is perfectly acceptable for types that adhere to the CLR's common type system. However, to allow compilers to support constructs that are not part of the CLR's common type system, such as multiple inheritance or templates, the CLR provides a mechanism for indicating that a type is opaque. **Opaque types** are just that: opaque. The metadata for an opaque type consists of nothing other than the size of an instance in memory. There is no metadata to indicate the fields or methods of the type. Additionally, opaque types are always value types, and that frees the implementation from needing to support the CLR's runtime type infrastructure or garbage collector.

C# and VB.NET do not support opaque types. In contrast, C++ supports opaque types by default. When one uses the /CLR switch, all C++ classes and structs are emitted as opaque types. The CLR does this to maintain strict C++ semantics, which allows any C++ program to be recompiled to a CLR module and just work. To indicate that a type is not opaque (sometimes called a managed type), the C++ type definition must use either the __gc or the __value modifier, depending on whether one

desires a reference type or a value type. When one uses either of these modifiers, the resultant type will no longer have pure C++ semantics. Rather,
issues such as order of construction, finalization, and other CLR-isms will
apply to the type.

To understand the difference between opaque types and non-opaque
types in C++, consider the following C++ type definitions:

```
template <typename T>
class Bob {
  T t;
  public: void f() { t++; }
  public: Bob() { t = 0; }
  public: ~Bob() { }
};

class Steve : public Bob<int>, public Bob<double> {
  float x;
  public: void g() {
    Bob<int>::f();
    Bob<double>::f();
  }
  public: Steve() {}
  public: ~Steve() {}
};
```

Because neither Bob nor Steve is marked __gc or __value, the C++
compiler will compile these types as opaque types, and they will have full
C++ semantics (deterministic destruction and base-to-derived construction). However, because these types are opaque, none of the fields of Bob
or Steve will appear in the metadata. In fact, the methods of Bob and
Steve will appear as module-scoped methods using mangled names. Also,
because the CLR does not support generics, the C++ compiler must explicitly instantiate the types Bob<int> and Bob<double> as distinct types in
the metadata.

The fact that the CLR does not know the fields of opaque types presents
a problem when one is dealing with object references. Because the CLR
must know the location of every object reference in order to implement
garbage collection, opaque types cannot have object references as fields. To
get around this limitation, the CLR provides a type, System.Runtime.

`InteropServices.GCHandle,` that supports treating object references as integers. To use a `GCHandle`, one must first explicitly allocate one using the static `GCHandle.Alloc` method. This method creates a rooted object reference and stores a handle to that reference in the new `GCHandle` instance, as shown in Figure 10.1. Any program can convert a `GCHandle` to and from an `IntPtr` (which is safe to store in an opaque type). The allocated `GCHandle` (and its rooted reference) will exist until the program makes an explicit call to `GCHandle.Free`.

The following opaque C++ class demonstrates how to use a `GCHandle` to cache an object reference as a field:

```
#using <mscorlib.dll>
using namespace System;
using namespace System::Runtime::InteropServices;

class OpaqueObjrefUser
{
  void *pvCache;
public:
  void SetIt(Object *obj) {
    GCHandle handle = GCHandle::Alloc(obj);
    pvCache = ((IntPtr)handle).ToPointer();
  }
  int GetHash() {
    GCHandle handle = GCHandle::op_Explicit(pvCache);
    Object *obj = handle.Target;
    return obj->GetHashCode();
  }
  void FreeIt() {
    GCHandle handle = GCHandle::op_Explicit(pvCache);
    handle.Free();
  }
};
```

Readers with a COM background will likely notice the similarity between the `GCHandle` type and COM's global interface table. To that end, the Visual C++ include directory contains a file, `gcroot.h`, that defines a smart pointer to simplify the use of `GCHandle` in opaque types. Given that header file, one could rewrite the previous example as follows:

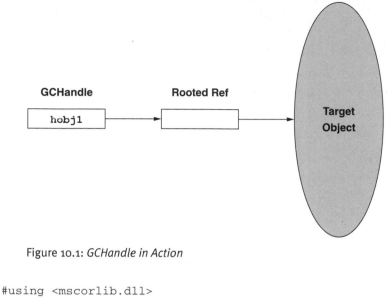

Figure 10.1: *GCHandle in Action*

```
#using <mscorlib.dll>
using namespace System;
using namespace System::Runtime::InteropServices;

class OpaqueObjrefUser
{
  gcroot<System::Object*> cache;
public:
  void SetIt(Object *obj) {
    cache = obj; // overloaded operator =
  }
  int GetHash() {
    return cache->GetHashCode(); // operator ->
  }
  void FreeIt() {
    cache = 0; // or let destructor do it...
  }
};
```

C++ programmers familiar with smart pointers should feel right at home with this usage.

Modes of Execution

The previous discussion regarding explicit access to memory illustrates how rich the CLR type system and instruction set are. The availability of managed and unmanaged pointers allows programs to gain efficient access to memory without sacrificing the services of the CLR. It is now time to turn our attention to exactly how the CLR supports those services and when (and why) one may need to bypass those services.

The CLR is based on a simple premise—that is, that the CLR is omniscient and omnipotent. The CLR needs the ability to know everything about a running program. This is one more reason why metadata is so important, because metadata is the key to the CLR's understanding the relationships between objects and values in memory. Moreover, the CLR needs the ability to manage and control all aspects of a running program. This is where managed execution comes into play.

The CLR supports two modes of execution: managed and unmanaged mode. In **managed execution** mode, the CLR is capable of interrogating every stack frame of every thread. This capability includes being able to inspect local variables and parameters. This capability includes being able to find the code and metadata for each stack frame's method. This capability includes being able to detect which object references on the stack are "live" and which are no longer needed, as well as to adjust the live object references after heap compaction. In short, managed execution mode makes your program completely transparent to the CLR.

In contrast, **unmanaged execution** mode renders the CLR blind and powerless. When running in unmanaged execution mode, the CLR cannot glean any meaningful information from the call stack, nor can it do much to the executing code other than simply suspend the running thread altogether. As far as the CLR is concerned, unmanaged code is an opaque black box that the CLR respectfully must ignore.

One alters the mode of execution based on method invocation. One can mark each method for which the CLR has metadata as `managed` or `unmanaged`. The VB.NET and C# compilers can emit only `managed` methods. The C++ compiler emits `managed` methods by default when one uses the `/CLR` switch. However, the C++ compiler also supports emitting unmanaged methods. The compiler automatically emits unmanaged methods when a method body contains either inline IA-32 assembler or `setjmp/longjmp` calls, both of which make managed execution impractical. You can explicitly control the mode of a method using the `#pragma managed` and `#pragma unmanaged` directives in your source code.

The CLR is blind to unmanaged methods, so methods that are unmanaged may not use CLR object references because the CLR garbage collector cannot detect their existence nor adjust them during heap compaction. That means that the following C++ code will not compile:

```
void f() {
// these statements require managed mode
  System::Object *obj = new System::Object();
  System::Console::WriteLine(obj->ToString());
// this statement requires unmanaged mode!
  __asm
  {
    push eax
    xor eax, eax
    pop eax
  }
}
```

To get this program to work, one would need to separate the two regions of code into separate methods whose mode would reflect the needs of the code.

```
#pragma managed
void f() {
  f1(); // call managed code
  f2(); // call unmanaged code
}
#pragma managed
void f1() {
  System::Object *obj = new System::Object();
  System::Console::WriteLine(obj->ToString());
}
#pragma unmanaged
void f2() {
  __asm
  {
    push eax
    xor eax, eax
    pop eax
  }
}
```

Note that the use of #pragmas is optional because the C++ compiler will set the mode based on whether or not the method body uses __asm or setjmp/longjmp.

There is no fundamental difference between the method body of a managed method and that of an unmanaged method. The methods' prologs and epilogs will look the same, as will the actual native code that will execute. What distinguishes managed from unmanaged methods is that the CLR can infer everything it needs to know about a stack frame for a managed method. In contrast, the CLR cannot infer much at all about a stack frame for an unmanaged method. It is important to note that the ability to infer rich information about a managed stack frame does not require additional instructions during method invocation. Rather, a call from one managed method to another managed method is indistinguishable from a classic C function call. However, because the CLR controls the method prologs and epilogs for managed methods, the CLR can reliably traverse the managed regions of the call stack, often (but not always) using the IA-32 ebp register used by most debuggers. Because the CLR needs this stack inspection only during relatively rare occurrences such as security demands, garbage collection, and exception handling, the common-case code path for managed code looks indistinguishable from the code generated by the classic C compiler.

As just described, homogeneous, same-mode invocation is indistinguishable from normal C-style function invocation. In contrast, cross-mode, heterogeneous invocation is not so simple. Cross-mode invocation happens when a managed method calls an unmanaged method or when an unmanaged method calls a managed method. In either case, the emitted code for the call looks considerably different from that of a normal same-mode call.

Cross-mode invocations need to perform extra work to signal the change of execution semantics. For one thing, the caller needs to push a sentinel on the stack marking the beginning of a new chain of stack frames. The CLR partitions the stack frame into **chains**. Each chain represents a series of same-mode method invocations. When the JIT compiler compiles a cross-mode call, it emits additional code that pushes an extra **transition frame** on the stack as a sentinel. As shown in Figure 10.2, each transition

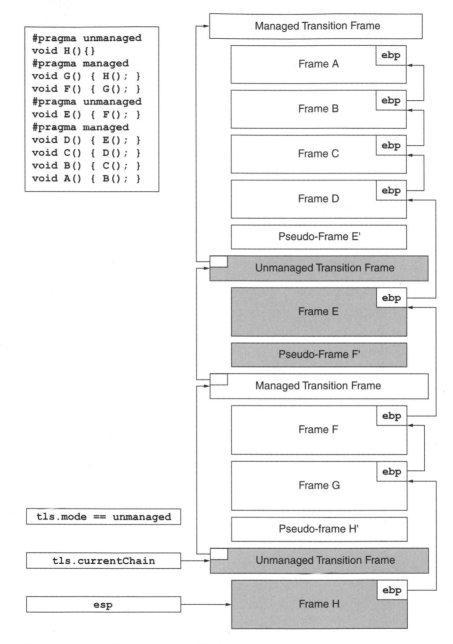

```
#pragma unmanaged
void H(){}
#pragma managed
void G() { H(); }
void F() { G(); }
#pragma unmanaged
void E() { F(); }
#pragma managed
void D() { E(); }
void C() { D(); }
void B() { C(); }
void A() { B(); }
```

Figure 10.2: *Transition Frames and Chains*

frame contains a back-pointer to the transition frame that began the previous chain. These transition frames allow the CLR to efficiently skip regions of the stack it doesn't care about—namely, the frames in unmanaged chains. After the transition frame is pushed on the stack, the caller then forms the normal stack frame that is expected by the target method. Note that this technique results in two stack frames for a cross-mode method call, one for each mode.

After the transition thunk prepares the stack for the cross-mode target method, the thunk must then adjust the execution state of the current thread to reflect the change in execution mode. Part of this preparation involves caching a pointer to the newly formed transition frame in thread local storage. Additionally, the transition thunk must toggle the bit in thread local storage that indicates which execution mode the thread is currently executing in. When this bit is set, the thread is running in managed execution mode. When the bit is clear, the thread is running in unmanaged execution mode. After the transition thunk has prepared the thread state, the thunk then jumps to the target method body. When the target method returns, it returns to additional transition code that resets the thread state and pops the transition frame from the stack. For calls with simple method signatures, the overall cost of making the transition is about 32 IA-32 instructions. Because making a cross-mode call requires setting up a second stack frame after the transition frame, the cost of cross-mode calls is dependent on the number and type of parameters passed to the method. The greater the number of parameters, the greater the cost of making the transition.

Unmanaged Modules

The discussion of unmanaged methods in the previous section assumed that the methods resided in an otherwise managed module and assembly. The CLR also supports calling code in unmanaged modules to allow the use of legacy C DLLs and API functions. One exposes this capability via a technology called P/Invoke.

P/Invoke is a superset of the managed and unmanaged transitions just described. P/Invoke provides a rich set of type conversion facilities to deal with the inherent differences between legacy C DLLs and the CLR. In addition to implementing the execution mode switch just described, P/Invoke performs a security permission demand to ensure that the security of the system is not compromised. Like the ability to execute nonverifiable code, the ability to call classic C DLLs is considered a highly privileged operation. To that end, the P/Invoke engine will demand the `UnmanagedCode` permission. Components that make any use of P/Invoke must be explicitly granted this permission. Moreover, components that make extensive use of P/Invoke should call `IStackWalk.Assert` prior to calling P/Invoke routines. This needs to be done not only to improve performance but also to guarantee that the P/Invoke call will succeed no matter what code path caused the current method to be called. An even better optimization would be to add the `System.Security.SuppressUnmanagedCodeSecurity` attribute to the type or method in question. The presence of this attribute suppresses the CLR's security demand altogether (provided that the assembly in fact has the `UnmanagedCode` permission). However, one should use this attribute with caution because it is a fairly coarse-grained solution, and careless use could weaken the overall security of the system.

Using P/Invoke is rather simple. P/Invoke allows one to mark methods as imported from a classic pre-CLR DLL. P/Invoke requires C functions exported from unmanaged modules to be redeclared in a managed module using special metadata directives. These directives indicate the file name of the DLL as well as the symbolic name of the entry point in the DLL. The P/Invoke engine then uses these two strings to call `LoadLibrary` and `GetProcAddress`, respectively, just prior to invoking the annotated method.

One can prepare methods for use with P/Invoke by using the language-neutral `System.Runtime.InteropServices.DllImport` pseudo-custom attribute. One must mark methods that use the `DllImport` attribute as `extern` and declare them with a method signature that matches the target function in the external DLL. Ultimately, every P/Invoke method has two signatures: the explicit one that is seen by managed code making the call, and the implicit one that is expected by the external DLL function. It is the job of the P/Invoke engine to infer the unmanaged signature based on default mapping rules and custom attributes.

The `DllImport` attribute takes a variety of parameters that customize how the external method and signature are to be imported and resolved. As shown in Table 10.1, the `DllImport` attribute requires that one provide at least a file name. The runtime uses this file name to call `LoadLibrary` prior to dispatching the method call. The string to use for `GetProcAddress` will be the symbolic name of the method unless the `EntryPoint` parameter is passed to `DllImport`. The following C# fragment shows two ways to call the `Sleep` method in `kernel32.dll`.

```
using System.Runtime.InteropServices;

public class K32Wrapper {
  [ DllImport("kernel32.dll") ]
  public extern static void Sleep(uint msec);
  [ DllImport("kernel32.dll", EntryPoint = "Sleep") ]
  public extern static void Doze(uint msec);
}
```

The first example relies on a match between the name of the C# function and the name of the symbol in the DLL. The second example relies on the `EntryPoint` attribute parameter instead.

Independent of how the entry point name is specified, one has to deal with the variety of name mangling schemes used to indicate calling convention and character sets. Unless one sets the `ExactSpelling` parameter to `true`, the P/Invoke engine will use several heuristics to find a matching entry point in the external DLL. When a P/Invoke method that uses strings is called, the entry point name will automatically have a `W` or `A` suffix

TABLE 10.1 DllImport Attribute Parameters

Parameter Name	Type	Description	Default
Value	System.String	Path for LoadLibrary	‹mandatory›
EntryPoint	System.String	Symbol for GetProcAddress	‹methodname›
Calling Convention	Calling Convention	Stack cleanup/order	Winapi
CharSet	CharSet	WCHAR/CHAR/TCHAR	Ansi
ExactSpelling	System.Boolean	Don't look for name with A/W/@	false
PreserveSig	System.Boolean	Don't treat as [out,retval]	true
SetLastError	System.Boolean	GetLastError valid for call	false

appended if needed, depending on whether the underlying platform is Unicode or ANSI-based. If the entry point still cannot be found, the runtime will mangle the name using the stdcall conventions (e.g., Sleep becomes _Sleep@4).

The P/Invoke engine has special facilities for dealing with errors raised by external DLLs. Because the P/Invoke engine itself makes system calls, it is possible that the error code returned by GetLastError may not be accurate. To preserve this error code, P/Invoke methods that map to functions that call SetLastError must be marked SetLastError=true. To recover the error code after making the P/Invoke call, managed code should use the System.Runtime.InteropServices.Marshal.GetLast-Win32Error method. Consider the following C# program, which calls CloseHandle via P/Invoke:

```
using System;
using System.Runtime.InteropServices;

class App {
  [ DllImport("kernel32.dll", SetLastError=true) ]
  static extern bool CloseHandle(IntPtr handle);

  static void Main() {
    if (!CloseHandle(IntPtr.Zero)) {
      Console.WriteLine("Error: {0}",
                         Marshal.GetLastWin32Error());
    }
  }
}
```

Note the use of SetLastError=true in the DllImport attribute. In this example, the program will print the following message:

```
Error: 6
```

This message corresponds to the Win32 error code ERROR_INVALID_HANDLE. Had the SetLastError=true parameter not been set, the program would have printed the following:

```
Error: 126
```

This message corresponds to the Win32 error code ERROR_MOD_NOT_FOUND. Unless one marks the method SetLastError=true, the P/Invoke engine will not preserve the value set by the CloseHandle function (ERROR_INVALID_HANDLE).

Another popular error-reporting technique from the past was to use numeric HRESULTs. P/Invoke supports two options for dealing with functions that return HRESULTs. By default, P/Invoke treats the HRESULT as a 32-bit integer that is returned from the function, requiring the programmer to manually test for failure. A more convenient way to call such a function is to pass the PreserveSig=false parameter to the DllImport attribute. This tells the P/Invoke layer to treat that 32-bit integer as a COM HRESULT and to throw a COMException in the face of a failed result.

To understand the PreserveSig option, consider a legacy C DLL that exposes the following function (shown in pseudo-IDL):

```
HRESULT __stdcall CoSomeAPI([in] long a1,
                            [out, retval] short *pa2);
```

One could import this function either with or without PreserveSig. The following import uses PreserveSig=true, which is the default for P/Invoke:

```
// returns HRESULT as function result
[ DllImport("ole32.dll", EntryPoint="CoSomeAPI") ]
public extern static int CoSomeAPI1(int a1, out short a2);
```

With this declaration, the caller must manually check the result of the method for failure. In contrast, the following import suppresses PreserveSig:

```
// throws COMException on failed HRESULT
[ DllImport("ole32.dll", EntryPoint="CoSomeAPI",
            PreserveSig=false)  ]
public extern static short CoSomeAPI2(int a1);
```

This code informs the P/Invoke engine to automatically check the HRESULT and map failed calls to exceptions of type COMException. Note that in the case of `OLE32Wrapper.CoSomeAPI2`, the method returns a `short` that corresponds to the underlying function's final `[out,retval]` parameter. Had the P/Invoke method been declared to return `void`, then the P/Invoke layer would have assumed that the specified parameter list matches the underlying native definition exactly. This mapping takes place only when the `PreserveSig` parameter is false.

As mentioned previously, each P/Invoke method has two method signatures: a managed signature and one that is expected by the external DLL. This is illustrated in Figure 10.3. Depending on the type of parameter, the P/Invoke engine may (or may not) need to perform an in-memory conversion. Types that can be copied without conversion are called **blittable** types. Types that require conversion are called **nonblittable** types. To risk stating the obvious, the performance of a P/Invoke call is considerably faster when one uses only blittable parameters because setting up the second stack frame typically requires only one IA-32 instruction per parameter. The same cannot be said when one uses nonblittable types.

Table 10.2 shows a list of the basic blittable and nonblittable types as well as their default mappings in C/IDL. You are free to override

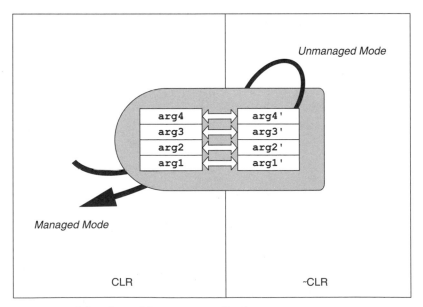

Figure 10.3: *P/Invoke and Parameter Duplication*

these default mappings on a parameter-by-parameter (or field-by-field) basis using the System.Runtime.InteropServices.MarshalAs attribute. This attribute indicates which unmanaged type to use when marshaling a stack frame using P/Invoke. As shown in Table 10.3, the MarshalAs attribute requires one parameter of type UnmanagedType. The UnmanagedType is an enumerated type whose values correspond to the types the P/Invoke marshaler knows how to handle. By applying the MarshalAs attribute to a parameter of field, you are specifying which external type should be used by P/Invoke. One can use additional parameters to MarshalAs to tailor the handling of arrays, including support for COM-style [size_is] using the SizeParamIndex parameter. Additionally, one can extend the P/Invoke marshaler by specifying a custom marshaler using the MarshalType parameter. This custom marshaler must implement the ICustomMarshaler interface, which allows the marshaler to do low-level conversions between instances of managed types and raw memory.

To grasp how the MarshalAs attribute is used, consider the following P/Invoke method declaration:

```
[ DllImport("foobar.dll") ]
public static extern void DoIt(
  [MarshalAs(UnmanagedType.LPWStr)] String s1,
  [MarshalAs(UnmanagedType.LPStr)] String s2,
  [MarshalAs(UnmanagedType.LPTStr)] String s3,
  [MarshalAs(UnmanagedType.BStr)] String s4
);
```

This method declaration implies the following unmanaged C function declaration:

```
void _stdcall DoIt(LPCWSTR s1, LPCSTR s2,
                   LPCTSTR s3, BSTR s4);
```

Note that the C function prototype uses const parameters. This is critically important given the semantics of System.String, which is that all instances of System.String are immutable. To that end, the CLR provides no mechanisms to change the contents of a System.String object. To

TABLE 10.2 Blittable and Nonblittable Types

	CLR Type	IDL/C Type
Blittable	Single	float
	Double	double
	SByte	signed char
	Byte	unsigned char
	Int16	short
	Uint16	unsigned short
	Int32	long
	Uint32	unsigned long
	Int64	__int64
	Uint64	unsigned __int64
	IntPtr	INT_PTR
	UIntPtr	UINT_PTR
	Formatted type containing only blittable types	Euivalent C-style struct
	One-dimensional array of blittable type	Equivalent C-style array
Nonblittable	All other arrays	SAFEARRAY or C-style array
	Char	wchar_t (blittable) or char
	String	LPCWSTR(blittable) or LPCSTR or BSTR
	Boolean	VARIANT_BOOL or BOOL
	Object	VARIANT

TABLE 10.3 MarshalAs Attribute Parameters

Parameter Name	Type	Description
Value	Unmanaged Type	Unmanaged type to marshal to (mandatory)
ArraySubType	Unmanaged Type	Unmanaged type of array elements
SafeArraySubType	VarType	Unmanaged VARTYPE of safearray elements
SizeConst	int	Fixed size of unmanaged array
SizeParamIndex	short	0-based index of [size_is] parameter
MarshalType	String	Fully qualified type name of custom marshaler
MarshalCookie	String	Cookie for custom marshaler

understand how this impacts P/Invoke, consider the internal representation of a System.String. As shown in Figure 10.4, System.String is a reference type, so all strings are compatible with the CLR internal object format. Additionally, all strings are prefixed with both a capacity and a length field. In almost all cases, these two fields are the same. Finally, the string object ends with a null-terminated array of System.Char, which is a 16-bit Unicode character.

Because the CLR does not allocate System.String objects using the SysAllocString API call, they are not valid BSTRs, and passing a string as

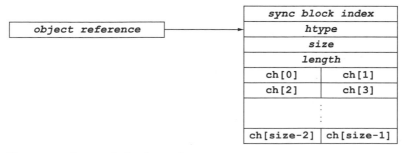

Figure 10.4: *System.String Internals*

a BSTR causes the P/Invoke engine to create a copy of the string. Similarly, because a System.String object contains Unicode characters, strings are considered nonblittable when passed as an ANSI string. These temporary copies of the string live only for the duration of the call, and the CLR will not propagate any changes back to the original string object. However, if one passes the string as a Unicode string (UnmanagedType.LPWStr), the P/Invoke engine actually passes a pointer to the beginning of the string's character array. This means that for the duration of the call, the external DLL has a raw pointer to the string's actual buffer. Because CLR strings are immutable, any changes made by the external DLL to the string will result in random and unpredictable errors. To avoid this, one should declare the external DLL's parameter as const wchar_t*. If one needs to pass a string to an external DLL for modification, one should instead use the System.Text.StringBuilder type. For example, consider the following Win32 API function:

```
BOOL __stdcall GetModuleFileName(HMODULE hmod,
                                 LPTSTR psz,
                                 DWORD nSize);
```

This function would require a P/Invoke prototype that looks like this:

```
[DllImport("kernel32.dll",
          CharSet=CharSet.Auto,
          SetLastError=true) ]
static extern bool GetModuleFileName(IntPtr hmod,
                                     StringBuilder psz,
                                     uint nSize);
```

To use this function, one would need to preallocate a string buffer using the StringBuilder class as follows:

```
static string GetTheName(IntPtr hmod) {
// allocate a 1024 character buffer
  StringBuilder sb = new StringBuilder(1024);
// call the P/Invoke routine
  if (!GetModuleFileName(hmod, sb, 1024))
    throw new MyException();
```

```
// harvest out the string
  return sb.ToString();
}
```

Note that the `StringBuilder` object keeps a private string object to use as the underlying character buffer. Calling `ToString` returns a reference to this private string object. Any future use of the `StringBuilder` object will trigger a new copy of the string, and it is this copy that the `StringBuilder` object modifies in subsequent operations. This technique avoids further corruption of the last string returned from the `ToString` method.

The `DllImport` attribute allows one to specify the default string format on a method-wide basis, eliminating the need for the `MarshalAs` attribute on each parameter. One can set the Unicode/ANSI policy for a method using the `CharSet` parameter. The `CharSet` parameter to `DllImport` allows you to specify whether Unicode (`CharSet.Unicode`) or ANSI (`CharSet.Ansi`) should be used. This is equivalent to manually marking each string parameter with a `MarshalAs(UnamanagedType.LPWStr)` or `MarshalAs(UnamanagedType.LPStr)` attribute, respectively.

The `DllImport` attribute supports a third setting, `CharSet.Auto`, which indicates that the underlying platform (Windows NT/2000/XP versus Windows 9x/ME) should dictate the external format of string parameters. Using `CharSet.Auto` is similar to writing Win32/C code using the `TCHAR` data type, except that the CLR determines the actual character type and API at load time, not compile time, allowing a single binary to work properly and efficiently on all versions of Windows.

When one passes object references other than `System.String` or `System.Object`, the default marshaling behavior is to convert between CLR object references and COM object references. As shown in Figure 10.5, when one marshals a reference to a CLR object across the P/Invoke boundary, the CLR creates a **COM-callable wrapper (CCW)** to act as a **proxy** to the CLR object. Likewise, when one marshals in a reference to a COM object through the P/Invoke boundary, the CLR creates a **runtime-callable wrapper (RCW)** to act as a proxy to the COM object. In both cases, the proxy will implement all of the interfaces of the underlying object. Additionally, the proxy will try to map COM and CLR idioms such as IDispatch, object persistence, and events to the corresponding construct in the other technology.

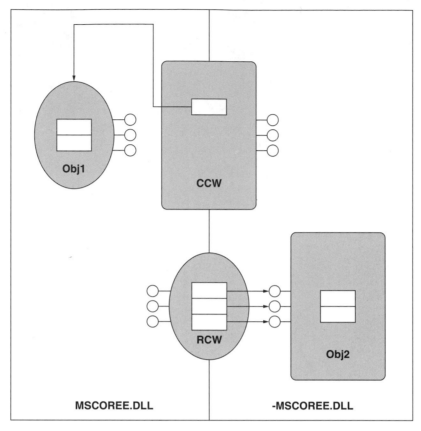

Figure 10.5: *RCW and CCW Architecture*

It is important to note that the presence of CCWs or RCWs (or both) can wreak havoc on the lifecycle management of the CLR and of COM. For example, the RCW holds `AddRefed` interface pointers to the underlying COM object. The CLR does not release these interface pointers until the RCW is finalized. Moreover, the CCW holds a rooted reference to the underlying CLR object, and that prevents the object from being garbage-collected as long as there is at least one outstanding COM interface pointer. This means that if cycles in an object graph contain CCWs or RCWs, one needs some mechanism to break the cycle. You can preemptively release an RCW's interface pointer by calling the `Marshal.ReleaseComObject` static method. You can also convert the rooted reference inside a CCW to a weak reference by calling `Marshal.ChangeWrapperHandleStrength`.

Like any other call to or from unmanaged code, a call to an RCW or a CCW triggers a mode transition. However, as was the case with P/Invoke, calls to an RCW also force a security demand because calling to unmanaged DLLs is a privileged operation. When one calls an RCW, the type conversion rules used for method parameters differ slightly from those used in P/Invoke calls. In particular, strings default to BSTRs, Booleans default to VARIANT_BOOL, and PreserveSig is assumed to be false, not true. To suppress the automatic translation of HRESULTs to exceptions, one must apply the System.Runtime.InteropServices.PreserveSig attribute to the interface method of interest.

For interfaces that straddle the P/Invoke boundary via RCWs or CCWs, the CLR relies on a set of annotations to the managed interface definition to give the underlying marshaling layer hints as to how to translate the types. These hints are a superset of those just described for P/Invoke. Additional aspects that need to be defined include UUIDs, vtable versus dispatch versus dual mappings, how IDispatch should be handled, and how arrays are translated. One adds these aspects to the managed interface definition using attributes from the System.Runtime.InteropServices namespace. In the absence of these attributes, the CLR makes conservative guesses as to what the default settings for a given interface and method should be. For new managed interfaces that are defined from scratch, it is useful to use the attributes explicitly if you intend your interfaces to be used outside of the CLR.

One can translate native COM type definitions (e.g., structs, interfaces, etc.) to the CLR by hand, and, in some cases, this is necessary, especially when no accurate TLB is available. Translating type definitions in the other direction is simpler given the ubiquity of reflection in the CLR, but, as always, one is better off using a tool rather than resorting to hand translations. The CLR ships with code that does a reasonable job of doing this translation for you provided that COM TLBs are accurate enough. System.Runtime.InteropServices.TypeLibConverter can translate between TLBs and CLR assemblies. The ConvertAssemblyToTypeLib method reads a CLR assembly and emits a TLB containing the corresponding COM type definitions. Any hints to this translation process (e.g., MarshalAs) must appear as custom attributes on the interfaces, methods, fields, and parameters in the source types. The `ConvertTypeLibToAssembly` method reads a COM TLB and emits a CLR assembly containing the corresponding CLR type definitions. The SDK ships with two tools (`TLBEXP.EXE` and `TLBIMP.EXE`) that wrap these two calls behind a command-line interface suitable for use with NMAKE. Figure 10.6 shows the relationship between these two tools.

In general, it is easier to define types first in a CLR-based language and then emit the TLB. For example, consider the C# code shown in Listing 10.1. If we were to treat this code as a "pseudo-IDL" file, we could run it through `CSC.EXE` and `TLBEXP.EXE` to produce a TLB that is functionally identical to the one produced by the "real" IDL file shown in Listing 10.2. The advantage to using the C# approach is that the type definitions are extensible and readily machine-readable, neither of which could be said for the TLB or IDL file.

Listing 10.1: *C# as a Better IDL*

```csharp
using System;
using System.Runtime.CompilerServices;
using System.Runtime.InteropServices;

[assembly: Guid("4c5025ef-3ae4-4128-ba7b-db4fb6e0c532") ]
[assembly: AssemblyVersion("2.1") ]

namespace AcmeCorp.MathTypes {
  [
    Guid("ddc244a4-c8b3-4c20-8416-1e7d0398462a"),
    InterfaceType(ComInterfaceType.InterfaceIsIUnknown)
  ]
  public interface ICalculator
  {
    double CurrentValue { get; }
    void    Clear();

    void Add(double x);
    void Subtract(double x);
    void Multiply(double x);
    void Divide(double x);
  }
}
```

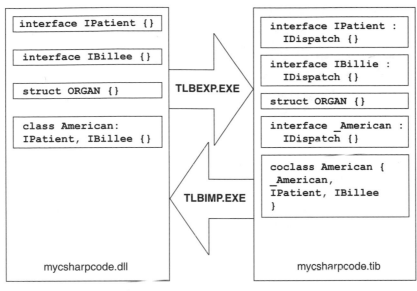

Figure 10.6: *TLBIMP and TLBEXP*

Listing 10.2: *C# as a Better IDL (Generated TLB)*

```
[
  uuid(4C5025EF-3AE4-4128-BA7B-DB4FB6E0C532),
  version(2.1)
]
library AcmeCorp_MathTypes
{
  importlib("stdole2.tlb");
  [
    object,
    uuid(DDC244A4-C8B3-4C20-8416-1E7D0398462A),
    oleautomation,
    custom({0F21F359-AB84-41E8-9A78-36D110E6D2F9},
           "AcmeCorp.MathTypes.ICalculator")
  ]
  interface ICalculator : IUnknown {
    [propget]
    HRESULT CurrentValue([out, retval] double* pRetVal);
    HRESULT Clear();
    HRESULT Add([in] double x);
    HRESULT Subtract([in] double x);
    HRESULT Multiply([in] double x);
    HRESULT Divide([in] double x);
  }
}
```

In an ideal world, there would be only one definition of a given type. Unfortunately, the realities of the COM installed base require two definitions to exist: one in CLR metadata and one in a COM TLB. If the COM TLB is the "authoritative" version of the type, there is a risk that multiple developers will import the TLB. Unfortunately, each of these imported assemblies will be different to the CLR, and this means that object references to COM components cannot be shared among multiple CLR-based components. This is especially problematic for shared COM components such as ActiveX Data Objects (ADO) because passing ADO recordsets as parameters was one of the defining acts of a VB programmer in the 1990s. To ensure that only one imported CLR assembly is used for each type library, the CLR supports the notion of a primary interop assembly.

One registers a **primary interop assembly** in the COM registry as the authoritative version of the TLB. When loading the CLR type for a type in a COM TLB, the CLR will defer to the type definition in the primary interop assembly. This ensures that only one version of a given COM type exists in memory at once. One sets the primary interop assembly using the /primary command-line switch to TLBIMP.EXE. When an administrator or user registers the resultant assembly using REGASM.EXE, REGASM.EXE will place additional registry entries under HKEY_CLASSES_ROOT\TypeLib that indicate that the imported assembly is the primary interop assembly for the COM TLB. To maintain consistency, all type libraries referenced by a primary interop assembly's TLB must also have primary interop assemblies. When the CLR is installed, REGASM.EXE creates a primary interop assembly for STDOLE.TLB, which is referenced by all TLBs.

The discussion of P/Invoke illustrated how one can access the classic Win32 loader transparently from CLR-based programs. The discussion of P/Invoke neglected to discuss another classic loader that dominated the 1990s—that is, COM's CoCreateInstance.

The COM loader translated location-neutral type names in the form of CLSIDs into DLLs that exposed the DllGetClassObject entry point. One exposed this functionality via a variety of API functions; however, the most popular was easily CoCreateInstance. Although it is completely legal to call CoCreateInstance via P/Invoke, most CLR-based programs will elect to use the System.Runtime.InteropServices.ComImport attribute.

The CLR treats CLR-based classes specially that are marked with the `ComImport` attribute. In particular, when a `newobj` CIL instruction is performed on a type marked `ComImport`, the CLR will read the type's globally unique identifier (GUID) from the metadata and will translate the `newobj` request into a call to `CoCreateInstance`. Types that use `ComImport` invariably use the `System.Runtime.InteropServices.Guid` attribute to explicitly control the type's GUID.

The following program uses `ComImport` to map a CLR-based type named `Excel` to the COM class for Microsoft Excel.

```
using System;
using System.Runtime.InteropServices;

[ ComImport ]
[ Guid("00020812-0000-0000-C000-000000000046") ]
class Excel {
}

class xx {
  static void Main()  {
    Excel app = new Excel(); // calls CoCreateInstance
    Console.ReadLine();
    Console.WriteLine(app.ToString());
  }
}
```

Note that the CLR's TLB importer will automatically generate `ComImport` types for each `coclass` in the TLB.

COM programmers often used monikers to place a level of indirection between the client and the target class and object. Programmers usually accessed this capability via COM's `CoGetObject` or VB's `GetObject` function. CLR-based programs can access this same functionality using the `Marshal.BindtoMoniker` static method.

Loading the CLR

Getting the CLR to call `LoadLibrary` or `CoCreateInstance` is fairly trivial and extremely straightforward. Going in the other direction—that is, allowing CLR-based code to be loaded from legacy code—is considerably more interesting.

Ultimately, the CLR is implemented as a family of Win32/COM-based DLLs. Although one can load these DLLs directly using `LoadLibrary` or `CoCreateInstance`, these are not the preferred techniques to use when one is loading the CLR into a new process. Instead, unmanaged programs are encouraged to use the CLR's explicit facilities for loading and hosting the runtime. The CLR exposes these facilities via a DLL called `MSCOREE.DLL`.

`MSCOREE.DLL` is sometimes called the "shim" because it is simply a facade in front of the actual DLLs that the CLR comprises. As shown in Figure 10.7, `MSCOREE.DLL` sits in front of one of two DLLs: `MSCORWKS.DLL` and `MSCORSVR.DLL`. The `MSCORWKS.DLL` DLL is the uniprocessor build of the

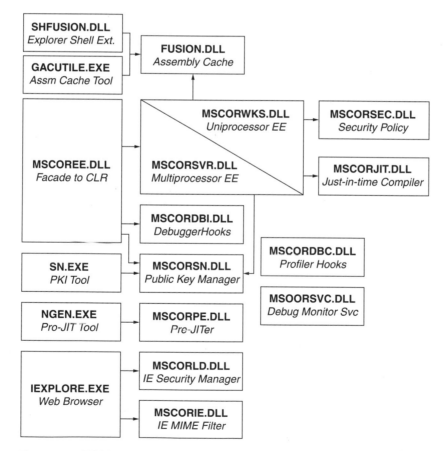

Figure 10.7: *MSCOREE and Friends*

CLR; `MSCORSVR.DLL` is the multiprocessor build of the CLR. The primary difference between the two builds is that the multiprocessor build uses one heap per CPU per process to reduce contention; the uniprocessor build has one heap per process. It is the job of `MSCOREE.DLL` to select the appropriate build based on any number of factors, including (but not limited to) the underlying hardware.

Of all the DLLs shown in Figure 10.7, only `MSCOREE.DLL` can be found in the `%SYSTEM_ROOT%` directory. To support side-by-side installation of multiple versions of the CLR, Microsoft has placed all other DLLs in a version-specific subdirectory. The CLR determines which version is selected based on a number of configuration options. The Everett release of the CLR (tentatively to be called the .NET framework Version 1.1) will be the first version of the CLR to actually support side-by-side versions of the CLR itself.

Several aspects of the CLR use a well-known registry key for global configuration information. The machine-wide settings are stored under `HKEY_LOCAL_MACHINE\Software\Microsoft\.NETFramework`. Per-user settings are stored under `HKEY_CURRENT_USER\Software\Microsoft\.NETFramework`. Additionally, one can override many of the settings stored in the registry by setting OS-level environment variables. For example, one specifies the default version of the runtime using the `Version` named value. That means that the following .REG file would set the default CLR version number to "v1.0.3215" for all users:

```
[HKEY_LOCAL_MACHINE\Software\Microsoft\.NETFramework]
Version=v1.0.3215
```

In contrast, the following `CMD.EXE` command would set the default version to "v1.0.3500" for all subsequent programs run from a particular command shell:

```
set COMPlus_Version=v1.0.3500
```

Note that one must prefix the name of the registry value with `COMPlus_` when one is using it as an environment variable. One uses this convention for most registry settings used by the CLR.

When trying to determine the name and location of the DLL that implements the CLR, MSCOREE.DLL looks at both the Version setting and the InstallRoot setting. The latter points to the base directory in which the various versions of the CLR are installed. For example, on the author's machine, the default settings are as follows:

```
[HKEY_LOCAL_MACHINE\Software\Microsoft\.NETFramework]
Version=v1.0.3705
InstallRoot=C:\windows\Microsoft.NET\Framework\
```

When looking for the CLR DLLs, MSCOREE.DLL simply catenates the two values and looks in the C:\windows\Microsoft.NET\Framework\ v1.0.3705 directory. You can programmatically construct this path by calling the System.Runtime.InteropServices.RuntimeEnvironment. GetRuntimeDirectory static method. Similarly, you can fetch the Version property used to load the runtime by calling the System. Runtime.InteropServices.RuntimeEnvironment.GetSystem-Version static method.

To determine the actual file name of the CLR DLL, MSCOREE.DLL looks for one more configuration property. If the BuildFlavor property is present in either the registry or the process environment variable, MSCOREE.DLL will take that string as the suffix of the file name and catenate it with MSCOR, producing either MSCORWKS or MSCORSVR. Note, however, that MSCOREE.DLL will never load MSCORSVR.DLL on a uniprocessor machine.

MSCOREE.DLL also supports the silent loading of newer versions of the CLR that are known to be compatible. The .NETFramework registry key contains a policy subkey that indicates which range of build numbers a given version of the CLR is compatible with. When loading the CLR, MSCOREE.DLL will consult this subkey and silently promote the requested version number if possible.

The Version setting just described is installation-specific. It is also possible to use configuration files to control which version of the runtime is loaded. If an application's config file contains a <startup> element, the version number found there overrides the version specified in the registry or in environment variables. Consider the following configuration file:

```
<?xml version="1.0" encoding="utf-8" ?>
<configuration>
  <startup>
    <requiredRuntime version="v1.0.2605"
                     safemode="false"     />
  </startup>
</configuration>
```

This file indicates that version `v1.0.2605` should be used. The `safemode="false"` attribute indicates that it is acceptable to apply version policy to select a higher (or lower) version number. To suppress this version policy mapping, one should set the `safemode` attribute to `true`. In this mode, the exact version of the CLR must be available; otherwise, `MSCOREE.DLL` will fail to load the runtime.

It is important to note that even though the CLR supports side-by-side installation of multiple versions of the CLR, one can use only one version within a single OS process. In fact, after the CLR has been loaded into a process, that process can use no other versions even after the original instance of the CLR is completely torn down. To support side-by-side execution of multiple CLR versions, one must use multiple OS processes, one per CLR version.

One additional process-wide setting that needs to be discussed is whether or not the concurrent garbage collector will be used. By default, the garbage collector always runs on the thread that triggered the collection. In contrast, the concurrent garbage collector will avoid this situation by allowing garbage collection to occur on other threads as well. The concurrent collector is suited to interactive applications in which the latency of running the garbage collector on the primary thread of the application is unacceptable. One specifies the use of the concurrent collector using the following configuration file entry:

```
<?xml version="1.0" encoding="utf-8" ?>
<configuration>
  <runtime>
    <gcConcurrent enabled="true" />
  </runtime>
</configuration>
```

The absence of this element (or setting the `enabled` attribute to `false`) will cause the CLR to use the normal garbage collector.

The discussion so far has focused on how `MSCOREE.DLL` determines which CLR DLL to load. What has yet to be discussed is how to instruct `MSCOREE.DLL` to perform this feat.

One can use `MSCOREE.DLL` in any number of ways. Managed executables implicitly reference it in their PE/COFF headers. In particular, a managed `.EXE` will forward its Win32-level main entry point to `MSCOREE.DLL`'s `_CorExeMain`. After loading the CLR, `_CorExeMain` simply traverses the program's metadata and executes the program's CLR-level main entry point. Similarly, DLLs forward their Win32-level main entry point to `_CorDllMain`. In either case, `MSCOREE.DLL` will change execution modes from unmanaged to managed prior to executing the main entry point of the target executable.

For COM compatibility, `MSCOREE.DLL` also exports a `DllGetClass-Object`. When `MSCOREE.DLL` is registered as an `InprocServer32`, `MSCOREE.DLL` expects to find additional registry entries that indicate the assembly and type name of the corresponding COM class. The `REGASM.EXE` tool writes these automatically. For example, consider the following C# class:

```
using System.Runtime.InteropServices;

namespace AcmeCorp.Utilities {
  [ Guid("2bb710e9-7cf0-46fa-91fe-94e46f44a76a") ]
  [ InterfaceType(ComInterfaceType.InterfaceIsIUnknown) ]
  public interface IOpener { void Open(); }

  [ Guid("5321aeb6-2a7d-43f1-a045-2392eb917f73") ]
  public class Pliers : IOpener  {
    public void Open() {}
  }
}
```

This class would cause `REGASM.EXE` to generate the following registry entries:

```
[HKEY_CLASSES_ROOT\CLSID\{5321AEB6-2A7D-43F1-A045-
2392EB917F73}]
@="AcmeCorp.Utilities.Pliers"

; all REGASM-ed components are in the ".NET Category"
[HKEY_CLASSES_ROOT\CLSID\{5321AEB6-2A7D-43F1-A045-
2392EB917F73}\Implemented Categories]

[HKEY_CLASSES_ROOT\CLSID\{5321AEB6-2A7D-43F1-A045-
2392EB917F73}\Implemented Categories\{62C8FE65-4EBB-45e7-
B440-6E39B2CDBF29}]

; here's the meat!
[HKEY_CLASSES_ROOT\CLSID\{5321AEB6-2A7D-43F1-A045-
2392EB917F73}\InprocServer32]
@="C:\\WINNT\\System32\\mscoree.dll"
"ThreadingModel"="Both"
"Class"="AcmeCorp.Utilities.Pliers"
"Assembly"="acme, Version=1.0.0.0, Culture=neutral,
PublicKeyToken=cf60c03991d9a41f"
"RuntimeVersion"="v1.0.3705"
"CodeBase"="file:///c:/mycode/acme.DLL"

[HKEY_CLASSES_ROOT\CLSID\{5321AEB6-2A7D-43F1-A045-
2392EB917F73}\ProgId]
@="AcmeCorp.Utilities.Pliers"
```

Notice that the Class and Assembly specify the fully qualified type name of the target class. Also note that the CodeBase entry provides the necessary codebase hint used by the assembly resolver. This codebase hint is critical because the COM client will not have a configuration file of its own. This codebase hint will be inserted into the registry only if the call to REGASM.EXE specifies the /codebase command-line option.

It is also possible to register a CLR-based type with the COM+ 1.x catalog manager. CLR-based types that wish to be configured with COM+ must directly or indirectly extend the System.EnterpriseServices. ServicedComponent base type. This base type ensures that the CLR-based object will have a COM+ 1.x context associated with it. For version 1 of the CLR, COM+ 1.x services are still implemented in unmanaged COM code. The use of ServicedComponent acts as a signal to the CLR to ensure that both a CLR and a COM+ 1.*x* context are available for the new object. When the CLR creates an instance of a serviced component, it ensures that there are proper COM+ 1.*x* catalog entries for the class. To that end, most of the COM+ 1.*x* catalog attributes are available as custom metadata attributes to allow developers to specify their COM+ 1.*x* service requirements at development time.

Finally, to avoid the need to use COM interop, the CLR makes available the facilities of `CoGetObjectContext` via the `System.EnterpriseServices.ContextUtil` type. At the time of this writing, the lone compelling feature of COM+ 1.*x* that would warrant the use of this plumbing is to ease the use of the distributed transaction coordinator (DTC). Applications that do not need DTC probably do not need COM+ 1.*x* either. See Tim Ewald's book *Transactional COM+* (Addison-Wesley, 2001) on why this is so.

The CLR as a COM Component

The uses of `MSCOREE.DLL` just described all take advantage of the CLR implicitly. It is also possible to use the CLR explicitly from unmanaged programs. When you use the CLR explicitly, your unmanaged program has considerably more control over how the CLR is configured within the process. To facilitate this, the CLR exposes a family of COM-based hosting interfaces that can be accessed from any COM-compatible environment. The most critical of these interfaces is `ICorRuntimeHost`.

`ICorRuntimeHost` is the primary hosting interface of the CLR. This interface allows programs to manage the AppDomains of the CLR as well as control how OS threads and fibers interact with the CLR. The simplest way to acquire an `ICorRuntimeHost` interface is to call `CoCreateInstance` on the `CorRuntimeHost` coclass. Consider the following VBA 6.0 code:

```
Private Sub Form_Load()
  Dim rt As mscoree.CorRuntimeHost
  Dim unk As stdole.IUnknown
  Dim ad As mscorlib.AppDomain
  Dim s As mscorlib.Stack

  Set rt = New mscoree.CorRuntimeHost
  rt.Start
```

```
      rt.GetDefaultDomain unk
      Set ad = unk
      Set s = ad.CreateInstance("mscorlib", _
                          "System.Collections.Stack").Unwrap
      s.Push "Hello"
      s.Push "Goodbye"
      s.Push 42
      MsgBox s.Pop()
      MsgBox s.Pop()
      MsgBox s.Pop()
   End Sub
```

Assuming that this code is in a project that references both MSCOREE. TLB and MSCORLIB.TLB, the new statement will cause MSCOREE.DLL to be loaded into the process. Note that there is an explicit Start method that one must call prior to using the CLR. This two-phase initialization allows the container to configure the default AppDomain's loader properties using an AppDomainSetup object. After the Start method has been called, the default domain of the process will have been initialized and made available via the GetDefaultDomain method. After the default domain is available, programming the CLR from the host application is extremely similar to programming the CLR from within. The primary difference is that the host application is unmanaged code, so the reference returned by GetDefaultDomain is a CCW to the underlying CLR-based object.

Using CoCreateInstance to load the CLR has two pitfalls. For one thing, you cannot explicitly control the version of the CLR that will be loaded. Rather, the CLR will use the Version property as described earlier. Moreover, using CoCreateInstance requires that you initialize COM in process. There are actually processes that do not use OLE32.DLL. To allow the CLR to be hosted in these processes, MSCOREE.DLL exposes a set of API functions that load the correct runtime without resorting to COM. The most flexible of these API calls is CorBindToRuntimeHost.

CorBindToRuntimeHost allows the caller to specify several parameters that control which build of the CLR is loaded as well as how it will be initialized. Here is the signature for CorBindToRuntimeHost:

```
HRESULT
CorBindToRuntimeHost(
    LPCWSTR pwszVersion,            // which Version?
    LPCWSTR pwszBuildFlavor,        // "wks" or "svr"?
    LPCWSTR pwszHostConfigFile,     // config file name?
    VOID* pReserved,                // must be zero
    DWORD startupFlags,             // see STARTUP flags
    REFCLSID rclsid,                // __uuidof(CorRuntimeHost)
    REFIID riid,                    // iid_is parameter for ppv
    VOID **ppv);                    // put the itf. ptr. here!
```

The first parameter overrides the `Version` property that may appear in the registry or an environment variable. The second parameter indicates whether the uniprocessor or multiprocessor build is desired. However, be aware that `MSCOREE.DLL` will ignore requests for `svr` when running on a uniprocessor machine. The third parameter is the file name of the application configuration file. This allows the host application to use whatever name it chooses for the configuration file. Finally, the fifth parameter is a bitmask taken from the following enumeration:

```
typedef enum {
    STARTUP_CONCURRENT_GC           = 0x1,

    STARTUP_LOADER_OPTIMIZATION_MASK = 0x3<<1,
    STARTUP_LOADER_OPTIMIZATION_SINGLE_DOMAIN = 0x1<<1,
    STARTUP_LOADER_OPTIMIZATION_MULTI_DOMAIN = 0x2<<1,
    STARTUP_LOADER_OPTIMIZATION_MULTI_DOMAIN_HOST = 0x3<<1,

    STARTUP_LOADER_SAFEMODE = 0x10,
} STARTUP_FLAGS;
```

The loader optimization flags correspond to the `System.Loader-Optimization` enumeration described in Chapter 8. The `STARTUP_LOADER_SAFEMODE` flag serves the same function as the `safemode` configuration file attribute and suppresses the default version policy applied by `MSCOREE.DLL`. Finally, the `STARTUP_CONCURRENT_GC` flag informs the CLR to use the concurrent garbage collector a la the `gcConcurrent` configuration file element. Finally, the last three parameters of `CorBind-ToRuntimeHost` match those found in a `CoCreateInstance` call and indicate which coclass and interface to use.

The presence of a configuration file influences the parameters to `Cor-BindToRuntimeHost`. In particular, the settings in the configuration file will take precedence over any parameters passed to `CorBindToRuntime-Host`. This is reflected in the overall version policy used to load the CLR, which is shown in Figure 10.8.

`MSCOREE.DLL` exports several variations on `CorBindToRuntimeHost` that accept fewer parameters. However, there are two functions that `MSCOREE.DLL` exports that bear further scrutiny: `CorBindToCurrentRuntime` and `ClrCreateManagedInstance`. The former function allows unmanaged code to access the `ICorRuntimeHost` reference to the runtime that is already initialized in the process. The latter function takes a fully qualified CLR type name and wraps the underlying calls to `CorBindToRuntimeHost`, `ICorRuntimeHost.GetDefaultDomain`, and `AppDomain.CreateInstance`.

The object returned by `CorBindToRuntimeHost` provides additional functionality beyond what has already been discussed. In particular, it gives host applications fairly fine-grained control over how the garbage collector and threads are managed. Figure 10.9 shows the overall object model. Be aware that none of these interfaces is documented; however, one can easily infer their usage through experimentation. The `ICorThreadpool` interface allows unmanaged code to access the CLR's process-wide thread pool. The methods of `ICorThreadpool` mirror those of its managed counterpart, `System.Threading.ThreadPool`. The `IGCHost` interface allows one to set various thresholds for the garbage collector's heap manager as well as allows one to examine heap usage information. The `IValidator` interface exposes the PE/COFF validation functionality of the CLR to allow arbitrary tools (such as `peverify.exe`) to verify CLR-based modules. The `IMetaDataConverter` interface exposes the TLB-to-CLR metadata conversion facilities to tools such as `TLBEXP.EXE`.

The CLR also allows the host application to register several callback interfaces to gain better control over how the garbage collector and thread manager work. The `IGCThreadControl` interface allows the CLR to notify the host application when the garbage collector is suspending or resuming execution of a given thread. The `IGCHostControl` interface allows the host application to control how fast and how far the garbage collector can allocate virtual memory for its heap. Finally, the `IDebuggerThreadControl`

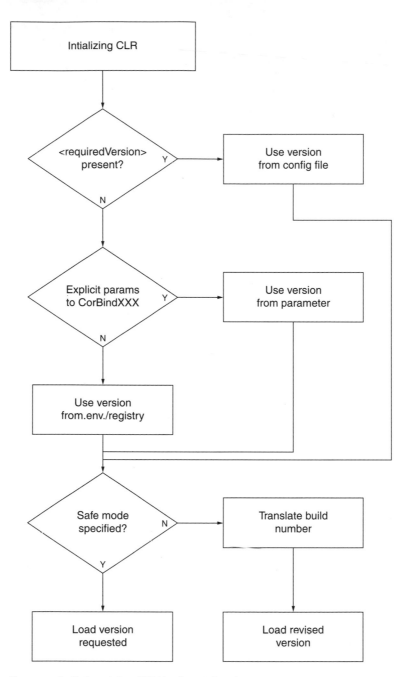

Figure 10.8: *Determining CLR Version at Runtime*

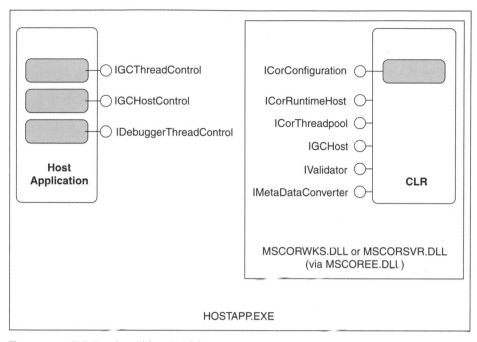

Figure 10.9: *CLR Hosting Object Model*

interface allows the CLR to notify the host when the CLR debugger is about to suspend execution of a given thread.

Independent of the hosting interfaces just described, the CLR provides a family of unmanaged COM interfaces that allow instrumentation, inspection, and intrusion into the CLR's execution engine. These interfaces are broken into two suites: one suite that is tailored to debuggers and another that is tailored to profilers. Between the two, however, one can expose virtually all aspects of the CLR to unmanaged code running just outside the CLR.

Figure 10.10 shows the CLR debugger object model. One can acquire the `ICorDebug` interface by calling `CoCreateInstance` on `CLSID_CorDebug`. This COM class is exposed by `MSCORDBI.DLL` and will hook up to the CLR running in any process. After being attached to a CLR instance, the debugger can register up to two callback interfaces. The CLR uses one of the interfaces, `ICorDebugManagedCallback`, to inform the debugger of relatively coarse-grained events that occur in the running program (e.g., loader activity, AppDomain creation and unloading) as well as debugger-specific events such as breakpoints encountered. The CLR uses the second event

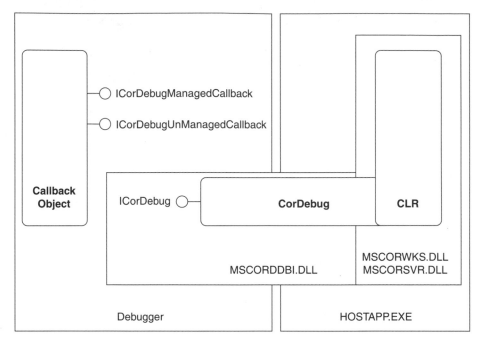

Figure 10.10: *CLR Debugging Object Model*

interface, `ICorDebugManagedCallback`, to signal classic Win32 debugger events. The CLR uses this interface only when the CLR debugger is also attached as the native Win32 debugger.

After your program attaches to a CLR as its debugger, the entire state of the running program is made available. Figure 10.11 shows the object model of the CLR as viewed through the lens of the debugging interfaces. This object model remains true to the conceptual model of the CLR but allows extremely fine-grained access to the execution state of a running program, down to the register level.

The events fired by the CLR debugging infrastructure are fairly coarse-grained. Programs that need finer granularity need to use the profiler interface suite. Upon initialization, the CLR looks for two configuration properties either in the registry or in process environment variables. One of the properties, `Cor_Enable_Profiling`, controls whether or not the CLR will load a profiler DLL to instrument the CLR. The second property, `Cor_Profiler`, indicates the COM CLSID of the profiler DLL to be loaded. As shown in Figure 10.12, this DLL must implement the `ICorProfiler-Callback` interface. Upon initialization, the profiler DLL must provide a

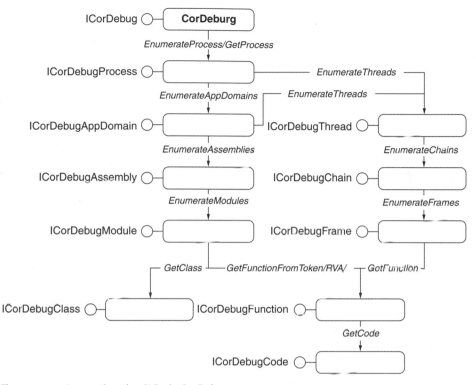

Figure 10.11: *Inspecting the CLR via CorDebug*

bitmask to indicate which event notifications it wishes to receive. Each possible event type has a distinct flag in this bitmask, allowing the profiling DLL to control how intrusive the instrumentation will be. Table 10.4 shows the family of profiler event notifications. Note that the finest-grained notification is MethodEnter and MethodLeave, allowing the profiling DLL to intercept literally every method call that occurs in the CLR.

It is difficult to talk about the profiling infrastructure without discussing **method inlining**. CLR modules carry a metadata attribute that controls how code will be generated. This metadata attribute is System.Diagnostics.DebuggableAttribute and is controlled via the /debug and /optimize command-line switches to your compiler. The attribute has two properties: IsJITTrackingEnabled and IsJITOptimizerDisabled.

IsJITTrackingEnabled informs the JIT compiler to emit perinstruction tables for the debugging infrastructure. This allows the debugger to do a better job of stepping through source code; however, it increases the in-memory size of the program. One sets this property to true using the

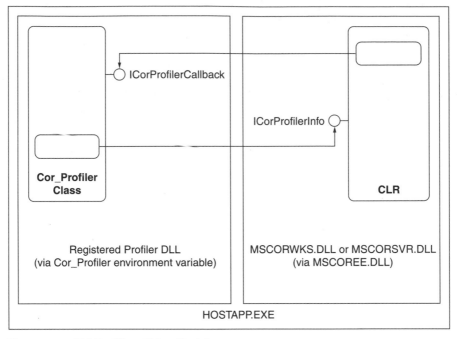

Figure 10.12: *CLR Profiling Object Model*

/debug or the /debug+ compiler switch. The property defaults to false, but one can explicitly set it to false using the /debug- or the /debug:pdbonly switch. The latter of these two options generates symbolic debugging information despite causing the JIT compiler to emit slightly less accurate debugging information.

IsJITOptimizerDisabled informs the JIT compiler to suppress inline expansion of method bodies. This allows the profiler to get a more accurate picture of which method bodies are actually the hotspots of a program. However, disabling inlining increases the impact of method invocation cost, which, for small method bodies, can be the dominant cost of a method. The IsJITOptimizerDisabled property defaults to true, but one can set it to false using the /optimize or the /optimize+ compiler switch.

Finally, one can override the per-module settings just described using a per-application configuration file. This file uses the classic Windows INI syntax and must look like this:

```
[.NET Framework Debugging Control]
AllowOptimize=1
GenerateTrackingInfo=1
```

TABLE 10.4 Profiler Notifications

MethodEnter	MethodReturn	MethodTailCall
AppDomainCreation	AssemblyLoad	ModuleLoad
AppDomainShutdown	AssemblyUnload	ModuleUnload
ModuleAttachedToAssembly	ClassLoad	ClassUnload
FunctionCompilation	FunctionUnload	JITCachedFunctionSearched
JITInlining	JITFunctionPitched	COMClassicVTableCreated
COMClassicVTable-Destroyed	UnmanagedToManaged-Transition	ManagedToUnmanaged-Transition
ThreadCreated	ThreadDestroyed	ThreadAssignedToOSThread
RuntimeSuspend	RuntimeResume	RuntimeThreadSusend
RuntimeThreadResume	MovedReferences	OBjectsAllocated
ObjectsAllocatedByClass	ObjectReferences	RootReferences
ExceptionThrown	ExceptionSearchFunction	ExceptionSearchFilter
ExceptionSearchCatcher	ExceptionOSHandler	ExceptionUnwindFunction
ExceptionUnwindFinally	ExceptionCatcher	ExceptionCLRCatcher

If the target executable is called `application.exe`, this file must have the name `application.INI` and reside in the same directory.

Where Are We?

The CLR is ultimately just a family of Win32/COM DLLs that one can load into any Win32 process. The primary facade to the CLR is `MSCOREE.DLL`, which acts as a lightweight shim in front of the actual runtime, which is implemented (primarily) in `MSCORWKS.DLL` or `MSCORSVR.DLL`. After the CLR loads your program, it is encouraged to stay within the confines of the CLR's managed execution model; however, you are free to leave at any time simply by invoking an unmanaged method.

Glossary

.NET Framework A set of technologies used to write CLR-based applications and XML Web Services.

.NET Framework SDK The freely downloadable software development kit for writing and debugging CLR-based applications and XML Web Services.

abnormal termination The premature exit of a method due to an exception being raised but not handled.

abstract type A type that can be used only as a base type and cannot be used to instantiate objects or values.

AL.EXE The assembly linker that ships with the .NET Framework SDK.

AppDomain The basic scope of execution in the CLR.

aspect-oriented programming (AOP) A programming technique based on factoring code based on separation of concerns, often using implicit execution based on out-of-band declarations and code injection.

assembly A collection of one or more modules that are deployed as a unit.

assembly loader The core piece of code in the CLR that maps assemblies and modules into memory prior to the use of a type.

assembly reference A reference to an external assembly, typically found in an assembly manifest.

assembly resolver The core piece of code in the CLR that locates assemblies by name prior to invoking the assembly loader to load them.

CASPOL.EXE A .NET Framework SDK tool used to view and control security policy.

CL.EXE The C++ compiler that ships with the .NET Framework SDK.

Common Intermediate Language (CIL) The architecture-neutral instruction set that is used by the CLI.

Common Language Infrastructure (CLI) A set of specifications ratified by ECMA that describe the public-facing aspects of the CLR.

Common Language Runtime (CLR) Microsoft's implementation of the CLI for Windows (specifically, Windows.NET Server, Windows XP, Windows 2000, Windows NT 4.0 SP6a or later, Windows 98, and Windows ME).

Common Language Specification (CLS) The subset of the CTS that all CLI-compliant languages must support.

common type system (CTS) The language-neutral type system that is used by CLI metadata and instructions.

Component Object Model (COM) A component technology used during the 1990s that added type to the loader and to component metadata.

constructor A method called automatically by the CLR to initialize a new instance of a type. Constructors are structurally only methods whose names are always .ctor.

contract The protocol describing the interactions between software components.

CORDBG.EXE The command-line debugger that ships with the .NET Framework SDK.

CSC.EXE The C# compiler that ships with the .NET Framework SDK.

DBGCLR.EXE The user-friendly debugger that ships with the .NET Framework SDK.

delegate An object that exists solely to invoke a specific method on a target object

event A named set of methods that represents a rendezvous point for registering event handlers.

event handler A delegate object registered with a CLR event.

evidence Testimony about the origins of an assembly that is gathered by the assembly loader and used to determine security policy for a given piece of code.

exception An object that signals an abnormal condition during program execution.

exception handler Code that processes an exception raised either implicitly by the runtime or explicitly by a throw statement.

field A named, typed unit of storage that is affiliated with a type or a module.

finalization The act of notifying an object that its underlying memory is about to be recycled.

FUSLOGVW.EXE A .NET Framework SDK tool used to view log files written by the assembly resolver.

GACUTIL.EXE A .NET Framework SDK tool used to manage the download cache and the assembly cache.

garbage collection An approach to resource reclamation based on automatic detection of unused resources by an omniscient piece of code.

Global Assembly Cache (GAC) A secured system-wide code cache used to permanently install shared components.

hard thread An operating system thread.

IEEXEC.EXE The host process used by Internet Explorer to launch CLR-based applications.

ILASM.EXE The CIL assembler that ships with the .NET Framework SDK.

ILDASM.EXE A .NET Framework SDK tool used to display the metadata and code of modules and assemblies.

Interface Definition Language (IDL) A text-based format for COM-based metadata.

JSC.EXE The JavaScript compiler that ships with the .NET Framework SDK.

loader A piece of code that locates and prepares chunks of code for execution.

metadata In the context of this book, metadata is information that describes components.

method A named, typed unit of execution that is affiliated with a type or a module.

Microsoft Transaction Server (MTS) An extension to COM that used AOP-like techniques to provide server-side services such as transaction management and declarative security checks.

module A file that contains code, resources, and metadata.

NGEN.EXE A .NET Framework SDK tool used to manage the cache of precompiled native images.

normal termination A method's successful execution of a return either explicitly or implicitly by reaching the end of its statements.

permission The right to perform a protected operation or to access a protected resource.

permission set An unordered set of permissions.

primitive type A value type whose value is atomic and is known a priori by the runtime to be one of the 12 intrinsic types (System.Boolean, System.Char, System.Double, System.Single, System.SByte, System.Int16, System.Int32, System.Int64, System.Byte, System.UInt16, System.UInt32, and System.UInt64).

property A named set of methods that represents a logical attribute.

public key A large, cryptographically unique number used to identify a user or organization. Used in the CLR to identify the developer of an assembly.

public key token A cryptographic hash of a public key that facilitates fast lookups and comparisons of public keys. Used in the CLR to reduce the size of a fully qualified assembly reference.

reference type A type whose variables are (potentially null) references to objects and not to values. All types that do not derive from System.ValueType directly or indirectly are reference types.

REGASM.EXE A .NET Framework SDK tool used to register CLR assemblies as COM components.

REGSVCS.EXE A .NET Framework SDK tool used to register CLR assemblies with the COM+ catalog manager.

RESGEN.EXE The resource compiler that ships with the .NET Framework SDK.

sealed type A type that cannot be used as a base type.

security policy The rules that determine the permission set to be granted to a piece of code based on evidence.

shadow copying A feature of the assembly resolver in which a copy of the assembly's files are loaded to avoid taking a read lock on the underlying files.

SN.EXE A .NET Framework SDK tool used to manage public/private keys and assemblies.

SOAPSUDS.EXE A .NET Framework SDK tool used to convert WSDL-based metadata for Web services to CLR-based metadata. See also WSDL.EXE.

soft thread A CLR thread object of type System.Threading.Thread.

strong name An assembly name that contains a public key (typically the public key of the component's developer).

termination handler Code that is guaranteed to run prior to leaving a protected range of instructions even in the face of exceptions.

thread local storage (TLS) Data that is specific to a particular thread.

TLBEXP.EXE A .NET Framework SDK tool used to convert CLR-based metadata to COM-based metadata.

TLBIMP.EXE A .NET Framework SDK tool used to convert COM-based metadata to CLR-based metadata.

type A named unit of abstraction.

type initializer A method called automatically by the CLR to initialize a type. Type initializers are structurally only methods whose names are always .cctor.

type library (TLB) A binary format for COM-based metadata.

uniform resource identifier (URI) A text-based name that uniquely identifies a resource. URIs are either uniform resource locators (URL) or uniform resource names (URN).

uniform resource locator (URL) A URI that contains location hints.

uniform resource name (URN) A location-independent URI.

value type A type whose variables are actual instances and not references to instances. All value types derive from System.ValueType either directly or indirectly.

VBC.EXE The Visual Basic.NET compiler that ships with the .NET Framework SDK.

version policy The set of rules that determines which versions of a component are substitutable for another.

Visual Studio.NET Microsoft's development environment that targets the CLR.

WINCV.EXE A .NET Framework SDK tool used to browse the type hierarchy of system assemblies.

WSDL.EXE A .NET Framework SDK tool used to convert WSDL-based metadata for Web services to CLR-based metadata. See also SOAPSUDS.EXE.

XSD.EXE A .NET Framework SDK tool used to convert between XML Schema-based metadata and CLR-based metadata.

Index

informIT

1325

Register
Your Book

at www.awprofessional.com/register

You may be eligible to receive:

- Advance notice of forthcoming editions of the book
- Related book recommendations
- Chapter excerpts and supplements of forthcoming titles
- Information about special contests and promotions throughout the year
- Notices and reminders about author appearances, tradeshows, and online chats with special guests

Contact us

If you are interested in writing a book or reviewing manuscripts prior to publication, please write to us at:

Editorial Department
Addison-Wesley Professional
75 Arlington Street, Suite 300
Boston, MA 02116 USA
Email: AWPro@aw.com

Addison-Wesley

Visit us on the Web: http://www.awprofessional.com